CW01315539

To Julian,
My new but valued friend,

THE GOING UP WAS WORTH THE COMING DOWN

IAN WATKINSON

With CHRIS PITT

Ian Watkinson.

Published by New Generation Publishing in 2021

Copyright © Ian Watkinson 2021

First Edition

Ian Watkinson asserts the moral right under the Copyright, Designs and Patents Act 1988 to be identified as the author of this work.

All Rights reserved. No part of this publication may be reproduced, stored in a retrieval system or transmitted, in any form or by any means without the prior consent of the author, nor be otherwise circulated in any form of binding or cover other than that which it is published and without a similar condition being imposed on the subsequent purchaser.

Paperback ISBN: 978-1-80031-126-8
Hardback ISBN: 978-1-80031-125-1
Ebook ISBN: 978-1-80031-124-4

www.newgeneration-publishing.com

New Generation Publishing

Every effort has been made to fulfil requirements with regard to copyright material. The author and publisher will be glad to rectify any omissions at the earliest opportunity.

Contents

Acknowledgements	iv
Foreword	v
Introduction	viii
1. The Fall	1
2. Getting Started	4
3. Greystoke	9
4. Giving Up	26
5. Coming Back	34
6. Recognition	46
7. Tingle Creek	66
8. Some Random Memories	78
9. Earl Jones	89
10. Some Other Trainers	96
11. Night Nurse and Sea Pigeon	101
12. Australia	112
13. The Women in my Life	124
14. Friends and Acquaintances	138
15. Tales From the Weighing Room	150
16. Back For Good	159
17. Epilogue	171
18. The Winners	176
Index	184

ACKNOWLEDGEMENTS

This book would not have happened without the insistence of my long-time and close friend Chris Pitt, who is also godfather to my son and reckoned that my mundane life might be of interest to other people. I was ably assisted by my new and dear friend Anna Scrase, who agreed with him.

Anna patiently listened to my random recollections as they came to mind, dutifully transcribed them, then sent them to Chris who put them into some sort of cohesive order and provided a story with a start, a middle and an end. In addition, Chris's wife, Mary Pitt, proof read the contents and provided helpful suggestions.

I would also like to thank my good friends Steve Smith Eccles, Derek Thompson and Harry Sidebottom for kindly providing the foreword and the introduction.

I am deeply indebted to many people including John Powney and Pat Moore for teaching me to ride; to Tom Robson for getting me going; and to Tom Jones for trusting me and giving me the chance to ride GOOD horses. Sadly, all four are now deceased but I will never forget and forever be grateful to them.

Happily, my closest weighing room buddies are still around. In addition to Steve's foreword, Bob Champion, John Francome and Brian Powell have each supplied a few memories for the book.

My thanks too go to David Walshaw of New Generation Publishing for their help and advice.

I was anxious not to turn what you are about to read into some sort of testimonial, but I did want certain people to contribute, not through self-interest or vainglory but so they could give their side of how it was to live with me or ride alongside me. I can only tell it as I saw it but those closest to me have their own versions and reminiscences which, I believe, need to be told to provide a balanced view. Thus, I asked my wives, former and present, my children and those aforementioned 'weighing room buddies' to share their stories and experiences. I hope this will give a fuller understanding of the life I've led, the sort of person I am and the reasons that led to some of my decisions.

As for the book's title, I chose a line from one of my favourite Kris Kristofferson songs called 'The Pilgrim, Chapter 33'. Not all of the song's lyrics reflect my roller coaster journey through life but perhaps these do:

From the rockin' of the cradle to the rollin' of the hearse,
The goin' up was worth the comin' down.

FOREWORD

By Steve Smith Eccles and Derek Thompson

I joined Harry Thomson Jones back in 1970 as an apprentice, working in the yard and aspiring to get rides and become a jockey. David Mould was first jockey at the time. I was young and ambitious and, like any jockey that really wants to make it, determined and competitive. I would say that Lady Luck has the most enormous part to play in the successful or not so successful career of jockeys. Ian came along around 1973/74, having been up north and he took his place in the yard above me, having already ridden winners. And when David Mould packed up, he became first jockey and I was second.

It is very difficult to explain to a non-racing person the relationship jockeys have with one another, as it is a unique bond within a working environment. It is such a rollercoaster ride of ups and downs. One minute you are on the crest of the wave having ridden a winner, the very next you are on the ground with broken bones and concussion. It is an extremely tough sport that is marked by rivalry yet camaraderie, and there was this knowledge amongst jockeys that while we were out there trying to beat each other and hoping to get on the best horses, we would help each other out, drive each other home or to hospital if necessary and look out for each other. You never knew when it would be your turn next. If you were to take the piss and cut people up, keep going up their inner when you shouldn't and being dangerous, you would be in big shit and would have to be punished.

Ultimately, you have to help each other out as it could be a matter of life and death out there. There would be fights in the weighing room – tempers can get high – but what went on in the weighing room tended to stay there. Obviously, some people got on better with each other than others.

So I was always on Ian's tail. He was my rival in the yard and I wanted his job. I didn't struggle with weight problems as much as he did. I was only ten to ten and a half stone naturally, but for Ian, when we had June and July off, his weight would sky rocket by a couple of stone and then come August, his torturous weight loss regime would begin.

We would travel to the races together. Bearing in mind the weather was warm then, he would be dressed in a sweat suit, the heating would be on full blast and I would be sitting beside him in my underpants. It was terrible. There were no motorways then and we would have to drive through Huntingdon and places to get out of town and we would get some very funny looks from truck drivers at traffic lights. After a two and a half hours' drive he would pull the string on his sweat suit and the sweat would literally gush out.

To take our mind off things we invented a game that involved earning points for abuse from other road users. Five points for a raised hand, ten for the finger, fifteen for a shaken fist – the most points if someone actually stopped their car to get out. I think Ian's record was 100 points before we even left Newmarket one day. How we didn't get killed I will never know. You would definitely not get away with it these days.

We did have a lot of fun and laughs along the way. We drank together – although Ian isn't a big drinker, couldn't really handle it – pulled the birds together and played lots of pranks.

The thing that finishes most jockeys off is the accumulative concussion. Apart from 23 broken bones I had seven bouts of concussion over the course of my career. That is to say, remaining completely knocked out for over 60 seconds ... and it builds up. It doesn't mean you have just taken a blow to the head either. When your body hits the ground at that speed the jarring goes right through your body and up to your brain.

After Ian had his final fall, he would sometimes ring me up at 3.00am and talk rubbish. He would ask me if I wanted to go to the cinema. He would talk about things that had happened years before as if it were yesterday. It did get quite wearing, but that could have been me, so I took the calls.

If I had to sum Ian up, I would say he is a bloody fearless lunatic. He just did not comprehend the term fear. He wouldn't refuse a ride and built up this reputation as 'Watty The Iron Man'. He would ride anything and didn't seem to know how to say no.

The silly thing is, he was getting rides on good horses and at that point most jockeys start to pick and choose a bit and leave the dodgy rides to the younger lads who are trying to get established. Not Ian, and consequently he suffered so many bad injuries that his career ended maybe sooner than it needed to, rather than him choosing to walk away on his own terms. I tried to work him out but I just couldn't. I've certainly never seen a soft side to him.

We see each other around the town every now and then and occasionally meet up for a drink. I do know that if I was in trouble and I needed help, I could ring Ian and he would be there for me.

Steve Smith Eccles
Newmarket
May 2021

I've known 'Watty' for far too many years and yet every time we bump into each other we have a laugh.

It's probably our way of dealing with getting older but even if he's in pain with a new hip or a new knee he still likes to tell me awful jokes and they are that bad they make me laugh. I even found a note on the windscreen of my parked car in Newmarket High Street recently saying it had been parked illegally and I would be prosecuted. Then, as I was swearing under my breath, I looked to the car behind and there was Watty laughing his socks off because he'd put the note on my car.

I remember him as a young apprentice up north all those years ago before he became a fully-fledged successful jockey and you can safely say the boy's done well. How you get from being a stable lad mucking out stables just outside Penrith to becoming number one jockey to one of the top stables in Newmarket cannot have been easy but he did it through determination, skill and a hell of a lot of hard work.

Watty would literally ride anything, yet somehow survived all those falls and broken bones to be able to ride Night Nurse and Sea Pigeon to victory on the same day.

At the other end of the scale, he nearly brought down Red Rum when the horse was going for his third Grand National win and also rode naked at Newmarket.

I'll let you enjoy his incredible life story put together so brilliantly by Chris Pitt and I can safely say – this book is a real winner!

Derek Thompson
Newmarket
May 2021

INTRODUCTION

By Harry Sidebottom

It is an honour to be asked to write a few words of introduction to Ian Watkinson's autobiography. Newmarket is the home of horse racing. A unique town where top jockeys have the same status as film stars or footballers in other places. And Ian Watkinson was one of the finest jump jockeys. In a career tragically cut short by injury, his record speaks for itself: two hundred and five winners, along the way partnering great horses such as Night Nurse, Sea Pigeon and Tingle Creek. The dangers they run make steeplechase riders a breed apart. None has been a finer horseman or a braver individual than Ian Watkinson, dubbed *The Iron Man* by the press, and affectionately known to some of his friends by the almost Homeric epithet of *The Bold Watty*.

This frank and often hilarious account takes the reader to the heart of racing: the cold early mornings of first lot, the endless work mucking out, grooming and schooling, the triumphs and the falls, the frequent trips to hospital, riding through the pain of broken bones, and the dark, gallows humour of men who risk death again and again in pursuit of their dreams.

Honour was not the only emotion I felt when Ian asked if I would write this introduction. There was also a keen apprehension, bordering on outright fear. Mischievous hardly covers Ian's attitude to extracting every drop of fun from life. Although his career was over by the time we met, we have been friends for more years than probably either of us can remember. In that time *The Bold Watty* has led me astray – obviously always totally against my better judgement – into innumerable scrapes and adventures. Which of those stories was he going to tell? So, it comes as a huge relief that not one of them is mentioned!

Courage and a heroic enjoyment of living are only two of the qualities that make up *The Bold Watty*. There is also a thoughtful and compassionate side to the hard man. When my father was terminally ill, we had made up a bed in his office on the ground floor overlooking the stables. Every day Ian would lead up one of his own horses from the yard and discuss its progress. It was a great kindness.

Another admirable aspect of Watty is a quite extraordinary ability to make friends, sometimes across language barriers. When Ian was buying his apartment in Torrevieja, we spent a memorable week in Spain. It was many years ago, but I still regularly get postcards from Carolina and the other girls we met in Club Los Moreras to see if I am coming back, and asking if I will bring my "dark-haired, good looking friend".

ONE

THE FALL

Wednesday, 7th March 1979 was like any other day. Nothing exceptional about it; no earth-shattering events. All in all, it was what you'd call a slow news day.

But it was different in the world of racing. Cheltenham was less than a week away, with anticipation growing by the day. And I was booked for the biggest ride of my life, on Night Nurse in the Gold Cup.

I'd stayed overnight with my good friend and fellow jockey Bob Champion, as we were planning to travel to the races together that day. It was a regular occurrence; all of us jockeys used to share transport to the races when we could.

That morning the phone rang while Bob was in the bath and he called out to me to answer it. It was Johnny Haine, probably the most stylish jockey I'd seen ride over fences before he turned his attention to training. He wanted to know if Bob was going to Towcester to ride in two days' time. I knew Bob wasn't going but I had one ride booked there and I told Johnny this. "Well now you've got three more," he said.

FRIDAY, 9th March, 1979: I set off as usual from Newmarket to Towcester and rode in a couple of early races, finishing third on the first of Johnny's and fifth on one for Bill Holden, a Newmarket trainer for whom I'd ridden many times. Next was the three-mile chase in which I was to partner a fine big horse of Johnny's called Regal Choice.

I'd never ridden him before. As we were coming up that steep Towcester hill for the final time, I can remember thinking, "This horse is a bit windy." In order to have any chance of victory, he was going to need a bit of encouragement from me to make his mind up over a fence.

I can remember giving him a clout or two going into the final open ditch. The horse never took off at the fence and gave me a bone-crushing fall.

I have no recollection of anything more from that day until June, three months later. I'd suffered a serious concussion which ultimately was to end my career.

After the fall I was transferred to Northampton General Hospital where I remained unconscious for three days. Then, at some point, my first wife Cathy – we weren't yet married at the time – took me on the train to London to Guy's Hospital, whereupon various clips and wires were attached to my skull and she was informed that my chances of becoming a vegetable for the rest of my life were acute. I was sleeping for 21 hours a day.

I was wheelchair-bound and because of the brain damage I'd suffered, I had to re-learn basic skills like brushing my teeth, shaving and using a knife and fork.

At some point between March and June they must have felt it was a good idea to take my car keys away from me. I'd made a few quid as a jockey and, a couple of years previously, I'd bought myself a Triumph Stag and had a Ford police car engine fitted in it.

Sometime in June I found the keys. Well, that was it. I was off for a spin up Windmill Hill near Exning. Unfortunately, a Mercedes was travelling equally fast towards me and we collided, ripping the sides off both cars. Amazingly, both were still drivable. I reckon the other fellow must have nicked the Merc because I never heard another word about it.

Anyway, Cathy wasn't very happy about that.

My other memory of June 1979 was when Harry Thomson Jones, the trainer by whom I was retained, summoned Steve Smith Eccles and me. We were to take Tingle Creek, by then retired, up north for the Royal Highland Show in Edinburgh to parade each day with some other famous horses.

My brain was still bruised and my balance was very poor. I could barely walk. I think I only managed to get round once so Steve did most of the leading.

We had a driver and, when the show was over, we decided to load Tingle Creek at midnight in order to get a good run home. The horse jibbed going into the horsebox so I chased him. He lashed out, I fell backwards and Steve said he missed kicking me full in the face by barely an inch. I hit my head on the ground and must have been unconscious for an hour or two because when I woke up, we were about 60 miles north of Newcastle. Steve and the driver had just loaded me into the box and set off.

So much of that time is a blur. I suffered dizzy spells, occasional double vision and loss of memory. I was told later that I used to ring Steve at three o'clock in the morning and ask him if he wanted to go to the pictures, but I simply don't recall it. However, I never for a minute doubted I'd be fit to resume riding once the new season was under way.

That summer I re-applied for my licence but it kept getting deferred. Eventually, I was passed fit following extensive tests at Guy's Hospital. Spurred on by the go-ahead, I shed a stone and a half through jogging and dieting. I also started riding out for trainers Ron Boss and Tom Jones. Pretty soon, I felt back in peak form.

It got to the beginning of August and I'd already got three booked rides for the following week at Market Rasen. I scheduled an appointment in

London with the Jockey Club's surgeon Frank D'Abreu, the man who had the final say in all matters medical.

I remember he asked me to stand in the middle of the room, close my eyes and put my index finger on the end of my nose. Try it ... I still struggle to do it now. My finger went in my eye, my cheek, anywhere but where it was supposed to go.

Frank told me that had the fall been a couple of inches one way I'd have been a goner. A couple of inches the other way and I might have escaped unscathed. The risk that another blow on the head could cause serious and permanent damage was, he reckoned, too great.

Then he looked at me and said, simply, "It's all over."

I was devastated. I'd thought it was just a matter of him signing a form to enable me to get my licence. But even if I'd disagreed with his decision, he'd instructed the Jockey Club not to grant me one.

It only took me an hour and a quarter to drive back to Newmarket. At that point I didn't care whether I killed myself or anyone else. Selfish, really. But I was so distraught I just didn't care. My career as a jockey was at an end.

TWO

GETTING STARTED

I was born in Newmarket on Saturday, 9th October, 1948, but my family had no connection with racing. My father, Eric, served in the Royal Navy and had ambitions for me to follow in his footsteps. He met my mother, Jill, after the war was over. My sister Aileen was born a year after me.

I was quite bright in primary school. I passed the eleven-plus and went to Newmarket Grammar School and ended up in the same class as Bill O'Gorman, son of the trainer 'Paddy' O'Gorman. Bill was an absolute genius at school; he had a photographic memory. When everyone else was revising, he'd be reading the Sporting Life, then he sailed through his O and A Levels, passing them all with flying colours without coming off the bit. As for me, I was useless at exams, mainly because after the age of fourteen my attention was all too easily distracted by other things.

My first recollection of an equine interest was my cousin Annie's pony. Her father, Joe Harrison, was a self-made man. He started a brick manufacturing business from a garden shed and by the mid-sixties had 300 people working for him.

I thought a lot of Uncle Joe. He used to take me and my cousin Robert water skiing at Lake Ullswater. (I wasn't a natural water skier, unlike my future weighing room colleague Bob Champion, who put on a magnificent display once in the sea on one of our summer jollies in Torquay.)

At that time there was a lot of talk in the northern press about Manchester removing a great deal of the water from Lake Ullswater to give to their residents. One of Uncle Joe's mates was a portly man, a decent water skier though, who cut an unenviable figure in a wetsuit. He sticks in my mind as one day I can remember him standing at the water's edge, unzipping his wetsuit and relieving himself into the lake, whilst exclaiming to his audience, "I hope the chairman of the Manchester council gets that cupful!"

After I'd starting riding, I didn't see Uncle Joe for many years. My last memory of him is the day I rode Night Nurse for the first time, at Ayr in the Scottish Champion Hurdle. I made the running but didn't go fast enough and came second, beaten half a length by Sea Pigeon, ridden by Jonjo O'Neill. Actually, Golden Cygnet would have beaten us both had he not fallen at the last hurdle. As I walked into the weighing room, Uncle Joe was in the doorway and he seemed so proud. I came out a minute or two later to chat to him and, sadly, that was the last time I saw him.

When I was about ten, I began working at weekends for two local trainers, Pat Moore and John Powney at Savile House. John owned the property, Pat trained there. I mucked out horses for Pat and pigs for John. They were both great people. They took the time to teach me to ride and, many years later, I would end up riding winners for both of them. Pat's son Colin was a top point-to-point rider until a nasty injury stopped him. I was twelve the first time I rode at a gallop – the horse bolted with me, but that didn't put me off. When I was thirteen I was allowed to school horses.

In 1964 Pat had a runner in the Grand National, Lizawake, to be ridden by Bobby Beasley, who'd won it three years earlier on Nicolaus Silver. On the Friday before the race, my mate Kevin Tuite, whose father was head groom to top Newmarket trainer Jack Jarvis, and I bunked off school and hitched a ride in the horsebox to Liverpool. It took all day to get there. No motorways in those days.

Kevin's parents had a lodger named Charlie Gaston, a former jockey. As an apprentice he'd won the Cambridgeshire and the Ascot Stakes. I remember he drove a Ford Corsair; it was the flashiest car in Newmarket. He had wooden blocks the size of house bricks attached to the pedals so he could reach them. He's still alive today and I occasionally see him around the town. Sometimes he remembers me, other times he doesn't.

Anyway, that Friday night a whole load of us boys, most of them older than Kevin and me, hitched a ride in the back of an empty coal lorry to the middle of Liverpool city. We couldn't get in to the Cavern Club as we were too young, only fifteen, but we loitered outside and listened to the music.

In those days you could get right up close to the Grand National fences, so on the day, Kevin and I made our way to the Chair to watch the action. As we stood there, Lizawake unseated Bobby Beasley. Then Paddy Farrell, riding a horse called Border Flight, crashed straight in to the fence giving Paddy the most horrific fall. He broke his back that day and was destined to spend the remainder of his life in a wheelchair.

Lizawake carried on loose, causing no trouble to anyone, jumping every fence perfectly and turning into the elbow going well. He even quickened going to the line and finished half a length in front of the eventual winner, Team Spirit. There's a well-known photograph showing the finish. It was a bit disappointing he didn't have a jockey on his back but he was such a grand old horse. He ended up show-jumping round a six-foot course at Wembley with top showjumper Tom Brake.

As for me, seeing the element of danger and the excitement involved sealed my destiny. I wanted to become a jump jockey.

The turning point came when I got a ride in a point-to-point at the age of sixteen. As a young teenager I always used to go to the point-to-points held at Cottenham and Moulton. The Moulton course is no longer there; it's now a private training ground for the Godolphin operation, but Cottenham is still going. In those days Bill O'Gorman and I often used to follow the Basset hounds on foot.

It was the very first meeting of 1965 at Cottenham and there was a mare called Moment Of Madness being led round by a Mrs Bailey, the Canadian wife of a lovely old fellow named Maurice Bailey. As the runners were about to leave the paddock, suddenly and without warning, 'Madness' reared up and went over backwards, breaking her jockey Philip Paxman's leg. There was the usual sort of commotion and I heard Mr Bailey muttering away as he led the horse back to the horseboxes, wondering to himself where and how he was going to run her next time.

My natural shyness deserted me momentarily and I jogged up behind him, tapped him on the shoulder and asked him, "What are you going to do now?"

"I wanted to run her next week at Moulton," he replied gloomily.

"Well, I'll ride her for you," I offered straightaway. The upshot of that was that Mr Bailey organised my licence for me and I duly lined up on the filly the following week at Moulton.

I'd been all booked in ready to follow my father into the navy. In fact, he'd already reserved a place for me at a naval training college on the Isle of Anglesey for two years ahead when I reached seventeen. But halfway round the first circuit, having jumped a few fences, I knew my naval career was over. The mare got tired and I pulled her up four fences out, but by then the writing was on the wall. Riding in races was what I wanted to do. I rode her a couple more times, once at Cottenham and the other back at Moulton. I didn't win, but it was more than enough to whet my appetite.

My parents were actually fine with my decision to go into racing rather than the Navy. Instead of going straight into stables, when I left school I joined the Newmarket Bloodstock Agency, run by Richard Galpin and his co-director Frank Dempsey. I rode out in the mornings and then headed off to work in the pedigree office. I did my best there but there was always the hankering to become a jockey. One day, Frank took me into his office and said, "Your mind isn't completely on this office work, is it? I'll tell you what: go away, break your bones, and when you've decided it's not for you, there's a job here for you."

I duly wrote the same letter to three trainers in my quest to get started as a jockey: Tom Robson, who trained at Greystoke in Penrith, Fred Winter in Lambourn, and George Owen in Cheshire. It was always going to be jumps racing for me as I was nine stone even when I was fifteen years old.

The first two replied and promised me rides, but Tom said, "If you're any good, I'll get you started. If you're not, you can go back to Newmarket."

My first point-to-point ride: Moment Of Madness at Cottenham.

Aged 15, at Branches Park, near Newmarket. I don't remember the horse's name.

That sealed it for me as I didn't see myself working as a lad for years in the hope I may get one ride. I figured if I worked hard for him, he might give me a chance. So that was it. I was going to Greystoke to work for Tom Robson.

Uncle Joe's business partner, Harold, gave me some sound advice when I left home to go up north. "Work hard while you're young, then you can enjoy your twilight years." I've never forgotten that and have passed the same advice on to my own son. Another piece of great advice I've never forgotten is something I read in a book by Phil Bull, the founder of Timeform: "Geese that lay golden eggs are never for sale." That has saved me a lot of cash over the years.

THREE

GREYSTOKE

When I arrived in Greystoke in 1966 to start work for Tom Robson, it was Grand National day. Anglo won it by twenty lengths. I'd driven all the way there from Newmarket by myself. I can remember saying goodbye to my parents. Mother was holding the tears back. Father was his usual stern, stoical self. We shook hands and his parting words were, "Just be careful what sort of girls you mix with, son."

I did take it upon myself to experiment with as many different types of girls as I could. Not at first of course, I was too shy and single-minded about becoming a jockey. I'd already realised at the age of seventeen that I'd have to make the choice between eating or riding.

Tom, who I always called 'Guvnor', was a lovely man. Strangely, the papers always referred to him as 'Tommy' but I never heard him called anything but 'Tom' or 'Guvnor'. He twice rode the winner of the Scottish Grand National: Queen's Taste in 1953, and Sham Fight, who he also trained, in 1962. He did well with horses he bought from Newmarket, Champion Hurdle winner Magic Court and Harvest Gold, who won the 1965 Ascot Stakes, among them. I'd been due to start work with him in the autumn of 1965 but, two or three days before I was due to set off up north, he was banned for six months over the running of one of his horses, Marsh King, so my start date was adjourned until March 1966 when he got his licence back.

The first person I met on arriving at Castle Stables was Eric Campbell, who was the stable jockey but still doing his two as was the custom. He viewed me with suspicion but let me look round the stables before taking me to the guvnor's house. The journey had taken me most of the day in the mini on the old A1, with frequent stops and sticking to 55 miles per hour. Over the next three years, Eric was to become a mentor to me and I don't think he would realise how big an influence he was to have been on me. Rough, tough, hard as nails, but if he said it was raining, you'd have to look out of the window to check.

The weather was rough. In the first week of April we were cut off from Penrith by snow. Raymond Titterington, the head lad, would speak to the boss on the telephone, write down his orders in a big diary and then see to it that we carried them out. Between first and second lot we'd have a coffee break and the flasks and sandwiches would come out. It must have been my landlady, Mrs Robinson, who used to make them for all the lads who lodged with her, myself included.

We'd have one Sunday off in every three and were paid £9 a week – and half of that went on paying for the digs. I worked from 7.00am to 6.00pm with only one hour off, accepting extra tasks in the afternoon. It was a hard life but it was the only way to get on.

Moving north and being away from home was a culture shock, but I kept myself to myself. Above the stables was a loft space including the racing tack room where we had our tea/coffee breaks. The tack room had a sprung wooden floor on which we'd stage occasional bouts of wrestling before we continued with the morning's work. Tom Wilson, from Ardrossan, in Scotland, didn't do very well as he was smaller than the rest of us, but he was certainly not a quitter.

The stable block at Greystoke was a beautiful old stone affair with a barn behind it and at the end of each row were bays for the hay and straw. We used to transfer bales from the barn to the bays so as not to litter the yard with straw. We'd roll them into the stables each week before cutting the wires off and placing them into some old rusty oil drums, which were known as the wire bins.

Well, on one occasion, someone had obviously been caught short and had done their business into one of these bins, much to the chagrin of the head lad, Raymond. He was so angry that he lined us all up against the wall and made us drop our pants and trousers to see if there were any rusty wire marks on the backs of our legs. He was raging about "some dirty dog having a shit in the bin."

In the fifties there was a black and white TV series about a famous Alsatian called Rin Tin Tin, who'd been a sniffer dog in the First World War. I'm not sure which wag came up with it, but forever after that incident the wire bin was known as The Bin Rin Tin Tin Shit In.

Christ, it was cold there! One part of the gallops was called Park House and Tom used to say, "Park Hoose is the coldest place in the wurreld." When it rained, it really rained and we didn't see anyone else apart from the farmhands, so no one cared what you wore. Eric used to wind thick grain sacks round his legs, secured with baler twine. Strange but waterproof.

Slowly, the weather improved. I was always watching my weight, just in case. Not exactly dieting but being very careful not to pig out. During this time I didn't have much contact with the opposite sex, apart from Friday and Saturday nights when the villages around Penrith appeared to take it in turns to hold dances. I don't remember the first few, I was extremely shy, but eventually things picked up. Even more so after I rode a winner on my first ever ride.

We had this little grey gelding called Charles Cotton. I didn't ride him much at home. Apparently, he had a small amount of ability but rarely showed it. There was a boys' race, a selling hurdle, at Hexham on 28th May 1966 – the Saturday of the Whitsun bank holiday weekend – and the boss said I could ride in it. I don't think the other lads were happy about it. I was given some real dirty jobs by Raymond during the days before the race, but I didn't care. He was due to carry 10st 13lb but my 7lb allowance would reduce that to 10st 6lb. I didn't have any trouble making the weight because I was always careful, plus working 24/7 helped.

The big day arrived and I travelled to the races over the Pennines to Hexham. My race, the Shire Selling Handicap Hurdle, was the first on the card and then I had to lead a horse up in a later race, an almost white grey called Tarquin Migol that Eric was riding. I didn't know much about him except that he was a bit odd and you didn't want to upset him. There was another lad with us too, Fred Ross, so I imagine we had other runners too.

I went into the changing room where the valet Pat Taylor, now sadly deceased, organised me. Not only did he look after me for my first professional ride, he would also look after me for the next thirteen years and for all the rides I had in between when we were at the same meeting. You could not meet a more efficient bloke, well taught by his father, Phil. He put up with a lot, as did his able assistant Arnie Robinson – not from me, I hope, because I treated them with the respect that they deserved. Arnie used to amuse us all by playing the 'castanets' with his false teeth!

I can't remember much about that first race except that Tom Robson said I should sit quiet up the short steep hill between the last two hurdles. Going into the last I was a few lengths behind Press Button B, ridden by Brian Fletcher. I felt then that 'Charlie' wasn't doing his best so I gave him a right belting and, lo and behold, he produced a turn of foot to snatch victory in the last few strides by a neck. Judging by the faded photos I have I was a bit bemused. I couldn't believe it; my first ride was a winner. I got changed and led Tarquin Migol up in the later race.

The next day, I received some advice that I've tried to live by all of my life. It was a Sunday morning and Reuben, the blacksmith, was shoeing Monday's runners for Hexham. He called me over and from underneath a horse he was shoeing, he said, "Well done, son. Be careful now who you fall out with on the way up the ladder, because you will have to look them in the eye on the way back down." Fantastic, sound advice that I have passed on to several young people including my own children. I hope I didn't let Reuben down.

He was right because racing can be, and usually is, a great leveller, as I quickly found out. Having ridden a winner on my first ride, I experienced the downside on the Monday of that same Hexham Whitsun meeting. I had my second ride in public on an odds-on shot of Tom's called Hy-Gocean in the selling hurdle. He was looking all set to win when he broke down close home and had to be put down.

After those two rides at Hexham, we had the summer break as racing in the north stopped at the end of May. I spent part of the summer working in the bar of a pub called the Queen's Head in the village of Tirril, at Lake Ullswater. The landlord, Malcolm Hunter, was a wonderful bloke.

May 28, 1966: A red letter day at Hexham. Being led in after winning my first race on Charles Cotton. (J. E. Hedley photo)

May 28, 1966: Winning on my first ride under rules on the grey Charles Cotton at Hexham, beating future three-time Grand National-winning jockey Brian Fletcher on Press Button B. (J. E. Hedley photo)

September 1966. Riding my second winner, Sundowner, at Hexham, thanks largely to Eric Campbell who impeded anything that looked like beating me! (J. E. Hedley photo)

I used to take him racing. He'd come out of the pub looking like a real country squire; big cigar, spotted bow-tie. Sadly, he died of cancer at just 38 years old.

On Sunday evenings the pub used to get swamped with university students who'd spent the day water-skiing on Lake Ullswater. They'd call in for a drink and something to eat before they drove back to Manchester. There was always a big demand for sandwiches. As well as serving the drinks and collecting the money, I also had to make the sandwiches. Malcom insisted that when I was adding the salad, I had to cut the skin off the cucumber. When I asked him why I needed to do that, he explained that it would show that I'd taken a bit of care with it. I could see what he meant.

The next National Hunt meeting wasn't until Sedgefield on 10th September. Eric rode a horse that day called Sundowner in the novice hurdle and finished third. Tom ran him again a fortnight later at Hexham and he became my second winner. I don't know why I was given the ride. I imagine Eric wasn't too pleased but he did at least make a few quid out of it. He finished second on a horse called Cosmo Walk. After the race he told me that he used the horse he was riding to bump and bore anything that looked like beating me because he'd told all his punters mine would win. Even a seventeen-year-old kid from Newmarket couldn't get it beaten with that sort of help. We won very easily by ten lengths. My mother could have won on it.

I finished second on Sundowner at Carlisle two weeks later, then next time out we were brought down at Newcastle, my first fall in a race.

I won on Charles Cotton again at Catterick in December, and then on a novice hurdler called Defender, owned by a Morpeth farmer named Charlie Brown, back at Catterick on 14th January. That earned me my first mention in the columns of the Sporting Life, with the northern correspondent Aubrey Renwick noting: "Ian Watkinson gained his fourth win on Defender. His previous success this season was also achieved here on Charles Cotton, and the other two at Hexham." Not much, I'll grant you, and almost right, but it was a start.

In the spring of 1967, I won three races on another of Tom's novice hurdlers, Champ, the first of them at Carlisle over Easter on atrocious going. They'd taken the last hurdle out because of the heavy ground. Carlisle, with that long, uphill finish, is probably the stiffest track in the country. Tom always said, "You have to go as far as you can as slow as you can, without losing touch. They'll come back to you on that hill". He was dead right. Turning for home, four and a half furlongs from the winning post, I was nearly 100 yards behind the leader and going nowhere and I thought about pulling up. Then suddenly, the field stopped dead in front of me and I went on to win easily. My mother was there that day, which made it extra special. One or two people said that I'd ridden a well-judged race. If only they knew!

I then won again on Champ at Hexham and Ayr. He was a lovely, big stamp of a horse. He certainly had the size and scope to make a chaser but I can't remember if we ever ran him over fences. Tom was adamant he was too windy to jump a fence.

April 1967: Head lad Ray Titterington leads me in after winning on Tom Robson's novice hurdler Champ, on whom I won three races in a row.

Tom restricted me to riding over hurdles for that first full season and all offers of outside rides were vetted by him. As I began to get a few more rides I felt I had to work extra hard to maintain respect in the yard. I was aware of a bit of resentment but I kept my head down and my mouth shut.

My social life picked up as I attracted the attention of some of the girls in the village of Greystoke. I was lodging by now with Ralph and Polly Banks and shared a room with a lad called Keith who slept with his boots on to save time in the morning. Eric Campbell lived in the street behind us and sometimes would walk to work with us, stopping en route to tickle a trout or two out of the stream. Totally illegal but he always swore they tasted better than bought ones.

As my rides became more frequent, I travelled to the races with Eric quite a lot. Most days I would drive home because Eric liked a drink or three with the owners after racing. One day at Catterick he drank himself into a coma perched on a barstool in the Bridge Hotel. People were walking round him on their way to and from the toilets. I wanted to go but didn't want to be berated for being a soft south country bastard, as had happened in the past. Somebody nudged him and he fell face first on to the carpet and was sick. I got him to the toilets for a clean-up then manhandled him to the car and drove him home while he slept.

He only lived a few hundred yards from my lodgings but as I parked the car and opened the door for him, he got out, marched up to his front door for his wife, Jean, to let him in and you would hardly realise he'd had a drink at all. He was made of iron ... with an enviable power of recovery!

Among the horses I used to ride for Tom at home was one named Vittorio. Prior to coming to Tom, he'd been trained by Harry Bell, who was known to be very hard on his horses. By the time he arrived with us he was very sour. He had loads of ability and he'd won quite a few for Harry Bell, but he was a bit of a specialist's ride and I wasn't allowed to ride him at first. Jack Berry used to ride him, as he had ridden him at Harry Bell's, and he ended up winning on him for Tom one day at Kelso.

Eventually I did start riding him at home, although he was still Jack's ride at the races.

One day at Haydock, Jack got hurt so Tom came to me and said, "Right, you're going to have to ride. Go into the ambulance room and see Jack and he'll tell you how to ride him."

Jack said, "You have to bring him in blind; don't let him see the hurdles. Stick him up someone's arse – he'll pick up when they do."

He was absolutely dead right. I duly shoved his head up the backside of the other runners. He couldn't see the hurdles and I couldn't see them either. But when the others picked up, so did he. The horse wasn't off that day so I finished where I was supposed to and all was well.

Vittorio was a tall horse but very fine, not a robust type. We all loved him; he was such a character. Some days he just would not go anywhere and there was nothing you could do. Tom would say, "Try taking him the other way but don't hit him." He was so good that, when he put his mind to it, he couldn't be beaten and he won all the races he was allowed to win, but I only rode him in that one race because he definitely needed knowing. I was still very young then and not first jockey. I remember one Sunday when Tom was going through the race plans for the week. He was telling us who could ride what. I happened to see Vittorio's name written there and couldn't help asking, "And Vittorio?" He looked at me. "Do you really think you're man enough to ride Vittorio?" He shook his head. He knew how to keep my feet firmly on the ground.

We had a small schooling ground, a long thin strip of ground between two dry-stone walls that was just wide enough for a row of fences and a row of hurdles. The field was part of Tom's farm and in the afternoons, my job was to take the tractor and trailer into Winfell Forest, which was near Cliburn where I lived. We had permission to cut the birch trees down right to the ground with a chainsaw. I built the fences then, using the trunks for the guard rails, put the birch into little bundles and tied them with ropes and stuffed them tightly into the rails. Then I trimmed them and by the time I'd cleared up all the mess it was time to start evening stables. Working flat out meant I never had problems with my weight then. I loved it. Great times.

One morning after exercise Tom said, "I think we will give that old bastard Vittorio a try over the fences," so a lad named Jimmy Newson and I – he was on an older horse, I was on Vittorio – showed the two horses the first fence. Vittorio looked at it and his ears went forward, then back, then forward, then back, working things out.

We rode back to the start and then cantered in to the first. The other horse jumped it. Vittorio stopped dead in front of it and I could see his eyes looking back at me as if to say, "You must be fucking joking!" Then Tom came over. "I thought he'd do that. Go on, put him back in his box." He knew there was no point getting after the horse. He still wouldn't have jumped it.

Local folklore had it that Harry Bell had a theory that if he had a doggy or recalcitrant horse, he would get it into water and apparently that would cure it. The story went that he tried it with Vittorio and the old horse climbed on top of him and nearly drowned him. I'm not sure if it's a true story but, knowing Vittorio, I can well believe it. And there's no smoke without fire.

Later in my career, I was booked to ride two of Harry Bell's one day at Kelso. The first one, a novice chaser, fell and a following horse took most of the knuckle off one of my fingers. You could see right down to the sinew. But when I told Harry I didn't think I could ride the hurdler, he said, "It's nobbut a scratch. Get weighed out." Tough bloke!

Another was a filly called Gongoozler. I rode her eight times during my first full season. What I really remember about her was her eyes. They stuck

November 1967: Future Grand National-winning jockey Maurice Barnes leads in Punion and I after winning at Wetherby. Punion was trained by Maurice's father Tommy and gave me my first four wins over fences.

out like a frog's. For a long time she suffered from an awful, snotty nose. Tom, being a vet, tried all different sorts of things without success. Eventually, they took a piece of bone out of her head the size of a half-crown. The bone had gone rotten; we had no idea what had caused it. But it solved the problem and whenever she ran afterwards, her breathing was much better. She was a pretty ordinary sort but I always thought she'd win a race. I looked like winning on her a couple of times, at Wetherby and Ayr, only to fall late on. In the end, the closest we got was fourth.

During my second full season, 1967/68, the guvnor moved stables from Greystoke to The Grange at Cliburn, between Penrith and Appleby. He also allowed me to ride over fences but only on the more experienced horses of ten years old and upwards; definitely no novices.

My first ride over fences was on an old horse named Red Rambler in a four-runner race at Ayr on 16th October for a small Scottish trainer, John McMurchie, who at the time had a good novice chaser named Devon Blue and trained him to win four in a row. Red Rambler ran okay to finish third of four but at least we completed safely.

I didn't have to wait long for my first success over fences. Just two more days, in fact, for I rode a horse named Punion, trained by Tommy Barnes, to win a selling chase at Newcastle. He was a dear little horse, always led up by Tommy's son Maurice, who would go on to win the Grand National on Rubstic.

I struck up a good partnership with Punion and won three more chases on him that season, at Wetherby, Sedgefield and Ayr. I have a picture of us being led in after one of them by Maurice.

Tommy Barnes was a small, wiry chap, an ex-jockey who trained nearby at Penrith. He'd finished second in the Grand National in 1962 on Wyndburgh and was the toughest bloke I ever met. He'd broken his back in a fall at Carlisle, yet just fourteen months later was outside in the farmyard loading fertilizer bags on to a trailer by hand.

My first four winners over fences were for him, all on Punion. The third of them, at Sedgefield on 25th November, 1967, was the last day before all racing was cancelled for six weeks as a precaution against the spread of foot and mouth disease.

One day in December, while I was working in the yard, I had a message from Tommy Barnes asking me to call him. He wanted me to go over and school a horse when I was free. I was working in the morning so by the time I got to his place was around 2.30, and at that time of year the light is fading fast. It was also freezing cold. A mate of mine, Bryan Clarke, came with me.

Tommy wanted me to school a horse called Rob Ricketts, who hadn't yet run over jumps. He was a very well-bred horse, a half-brother to that year's champion hurdler Saucy Kit. He was a year younger than Saucy Kit but, unfortunately, he didn't share a fraction of his sibling's ability.

"Ah," said Tommy, "we school in that field over there. Maurice is just warming him up for you."

Maurice rode the horse over to us and legged me up. I looked round the field that Tommy had indicated but I couldn't see anything to jump. Then Maurice reappeared, driving a tractor and trailer full of straw bales, which he proceeded to lay upright to form a schooling jump, with the wire fence used as one wing and the trailer used for the other. It was starting to snow by this time; you could just see ice forming on the grass in the dusk.

Now, Rob Ricketts was a bit free in his way of going, so we charged into the 'fence' and he slipped on landing and fell. As I rolled over, I heard Tommy shout, "Catch that horse, Maurice," before he helped me to my feet. I shook my head before they legged me back up a second time. Lo and behold, he fell again, but this time, as he got up, he put his leg out and stood on my face, breaking my nose. I could feel the blood running down my face. I also became aware of Tommy rummaging round in my pockets as I lay there. He pulled out a hanky, ripped it in half, made two balls then shoved them up my nostrils.

It was almost dark by this time but they legged me up again and this time he jumped it and stayed upright. I was feeling groggy from the second fall but, luckily, Bryan was there to drive me home as I still had to do evening stables. Whenever I see Bryan, he always reminds me of it.

Nor did the story end there. I rode Rob Ricketts later that season in a hurdle race at Ayr and we fell. The fall knocked me unconscious and put me in hospital. They kept me in overnight but, as would become usual, I discharged myself and somehow got back to Penrith by train and taxi. I know I eventually got back to the yard but I honestly couldn't remember doing it.

Racing resumed on the first weekend of January 1968 following the six-week layoff for foot and mouth. I'd got three booked rides at Teesside Park including my old friend Charles Cotton in the handicap hurdle and Bob's Brae in the novice hurdle. The going was heavy and the hurdles course was just about raceable. However, the ground on the chase course was treacherous. Furthermore, it was the first season of jump racing at Teesside – just their second meeting – and they'd made the tops of the fences too wide. They ran the novice chase, the second race on the card, and only three of the sixteen runners got round. Six of them came down at the first fence. There were loose horses everywhere.

Having witnessed the carnage, the stewards wisely decided to abandon the day's other two chases. By that time, I'd already weighed out for the third race, a valuable handicap chase sponsored by a local country club, in which I was due to ride Punion. The rules of racing stated that once a jockey had weighed out, he was entitled to his riding fee irrespective of whether the horse ran or not. On hearing the race had been abandoned, I was congratulating myself on the easiest riding fee I'd ever earn. Except that

Tommy Barnes came into the weighing room to bring the saddle back and said, "You don't have to give me back the riding fee – but if you don't, you'll never ride for me again!"

The following month I rode in a 24-runner novice hurdle at Catterick. I'd only ridden nine or ten winners by that time. During the course of the race, I got in the way of David (The Duke) Nicholson, who was riding a fancied one for Willie Stephenson. After the race he gave me a right bollocking. I must have looked visibly upset because Tom Robson came to collect a saddle from me and asked me what was wrong. I told him and he stormed along to the doorway of the jockey's changing room and tore a strip off David in front of all the jockeys for berating a young kid.

Soon after that, David started speaking to me, and when I later moved south he became a great friend. I thought a lot of him. Tall as he was, I saw him ride at 10st 4lb one day. In fact, I had a tremendous respect for David both on and off a horse, along with jockeys such as David Mould, Richard Evans, Jack Berry, Gerry Scott, Jeff King and the late and much missed Johnny Haine, Gerry Griffin, Pat McCarron and Terry Biddlecombe. They were all shining examples of how jump jockeys should ride and behave, and they were the jockeys I tried to imitate.

Gerry Scott was outstanding over fences, as was Johnny Leech. And when I first started riding for Tom Robson, he used to send me down to the last fence to watch George Milburn, who was nearing the end of his carer by then but still had it all.

Gerry Griffin was the best hurdle jockey I ever saw; he was brilliant. He rarely rode over fences but I used to have a photograph of Gerry, myself and half a dozen others jumping the first fence in a three-mile novice chase at Carlisle. Gerry is sat on the horse's neck as though he was on a good, experienced hurdler. He's sat perfectly whereas I look like a bloody farmer!

As for toughness, I remember one day at Kelso, seeing Jack Berry weighing out for a race. His nose was at an angle and blood covered his face as the result of a fall in the previous race. The clerk of the scales passed him and said, 'Righto Berry, but wash your face before you go out". I looked at Jack and I hoped that I'd be half as tough as him one day.

Once or twice at lunchtimes I saw Eric on a horse going through the village. He trained horses for two or three other people – not strictly legal but this was in the 1960s. He kept them in the cellar of an old pub just outside the village of Greystoke. I think the owners got the horses to the races and thereafter it was down to Eric.

One time he fell out with the owner of a small, weedy mare called Straight Sailing. The owner thought that he was wasting money as she hadn't shown much over hurdles. Eric knew she was going to leave so, to keep her two or three more weeks and get another riding fee, he suggested that she ran in a novice chase, at Kelso of all places. Eric told me that the owner

Early days but already having weight trouble. I'd just lost 12lb in three days to ride one for Tom Robson. No wonder I look gaunt!

agreed to the plan because there wasn't a hope in hell of her completing the course. Kelso was the only place where Freddie had fallen – and he'd twice been second in the Grand National. The owner, who felt that Eric had been conning him about the little mare, thought he'd get hurt and seemingly get his just desserts.

Eric never even showed the mare a fence before she ran in the novice chase. When I asked him about schooling her, he just said, "She'll be alright."

The day arrived. I was in the race on a big, hard-pulling grey horse that was wearing a rubber bit (I don't know why either). Eric and I cantered down and looked at the first fence together. The mare could hardly see over it and was spooking at it, understandably as it was the first fence she had ever seen. We set off in the race; I was in the front two or three for over a mile. The horse was hard to steady and was running into the bottom of the fences or just launching himself at them. I was hoping he'd fall just so I could get out of it but he completed the course. When I got back to the changing room, Eric was there and I asked him what had happened. "You wouldn't believe it," he said. "She ran out at the first fence and the owner called me a crook!" That wasn't the exact word he used but it did begin with the same letter.

In the spring of 1968, I rode a winner for Tommy Shedden, a horse called Marcello. I rode it once more after that. The next ride I had off him was a 'spare' at Wetherby on a horse called Boy Marvel. That won as well – but there was a nine-year gap between the rides!

By then I was riding a few for Peter Chesmore, who trained at Ayr. One day I rode one of his horses that was being led round by a beautiful, dark-red-haired girl named Margaret. I asked her where she lived. She said Ayr, so I badgered her to join me for dinner that night if I stayed, rather than driving back to Penrith. We had to do two circuits of the paddock before she eventually agreed, and even then I had to tell the paddock steward I needed a bit more time to adjust my irons.

The horse finished sixth or seventh. On my way back to the weighing room I was accosted by a large Glaswegian who, having listened to me trying to persuade Margaret to meet me, accused me of throwing the race away. "If you were thinking aboot the race rather than ye dick ye coulda won that," he fumed. Shocking!

Anyway, the lovely lady in question and I had a grand evening and I dropped her home at about 2.00am and got back in time to start work. We were an item for quite a while. She'd been crowned Miss Kilmarnock that year and she was the most beautiful girl I'd ever seen. I did want to marry her but I was only nineteen and far too young.

On the first day of May 1968, I rode a horse named Trespasser for Pat Moore in the last race, the 8.30, at an evening meeting at Wetherby. The horse was set to carry a massive 12st 13lb but my 5lb claim reduced it to

12st 8lb. Despite that welter burden, he was sent off the hot favourite. I was disputing the lead with two others when he fell at the last and I broke my left wrist and my nose.

I was carted off to Leeds Hospital. I remember sitting there in the casualty department, nursing my broken wrist and nose. I didn't get seen till half past eleven. Luckily, the amateur rider Jeremy Fawcett very kindly collected me from hospital, took me to his place in Wetherby and I stayed there overnight. Somehow, I don't know how, my car was there as well, so the next morning I drove back to Penrith with my left arm in a sling and a plaster across my nose.

After I got back, I hung around for a few days and then decided I felt alright to drive up to Ayr to see Margaret. I knew it was risky with an arm in a sling, driving with one hand, so I thought I'd be clever and drive through the night. I left Penrith about eleven o'clock. Just after the A74 turn-off where you go towards Ayr, you come to a place called New Cumnock, and that's where it all went wrong.

There was a group of four lads, aged about fifteen or sixteen, completely pissed, staggering about in the road, and I hit three of them before I saw them. The other saw me over his shoulder and dived into a hedge. The result was a total of four broken legs and a fractured skull; pretty horrific injuries. The impact smashed my car to pieces. A house nearby called the police and an ambulance. Luckily for me, the lad who'd dived into the hedge admitted to the police they were drunk and all over the road, which was obviously what saved me, or I could have ended up in clink. The police threatened me with prosecution but I got a letter a few weeks afterwards confirming there would be no further action.

I stayed a few days at Ayr with Margaret and her mother and sister. It was awkward for Margaret because the family was shunned when it became known that the teenage lout who had knocked down four local boys was connected with the family.

As there was no racing up north from the last week in May to September, I left her for the summer to return to Newmarket and ride out for Pat Moore, who had been instrumental in teaching me to ride in the very beginning. While there, I developed a special friendship with another beautiful girl, Kathleen.

I returned north in time for the start of the season. One day, Margaret and I were sitting by the seashore listening to Radio Luxembourg and having a bit of a kiss and cuddle when the DJ announced he had a special request for a northern-based jockey. "Oh, turn it up," said Margaret. "We may know him."

Imagine my horror when he announced that it was a special song "for Ian Watkinson from Kathleen to say thank you for the very special weeks we spent in Newmarket that summer". There was a splash. That was the ring I'd given Margaret being hurled into the sea.

Our relationship finally ended when her inquisitive younger sister made advances on me. She was a big, strong girl who overpowered me easily, and then thought it would be a good idea to confess to Margaret. A real shame, but we were very young at the time. And I still maintain that Margaret was one of the most beautiful girls I've ever seen in my life.

And there was a sequel to the car accident. About eighteen months later I was riding at Ayr. I was legged up and the lad leading me round the paddock looked up at me and said, "You don't recognise me, do you?"

"No, should I?" I replied.

"Yes," he said. "You ran me over and broke both my legs."

"Well, you look sound enough now," I responded.

As he let me go to canter down to the start, he said, "I hope you break your fucking neck!"

FOUR

GIVING UP

Prior to the start of the 1968/69 campaign, Ken Oliver, who trained at Hawick, offered me the job of riding as second jockey to Barry Brogan. Tom Robson said I should take it because he was in the process of winding down. I'd had a spare ride for Ken at Wetherby the previous season on a one-eyed hurdler named Fooasaboot, a Scottish term for being 'Brahms and Liszt'. Because I hadn't had any notice, I had to put up 12lb overweight to ride at 10st 5lb. He ran alright and finished fifth or sixth, which was a reasonable effort considering the overweight.

In October 1968 I won the Melleray's Belle Challenge Cup Chase at Ayr for Ken on Darkwood and finished second on another of his horses, Choir Boy, the same day. I only got those rides because Barry was suspended for cheating with his weight, and Darkwood was the only winner I ever rode for him.

Ken always rode out first lot and then went to his office in Hawick, because in addition to holding a trainer's licence and farming, he was also a livestock auctioneer, estate agent and heavily involved with Doncaster Bloodstock Sales. He left the supervision of the yard to his wife Rhona and their wonderful head lad, George Hogg. Barry and Rhona were, you might say, very close, and Barry used to more or less run the show. He had a very big say in the declarations. He engineered it so that all the runners went to one meeting, to make sure there was nothing he couldn't ride, so myself and another young jockey who was there, John Wilkinson, hardly got anything. We were doing all the schooling and sweeping up the yard but not getting any rides.

My main memory of being at Ken's is that he was then training Flyingbolt, who had once been rated within a pound of Arkle when they were both trained by Tom Dreaper. At Cheltenham in 1966 he'd won the Two-Mile Champion Chase by fifteen lengths, then turned out the next day and finished third in the Champion Hurdle. Next time out he won the Irish Grand National carrying 12st 7lb.

I used to ride him out virtually every day. He was on the downhill slide by then but what a fantastic machine he must have been in his prime. He was a great big strong horse who could really pull. He had a temper too – he was dangerous at both ends and uncomfortable in the middle – but I'd have given anything to have ridden him in a race.

One of the horses I looked after at Ken's was a lovely horse called Billy Bow. Barry rode him in the Ladbroke Handicap Hurdle at Newcastle in November 1968. I rode in the same race, a horse named Flatbush, trained by Peter Pittendrigh. I got knocked over at the bend past the stands, so I watched the rest of the race on my feet. Billy Bow won by a length. I was walking in behind him towards the winner's enclosure when he dropped dead in front of me. I was gutted. He was such a dear old horse and I thought the world of him. For many years thereafter, Ladbrokes sponsored a race in his memory at Newcastle, the Ladbroke Billy Bow Handicap Hurdle. Not many horses, apart from the great champions, are commemorated for so many years after their deaths.

Once or twice, Barry and I used to go from Hawick to Newcastle for a night out. I blame him for leading me astray, as he liked a glass or three. It was a shame that a combination of drink and gambling spoilt his career. He went out to Malaysia in 2001 and trained there. Then, a horse he was galloping suffered a massive heart attack, Barry went over his neck and fractured his spinal cord in two places. He's back in Ireland now. I had a day with him in July 2019 at Shannon. He can't walk very well but he's still the same bloke.

I remember one day riding out at Ken's, along with his wife Rhona among others. At the bottom of his drive the road fanned out and we'd walk around, twelve or fourteen of us in a circle, waiting for instructions. Ken was on China Cloud. The horse started messing about and then slipped over. While in the process of scrambling to its feet he put his foot right in Ken's crown jewels.

As he limped gingerly across to try and catch the horse, Rhona called out to him, "Did he stand on your leg Ken?" to which Ken muttered, "Nearly … fucking nearly!"

On another occasion riding out with Ken he told me about a day when he rode at Rothbury in the fifties. He'd ridden as an amateur before becoming a top trainer – he won the 1950 Scottish Grand National on Sanvina. He told me they raced downhill and round a bend before the last fence and up ahead of them was a river. Suddenly, his bridle fell apart and, with no steering or brakes, he found himself heading towards the aforementioned river. He bailed out and broke his collarbone. "That was careless," I remarked, to which he replied, "As I couldn't swim, I thought I'd recover a lot quicker from a broken collarbone than I would from drowning!"

I love stories about the old, long gone racecourses. Sadly, or perhaps luckily for me, Rothbury closed in 1965, just before I got started, so I never got chance to ride there.

Due to the lack of riding opportunities, I didn't stay very long at Ken's. Earlier that season I'd won the Anthony Marshall Trophy at Kelso on Altirio for Peter Pittendrigh, who trained near Bolden Colliery, in County Durham. He had quite a few horses and one or two decent ones including one called The Celestial Traveller. He persuaded me to join him as his stable jockey. I did ride a few winners for him but the whole set up was roughshod and very

March 1969: Being led in on Freddie Milburn's chaser Impeachment after winning at Sedgefield.

different to what I'd become used to. On reflection, I should have stayed where I was but hindsight is a wonderful thing.

Among Peter's horses were Tipperwood and Impeachment, owned by Freddie Milburn, who had a farm at Riding Mill, between Hexham and Newcastle. I won on both of them that season.

Tipperwood was a good little horse. I won a novice hurdle on him when he was a four-year-old, then they decided to send him chasing in the spring, which, in my opinion, was a year too soon because he was still a bit weak and unfurnished. He could fall a bit too – he broke my nose twice within six weeks – but I managed to win a late-season novice chase at Sedgefield on him. The following season, Freddie moved his horses to his farm and employed a private trainer named Peter Scott. Eventually, Tipperwood ended up with Harry Bell, for whom he won a few more races and finished second in a Scottish Grand National.

Freddie owned some decent horses which he never ran out of their class and he enjoyed a fair bit of success. However, he was universally disliked by the jockeys for his habit of blaming them for everything that went wrong, and also for his miserly nature.

One day I travelled to Catterick with Tom Robson's then stable jockey Eric Campbell as I had a ride in a hurdle in the middle of the card. When I arrived, I saw Freddie and he asked me to ride his novice chaser in the first race. He also had one in the last, a hurdle, and when I asked what his plans were for that, he replied to the effect that he would see how I fared in the first race before he made his decision. In those days, jockeys didn't need to be declared until three-quarters of an hour before the race.

Unfortunately, the horse I rode for him in the first collapsed and died of a heart attack between the second and third last fences. I pulled my tack off it and walked back to the weighing room. After my next ride I didn't get changed but sought out Freddie. "Excuse me, sir, will that horse run well in the last?"

"He should run well," Freddie replied. "Roy Edwards is riding him." That gave me my answer. I duly went and got changed.

As I went to leave, I saw Freddie coming off the course. His horse hadn't run at all well and I couldn't resist saying, "That horse didn't run too well, did it, Mr Milburn?" Freddie looked at me and, in his squeaky voice, retorted, "At least the jockey didn't kill it!"

In 1969 Weatherbys changed how they paid the jockeys. Previously, it was customary for owners to give their jockeys 10 per cent of any winnings, but it was purely discretionary. This, of course, resulted in a few jockeys not getting anything at all, or far less than was recommended. I think it was towards the end of the season, in May, that the rules changed and it became compulsory for owners to give their jockeys 7½ per cent of the winnings. A fair few owners would top it up to the previous 10 per cent. Not all would do that, mind you, but most would.

I'd ridden a winner for Freddie at Sedgefield and then, as it was the end of the season, I headed off to Calpe, in Spain, with my mates Bobby Greig and Stuart Oliver. It took us nineteen hours to get there … and about three weeks to get back!

Freddie had given me a cheque for £20 and eight shillings as my percentage. Then Weatherby's automatically deducted the 7½ per cent on top, so I ended up with 17½ per cent of the winnings. Freddie, who was well-known for being pretty careful with his money, was horrified and was going mad trying to get hold of me to get the money back.

Once I returned, I heard about this and sat down and wrote him a cheque for the £20 and eight shillings, along with an explanatory note to say thanks very much but I'd already received my 7½ per cent. Well, after that, Freddie thought the sun shone out of my backside and I rode virtually all his horses.

I remember one particular race I won for him on Tipperwood. Freddie was fairly frail by this stage, but on our return to the winner's enclosure he was beaming and said, "You've saved my life by winning today." John Leech happened to be walking past at the time on his way to the scales. He said to me afterwards, "If we jockeys had known he was that ill we'd have had a whip round to get you to stop it!"

Sadly, Freddie died shortly after that. Peter Scott had brought a horse out into the yard and Freddie was there. He said, "What are you going to do today, Peter?" Peter hopped on the horse and then Freddie just collapsed and died on the spot. Peter dragged him back to the house and, on hearing the commotion, two lads who were working in the yard came running over to see what was happening. Peter explained that poor Freddie had dropped dead and that he had just manhandled him up to the house. As I said before, Freddie was known to be careful with his money. One of the lads asked, in all seriousness, "Did you go through his pockets first?"

By now I was riding virtually all Tom Robson's horses, including his Ascot Stakes winner Harvest Gold. He'd been a decent stayer on the flat and then became a top-class hurdler, winning at Cheltenham twice. I won a chase on him at Kelso in April 1969. He wasn't very big but had a beautiful action. I have a photo of me being led out at Newcastle by Mick Clancy and the old horse is looking straight into the lens of the camera. Amazing!

Another of Tom's I won on was a mare called Pampered Queen. She was closely related to the Champion Hurdle runner-up Drumikill but nowhere near as good. She had a novice chase presented to her one evening at Hexham by horses falling in front of her. She was owned by lovely people, the Scotts, who had the most beautiful daughter, but she didn't win again.

I rode what would turn out to be my last winner for Tom on a three-year-old hurdler called Ticket o' Leave at Cartmel's 1969 August bank holiday meeting. He finished training later that year and his former head lad, Raymond Titterington, began training a handful of horses the other side of Penrith at Skelton.

I'd kept the ride on Tipperwood and rode him to win Ayr's Melleray's Belle Challenge Cup. I won twice more on him, firstly at Hexham in November and then at Catterick in January 1970. Little did I know that that Catterick victory would be my last for more than a year.

I'd ridden nine winners from 119 rides in 1968/69, eight from 127 in 1969/70. Not spectacular, I'll agree, but steady. But with Tom having retired, my main source of rides dried up. Having virtually no rides, I put on weight and I was also nursing a knee injury. With no more winners in the last four months of the season, it was a point in my life when my career wasn't going well. It felt like I was back at the bottom of the ladder and this time I couldn't even see the first rung. I became totally disillusioned.

Occasionally in my youth I'd ridden for a big farmer who held a permit. He had a top-class bloke called Alan who trained the horses for him. I'd won on one of his, Sea Romance, at Carlisle in 1968. It was the first time I'd ridden him. An amateur rider had been stopping him for two years, then they entered him in a boys' race and we won comfortably, thanks in part to my good friend the late Graham Lockerbie, who was leading going into the straight and kindly letting me in up his inner when I called to let him know I was there. Then he shut the door, making the rest go round him. On tacky ground at Carlisle, the stiffest course in the country, that was a big help to me.

Anyway, it was while I was going through this pretty grim time in my life, dispirited with everything and barely getting rides, that I was offered the mount on another of his horses at Perth in a novice chase. She was a twelve-year-old mare, the dam of three foals, but she'd then proved barren and was being trained again, poor old girl. This was to be her first run over fences. She'd jumped a few hedges at home but not a proper fence. I was desperate for rides at this stage but I realised I couldn't get anywhere near the 11st 9lb weight required so, two days before, I took laxatives, starved and just drank water then took a pee pill so I was empty. They're best taken in the morning but I knew I was travelling up with the permit holder and he'd have moaned about having to stop every half-hour to let me get out for a pee. I felt dreadful, made worse by having arrived punctually at the time he said, waiting in his kitchen/diner while he ate a full English breakfast, washed down by a gallon of tea, before we set off.

I just survived the journey without an 'accident', suffering the most awful stomach cramps, and rode her to finish way back in the field. We returned home with me wondering what to do next. I couldn't go on like this.

The farmer put that old mare back in foal and I heard from a pal in the village a couple of years later that, in search of food, the mare and her new foal broke the fence down and ended up on the road, where they were hit by a car in the early hours and both had to be put down. That broke my heart.

Not having a plan in mind, I left racing for six months and basically became a beatnik, grew my hair long and followed the trend of the time of putting flower transfers on my car. I also put on more weight. I still had a few quid in my pocket from some earlier success so I just dropped out of life. I'd get up at the crack of noon each day, go into Penrith and meet a mate for a liquid lunch and then lunch would drag into evening.

I still remember that feeling of being on the bottom rung; a Chinese takeaway consumed in my car on Christmas Day in a car park in Carlisle. Fortunate to have had a car, I suppose.

During that time I was living in Cliburn, near Penrith, lodging with a lovely old lady. I had my own room and I could get in without anyone knowing. I remember waking up one morning and coming face to face with a girl in my bed and I can honestly say I had no recollection of ever having seen her before in my life. I think I may have decided at that point to get a bit of a grip.

Decimal currency entered our lives on Monday, 15th February, 1971. The following Saturday I happened to be working as a barman in a rather nice country house hotel called Edenhall, near Penrith. The bar in the hotel was only small, with just enough room for one person serving behind it. The hotel catered for a rather distinguished clientele. It offered salmon fishing, rough shooting and the like. It also produced its own local venison from deer that grazed in the hotel grounds.

I wasn't looking forward to that Saturday evening and my fears proved true. I had to take the cost of the drinks in old money then convert it to new money and hand the change back to them in new money, and the local folk were notorious for being thrifty, so without exception every bloody customer would stare at the coins in the palm of their hand and demand an explanation. Now that is the stuff nightmares are made of.

The upside of working there was a very attractive head waitress. She'd been a beauty queen in the local pageants and this was a time when girls wore mini-skirts that resembled pelmets. I would be down in the cellar fetching bottles of wine and changing beer barrels in the mornings and she would come and stand at the top of the stairs, notepad and pen in hand, with a list of what people wanted to drink. She had the most incredible legs and I was staring up at them every day. I'm not going to name her – she was a little bit younger than me – but she did resist my advances for a few days until she succumbed, and then she became insatiable. Eventually, I left there and we both moved on.

Even though at that time I had a lovely girlfriend, Jossie – her real name was Josephine – I was still very disillusioned with life up north. Jossie was always wearing the tiniest of mini-skirts, as was the fashion back then. She wore cotton pants, dark tights over and then white knickers over the top to hold them up. I met her parents. When her Dad asked me what I did, I explained I rode racehorses. "But what do you actually do for a living?" he wondered.

Jossie was a lovely, down to earth girl, a great dancer. When we parked up outside the pub, all the lads would come over to say hello as she climbed out of my MG. I thought they were admiring my car but it transpired it was Jossie's legs they came for.

It was about 3.00am one night when a mate of mine, Fred, admitted he too was fed up with life up north, so we did a moonlit flit back to Newmarket. I did ring Jossie to let her know I wouldn't be back until about a week later. She understood, I think. I went back to see her a bit later but my heart lay back down south.

FIVE

COMING BACK

Looking to rekindle my enthusiasm for racing, I joined Peter Ransom, who trained at Wigmore, near Ludlow. It certainly rekindled my enthusiasm alright, and I also found out what hard work was. We did the horses all morning, haymaking all afternoon, then back for evening stables. Mr Ransom was a grand bloke who called a spade a spade. He was a hard task master but fair, and that helped to give me the impetus again. Chris O'Neill was working there then. Some years later, his father would train the last winner I ever rode.

I only had two dozen rides all that season, and fourteen of them fell. I didn't get badly hurt but had annoying little injuries that niggled away at me. I had a couple of rides for Mr Ransom, one of which gave me my only winner, Frontiersman, in a novice chase at Southwell on the Saturday of the Easter bank holiday weekend.

When I first moved there I lived in a B and B with a religious couple who frowned at me for laughing at the jokes on the Benny Hill Show. From there I moved in with a Welsh couple, Mr and Mrs Pugh. I remember Mrs Pugh never used an alarm clock. If she needed to get up early, she'd drink a large glass of water just before bedtime.

Chris and I used to eat our lunchtime sandwiches sitting on the floor of an old railway carriage in the corner of a field surrounded by rat holes. We used to put the crusts near the entrance then shoot the rats as they came out to dine. One day, we had a rat caught in a trap by his head and the others ate him, all of him bar his bones, head and front feet that were caught in the trap. Disgusting creatures.

I moved digs again, this time with Chris to a pub called the Aymestrey Inn, in the hamlet of Aymestrey, about a mile and a half from Wigmore. It was pretty basic; we had to make sure we wore socks to avoid getting splinters from the bare floorboards. One night Chris overdid the drink. I wasn't as pissed as him as I was driving. He'd eaten rather a lot of cashew nuts. We returned to our lodgings and when we woke up in the morning the room absolutely stank as he'd been sick all over the wall. And to make matters worse, the wall was pebble-dashed with regurgitated cashew nuts. We went off to work and, on our return, we found that we were homeless.

We managed to rent a quaint little cottage in the hills near the border of Wales, just a couple of miles from the yard. As the owner showed us round I asked him where the bathroom was and he pointed to a sink, a feed bowl and a big tray to stand in. You had to pour water over your head, soap yourself, then repeat the dousing. Rough, I know, but when you're young...

Then he said, "Follow me," at which point he led us down to the bottom of the garden to a chemical toilet with wooden walls and a tin roof. I couldn't help myself and said, "There's no lock on the door." He just looked at me and said with a completely straight face, "I wouldn't worry about that. No one has stolen a binful yet!"

We stayed there a while. Yes, it was primitive but at £1.50 a week it was great value. As we were used to filling ourselves up with alcohol most nights, weight wasn't so much of a problem for me then. Furthermore, it was hard to find the time to eat and our catering was a bit hit and miss.

Because of the liquid we consumed in the evenings, we didn't like to waste time going downstairs to have a pee. On the landing between the two bedrooms was a little window, like a small porthole, circular, about a foot across but only about two feet from the floor. We got a length of hosepipe, jammed a fuel funnel in to the end of it and draped the other end out of the window each night. The weeds below were kept well fertilised by alcoholic urine and we lost very little sleeping time.

It was a great summer. I always felt Peter Ransom should have been more successful than he was. He did everything right. Most importantly, he got a good foundation of fitness into the horses before he started cantering. We would trot them for miles every day.

Mr Ransom owned and trained a horse called Royal Emblem, who by this time was eleven years old. He'd won a few on firm ground. On the August bank holiday weekend I was booked to ride him in a three-runner two-mile chase at Warwick. He clouted the second fence hard – I actually have a picture sequence of events and it looks like he was diving down a rabbit hole before sliding along on his belly and then managing to get to his feet again. I followed the other two round for a few fences but then he fell properly later on and got loose.

For anyone not familiar with Warwick's racecourse, it's right in the centre of the town. The stables used to be way past the winning post on the bend next to the water jump – not any more, there are flats there now. Well, Royal Emblem headed off towards the town but, luckily, someone just managed to shut the gate before he escaped from the course. They caught him and handed him over to Mr Ransom, who then proceeded to flag down the ambulance in which I was getting a lift back. "Get back on him," he cried. "If you canter down to where you fell and complete, we can collect third prize money."

So I jumped on the horse, hacked back to the fence where we'd fallen, jumped the rest and completed the course to the usual derisory cheers from the crowd when that sort of thing happens. I returned to the weighing room fourteen and a half minutes after the start of the race. "You're lucky," remarked the clerk of the scales, looking at his watch. "You're only allowed fifteen minutes from post time to weigh back in." Lucky indeed, and we collected the prize money for third place.

In the autumn of that year, 1971, I returned to Newmarket and rode out for my old friend Bill O'Gorman, who was then training a mixed string, flat and jumps. His father, Paddy, a wonderful, brilliant horseman, had died and Bill took up the reins, so to speak, a little earlier than he'd intended. Bill has always been a great mate, right from when we passed our eleven-plus and ended up in the same class at grammar school.

Having had experience of the pub and hotel trade, I still fancied doing that rather than riding horses. I'd got very disillusioned with everything. I was heavy and half the horses I was riding fell. I remember saying to Bill, "You know, I've a good mind to go and become a bar worker." But he suggested that I joined him and he'd let me ride some of his in races. That was the best decision I ever made. Thanks to him, I got the racing bug again, and it's Bill who was instrumental in giving me a 'second coming'. We had a lot of fun and I managed to ride a couple of winners for him.

One of them was a four-year-old colt called Luck Of The Game in a selling hurdle at Doncaster. It was his first time in a seller. Bill was keen not to lose the horse at the auction so on the morning of the race he drained a syringe full of blood off one of his other horses and gave it to Luck Of The Game's lad, Dave Briggs, with the instruction to make sure he wore a light-coloured jacket. Dave took the syringe with him to the races. When the horse won, Dave walked out onto the course as we were pulling up and squirted blood up the horse's nose so it would blow it straight back onto his jacket. It worked a treat. When potential purchasers saw blood from the horse's nose on Dave's jacket, they were put off and he never got a bid.

Three weeks later, Bill rode the horse himself in a seller at Warwick and won that one too. He did exactly the same trick with the same result. That's how he managed to retain him. I often wonder if he ever paid for the dry-cleaning jobs on Dave's jacket.

On one occasion, in a hurdle race at Southwell, I got run out of it late on. Bill later showed me that he'd backed the horse to the tune of £25 at 33-1. This was in the early seventies, so he'd stood to win an astronomical sum of money.

Bill's mother was a great character. She was still driving quite late on in life and I recall she used to drive a Morris 1100. I remember one day in our late teens, Bill and I were riding out for his father, and there was a traffic jam on the High Street in Newmarket.

Bill was quite scathing about women drivers in general. "You know," he observed drily, "whenever there's a traffic jam, there's usually a woman in the middle of it. And whenever there's a traffic jam in Newmarket, it's usually my Mother in her 1100!"

I became a bit of a regular at the Kings Head at Dullingham, a village just outside Newmarket. They held parties there often. An extremely beautiful girl had caught not just my eye, but several lads' eyes too. Unfortunately, she happened to be married to a very tall rugby player. We knew her from riding out but she also worked as a hairdresser after first lot.

One night there was a party and this rugby player nodded at me. "Here," he said, "do us a favour, would you? Would you dance with my wife? She loves dancing but I don't dance and there's a few mates here I want to talk to." Well, I'm always happy to help people out, so I duly spent the evening dancing with Erica. It was my pleasure.

It was before the days of drink driving. After a while we all headed over to the White Horse in Exning. There were about fifteen of us – one of the lads' parents owned the pub – and it got to about 3.00 or 4.00 o'clock in the morning. Erica and I were sitting closely together at the bar. The rugby player clapped me on the shoulder. "Thanks mate, for looking after my wife. I've had a great evening," he said. Unbeknown to him, I had her phone number.

Thereafter, two or three mornings a week, instead of going to ride out she would hop through the window of my flat and we enjoyed some unbridled passion. She blew me away, actually. She was not only gorgeous; she was great company too and I was pretty smitten.

One day I met her and her husband in the High Street and he got me by the throat, warning me off. Erica told him if he didn't leave me alone, she'd leave him there and then, so he let go. It got to the stage where we began to plan to run away to Lambourn together and I happened to mention this to my good friend Brian Higgs (Higgsy) when I saw him.

He shook his head. "Don't be so fucking stupid," he said exasperatedly. "That girl will ultimately break your heart, you mark my words. Your future is here in Newmarket. You will have to start all over again in Lambourn."

I have to say here and now that Brian effectively saved my career. If he hadn't intervened, I certainly wouldn't have had a 'second coming'. I saw the error of my ways and Erica and I stopped seeing each other. I stayed in Newmarket and she went off to Lambourn with an Irishman. And she's now on husband number four in America.

In February 1972 I managed to win a three-runner novice chase at Plumpton despite remounting twice during the race. I was riding a horse called Carlton Hill for Eddie McNally, who trained near Findon. I remember that some of the fences had been rebuilt and were rock hard. Some of the jockeys went on strike and refused to ride over them, but I was going to ride either way. Both my rivals came down four or five fences from home, leaving me on my own. My horse then fell twice, the second time was at the last fence, but I remounted – which, of course, you can't do nowadays – and finished alone.

The best thing about Plumpton was the shellfish stall at the back of the stands, which was patronised by the top jockeys of the day like David Mould and Terry Biddlecombe.

I can still recall riding down south for the first time, at Sandown Park. I was sat in the corner of the weighing room, staring at all those famous jockeys: Biddlecombe, Mould, Jeff King, Johnny Haine and Paul Kelleway. Paul was holding court and the younger jockeys were complaining about the first fence in the three-mile chase, racing downhill away from the stands. Paul piped up that he'd rather jump that fence ten times than go round the bend after it once. "It's fucking deadly at speed," he observed.

I won on a couple of Pat Moore's novice chasers and finished that 1971/72 season with five winners from 85 mounts. I was still finding it an uphill struggle so I decided to try my luck in America as a work rider. I left for New York in May, arriving at Belmont Park, where I shared a room with an American guy named Jim. Breakfast at the track was fried eggs and pancakes with syrup all over them. Revolting!

I worked for Paul Mellon's trainer Elliott Burch, whose assistant at the time was John Veitch, who would go on to train that great horse Alydar. Because of my weight I could only ride slow work. I rode five or six a day, doing slow stuff at the track. My best memory of that time was seeing the great Secretariat. His trainer, Lucien Laurin, had his barn a couple of hundred yards down the road.

He was only a two-year-old at that time and I didn't see him every day but there was always a bit of buzz when he was being led up. He passed within feet of me, going out onto the track as I was coming back in. Laurin was pretty hard on him; one day he did a fantastic time for five furlongs. He was a beautiful horse and it was a privilege seeing him.

However, I didn't really enjoy Belmont and didn't stay long, only about a month. It felt just like a galloping factory and the way they treated their horses made me sick. Also, I was missing the jumps.

I went back to Newmarket. I was fat – my weight had soared to 12st 9lb. Again, the first person I went to see was Bill O'Gorman. I also started riding work for Dave Thom.

Dave was a fantastic bloke whose methods of training were what could be described as unorthodox. He was a very wiry man – he used to be in the SAS. He trained at Harraton Court Stables, over in Exning. In those days the bypass hadn't been built. When it was, they created a special tunnel so that the Exning horses could get to the Heath safely. It was an awful long walk from the yard to the gallops, particularly for two-year-olds, so the Exning horses had special permission to walk across the gallops as long as they didn't go single file and make a track. It was a huge patch of ground we crossed to the two-and-a-half-mile oval canter, and nesting in the grass were all these tiny peewits. As we rode through, they would squawk and dive bomb us.

Dave's head lad was a great girl named Linda Bush. On my first morning, the three of us were riding along in a line together. As the peewits swooped and dived at us, Linda exclaimed, "Oh, that was a close one. It was only an inch or two away from my arm!" to which Dave replied, "Well, I had one once where the wing scraped my jacket."

"Really?" asked Linda, conversationally. "They don't usually go that close."

It was an innocent remark but Dave absolutely exploded. "Are you calling me a liar, you fucking cow?" he bellowed at her.

I thought to myself, "Christ, what have I done here?" But by the time we got to edge of the canter they were conversing normally again. I couldn't help asking Linda later on if it bothered her, him raging like that, but she just shrugged and said, "No, not at all. He's always blowing his top and then it's all forgotten two minutes later."

Sadly, Linda died of cancer at a fairly young age, which I was so sorry to hear.

Dave only had a smallish string but he gave his horses individual attention and his methods worked. He'd feed them four or five times a day. If one didn't eat up he'd take the food away an hour later. I asked him about this and he said, "If your grub got taken away from you, when it was brought back again you'd make sure you ate it, wouldn't you?"

One day he was in the box with a little mare and I poked my head over the door. She put her ears flat back and roared at the door to bite me. Dave thought that was hilarious. He certainly knew how to bring the best out in them.

He could be very stubborn and he was a hard task-master He put me in charge of his pigs. Each day I'd work the horses, then in the afternoon I'd put a sweatsuit on and muck out all his pigs. In the end, I had the pigs looking cleaner than the horses. Sometimes I'd walk or jog from Newmarket to Exning. Because of that, but mainly due to the pig work, I managed to take off nearly three stone and get down so I could ride at 10st 1lb or 10st 2lb.

He had a sauna there, up in a loft, attached to his spare bedrooms. His conversions were ongoing at the time so there were no walls just baths and toilets. Even after I was no longer working there, he let me and my mate Jeff Barlow use it. Jeff didn't need to but he used to keep me company, which was good of him. We'd sweat in there then run naked down to the yard and chuck a couple of buckets of cold water over each other before going back in to sweat a bit more.

It was a lovely big yard with a short drive that led on to one of the streets in Exning. There was a large converted barn which was used for lunging, backing youngsters and so on. The doors to this were always left open, apart from the occasion when we saw Dave in his white E-type Jag roar into the barn, leap out and shut the doors behind him. Not long after, a police car arrived – the dust from Dave's tyres was still in the air.

"Have you seen a fellow in a white E-type Jag," the copper asked us, but we all shook our heads. "No officer, we haven't seen anyone."

He looked mildly perplexed but then went on his way. We didn't ask any questions and we never knew what it was all about.

I remember an occasion when we went racing up to Market Rasen, Bill O'Gorman drove the three of us. On the way back we stopped at the racing fraternity's regular watering hole called the Norman Cross, which was about an hour away from Newmarket on the A1. On the bar they had bowls of cheese and nuts and also, on this occasion, a bowl of fresh raw chopped onions. Dave ate the lot, then washed it down with a pint or two of Guinness.

There were two routes from there back to Newmarket, the main road way or a shorter but twisty bumpy road across the fens. Bill took the main road and Dave questioned him, "Why don't you go across the fens?" to which Bill replied drily, "Having just seen you eat raw onions and drink Guinness all night, I'm not risking it!"

Bill and Dave both put me up on early winners. Bill's was a horse called Strong Heart, over hurdles at Southwell. Strong Heart was a four-year-old colt. Although he'd won at Southwell, he was too high in the handicap for the type of race he had to run in. He wore blinkers as well. Bill asked me if I thought he would jump fences. I said, "Once maybe ... before he gets fed up with having his undercarriage scratched by birch."

Bill cleverly selected Nottingham for Strong Heart's debut over fences, one afternoon in December. The long run-in there in was important as I felt sure he wouldn't have been very quick over the last few fences, losing a length or two over every obstacle. That was how it turned out; slow over the fences but plenty of speed in between them to keep tabs on the leader.

Jeff King, riding one of John Edwards horses, was attempting to make all the running. I was still five lengths down at the last but got up to beat him close home. As I crossed the line, I heard – as indeed probably the entire population of the stands did – Jeff King shout, "Well done, fuck you!"

As I pulled the saddle off, Bill asked, "Would he do that again?" I told him I didn't think we'd even get him to the start again. He'd won four hurdle races and a chase but he was small. Bill never ran him over fences again and I think he found him a job as a stallion somewhere.

Bill would, of course, go on to become a top-class flat trainer, excelling with two-year-olds such as Superlative, Provideo, Brondesbury and Timeless Times, along with sprinters like Sayf El Arab, Mummy's Game and Reesh. But that was all in the future. Strong Heart was the only horse he ever ran in a chase, so he has a 100 per cent record over fences – and I was the man who rode his winner.

I rode seven winners from 136 mounts that season, then six from 75 the next. They were mostly for local Newmarket trainers such as Bill, Dave, Neville Callaghan, Bill Holden and Fiddler Goodwill.

I joined Harry Thomson (Tom) Jones at Green Lodge, The Severals, in the autumn of 1973, effectively as a stable lad. Although I still held a jockey's licence, I had no real thought of getting rides. It was a mighty stable, over sixty horses all told, a roughly fifty-fifty mix of flat and jumps. When I arrived, his jumpers included such good chasers Clever Scot, Foreman, Garnishee and French Society.

Tom had been Newmarket's youngest trainer, in his mid-twenties, when first taking out a licence in 1951. He'd served with the Royal Dragoon Guards during the war and afterwards worked as assistant trainer to Bob Featherstonhaugh at the Curragh and Sam Armstrong at Newmarket before setting up on his own, initially at Woodlands Stables. His first good horse had been a two-year-old filly named Our Betters, who he trained to win the Lowther Stakes at York in 1954. His first top-class jumper was Frenchman's Cove, winner of the King George VI Chase and the Whitbread Gold Cup in the early 1960s.

December 1972: Going to post on Bill O'Gorman's Strong Heart. This was the only occasion on which Bill ever ran a horse in a steeplechase and I was the man who rode him to win. Hence, Bill has a 100 per cent record over fences!

Tom knew I had a jockey's licence and let me school some of the horses, but I had to prove myself first. I looked after two horses and the hack, a former show-jumper called Cedric, who was just about as white as you could get.

I remember an occasion a few years later – actually it was in 1977, the year of the Queen's Silver Jubilee celebrations. The Duke of Norfolk held a big do at Arundel and Tom Jones came to me and said, "I'm going to enter in the trainers' and jockeys' show-jumping. You and I will go as a pair."

So off we went to Arundel with Cedric. Tom rode first and went round at a steady trot. He had one stop, then came out and handed the reins to me. I went round like a scalded cat and achieved a clear round. As I came out I heard Mrs Thomson Jones say, "Didn't Cedric do well?" to which Tom retorted, "So he bloody should. I schooled him, didn't I?" Funny but we still didn't win. Brough Scott won it instead.

The compulsory wearing of crash helmets didn't come into force until the late seventies and we all wore these check cloth caps with a bobble on the top. I actually still have mine. Tom would turn his round when going up the canter so the wind wouldn't get under the peak and blow it off.

March 1973: Left to right: Black Secret (Taffy Davies), Charley Winking (Derrick Scott) and me on Te Fou in the three-mile five-furlong King John Handicap Chase at Worcester. We pulled up when out of contention.

I didn't ride my first winner of the 1973/74 campaign until February, when I won a Leicester novice chase on a mare named Sammy's Girl for Rosemary Lomax. Mrs Lomax was Peter Ransom's sister and trained at Baydon, near Marlborough. They were the children of a big Lincolnshire landowner, Bill Ransom, who owned Sammy's Girl.

Richard Pitman put me in for the ride. He'd finished second on her at Huntingdon but she'd fallen next time out. He was due to ride Pendil the following week and couldn't risk taking the ride on her. She was a bit flighty but I nursed her round and she won, beating Terry Casey on Count Varano. After the race, Bill Ransom said to me "It's a good job you won. If you hadn't, I was going to put her down tonight."

I've no idea if he was joking or whether he really meant it.

The following month I won a sponsored race on TV, the Ladbroke Spot-Ball Handicap Hurdle at Market Rasen, on a horse of Bill Holden's called Anaval. He supposedly wasn't off, not in a crooked way but Bill didn't think the horse was fit enough and reckoned he'd be happy if he finished fifth or sixth, so he told the owner not to back it. Anaval was a big, nervous horse who was inclined to take a pull and do too much at home. He was obviously fitter than Bill had thought because I found myself in front after the first flight and we made the rest, holding on to win by three-quarters of a length. Halfway down the backstraight, conscious of what Bill had told the owner, I was thinking, "I'm in trouble here," but I had to make a bit of an effort, otherwise I'd have been in even bigger trouble with the stewards.

Bill was as good as he could be about it but the owner wasn't pleased at all. He thought Bill had put him away and told him in no uncertain terms that he'd be taking the horse away and putting him with another trainer. Poor Bill, within the space of half an hour he'd won a decent sponsored race and lost the horse. He was remarkably philosophical about it. "I may have lost the horse," he observed, "but at least I've still got my licence."

When Bill retired, many years later, he went to live in Spain. Before deciding to emigrate, he'd stayed a couple of times at a flat I'd bought in Torrevieja on the Mediterranean coast and had fallen in love with the place. Unfortunately, he made the mistake of selling all his property over here, so he had nowhere to stay when he used to come back twice a year for medical treatment. I'd pick him up at Stansted Airport and put him on the plane when he went back. Eventually his health deteriorated and he returned to England and lived in a care home near Yarmouth. I used to go and see him regularly. He loathed being on the downhill slide, hated being immobile after he'd led such an active life, and he was really just waiting for the end to come. That time came in May 2020. He'd made it to ninety years old so he'd had a good innings, but it was a shame that the last years of his life were so depressing for him.

May 1973: Returning on the John Webber-trained Foursquare, on whom I won two novice chases. Mrs Scott, the owner, is leading me in.

October 1973: I'm on the left on the Derek Weeden-trained Racer Jess jumping the last fence at Huntingdon. A moment later we were on the floor. Robin Griffin, wearing Jakie Astor's light blue silks, won it on Ashwell Street.

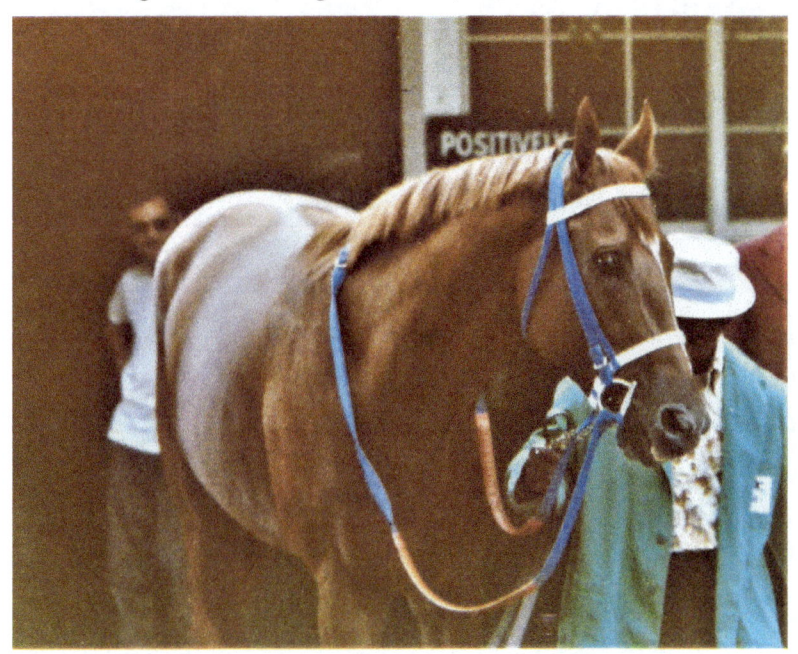

My photo of the great Secretariat at Belmont Park, New York.

SIX

RECOGNITION

October 26, 1974: The second and third legs of a treble at Huntingdon. (Top) Fiddler Goodwill's juvenile hurdler Speed Cop. (Bottom) John Webber's novice chaser Hezelestyn.

On 26th October 1974 I rode a treble at Huntingdon. I won both divisions of the three-year-old hurdle for Fiddler Goodwill on Golden Days and Speed Cop and the novice chase for John Webber on Hazelestyn. Mr Webber had two runners in the race and his son, Anthony, took the ride on the fancied one. What sticks in my mind most about that day was that I had rides in all seven races, with three of them set to carry ten stone, and I was able to do ten stone without cheating. I was 9st 8lb at the end of the day – but I didn't feel too great.

There was a piece in the race report afterwards that mentioned my weight. That was subsequently picked up by Eve Pollard of the Daily Mirror, who wrote an article entitled 'Success is the spur' about my weight reduction. It said that I'd started a diet recommended by a doctor but I'd only lost about 4lb in two weeks, so I'd followed my own diet and the pounds fell off. At the bottom of her article there was a footnote from a doctor, warning overweight people not to "try this at home" as my diet was too restrictive and would store up problems later in life.

My beautiful girlfriend of the time, Angela, was responsible for finding me a private doctor in Warwickshire, Dr Jennings, who was able to prescribe me appetite suppressing pills from 1974 until the end of my career. Apparently, Dr Jennings died shortly after my last fall. That would have been a real problem for me because I couldn't get the pills through an NHS doctor. Dr Jennings thought process was, "I'm in private practice and I can prescribe what I like." A great man; I owe him a lot.

Three weeks after my Huntingdon treble, I rode a winner for Gerry Blum at Stratford called Rapid Pass. Although Gerry trained in Newmarket, I'd never met him before bumping into him one day in Brian Scrivener's saddlery shop, just off the High Street. I didn't know him as such but I knew who he was, and he probably knew who I was, so I nodded amiably and said "Alright, Gerry."

"No, I'm not alright," he grumbled. "I've got a bloody good three-year-old hurdler whose fallen at the first three times in a row. Martin Blackshaw's ridden it twice, Graham Thorner's ridden it once, and they couldn't get it beyond the first flight. I can't understand it. And I've got no one at home who can ride him. Nobody can hold him and he keeps running off with them."

I asked him if he wanted me to have a school on him at home. Gerry hesitated. "You'd expect to ride it in a race then, wouldn't you?"

"Yes," I replied.

"Hmm, I don't know," he pondered. "I normally only use good jockeys."

In fairness, this was before I'd ridden many winners, so I wasn't as well-known then, but I was desperate for rides, so I said, "Just let me ride him the first time he runs. You don't have to use me again after that."

November 1974: On Gerry Blum's Rapid Pass after winning at 20-1 at Stratford. Gerry won a packet that day!

I went over and rode him. He was a big, strong horse by Ribero. It took me a bit of time to get him up to the schooling ground because he kept trying to run off in the wrong direction.

I met Gerry up there and he told me to pop the horse over the three small hurdles that were alongside the three fences. I jumped him over the three hurdles and he kicked two of them out of the ground. I went back to Gerry and said, "He's got no respect at all for them." He asked me to try again when the groundsman had put the hurdles back.

He did exactly the same thing to the first hurdle, clattered through it, so I switched him across and headed towards the second of the fences. I could hear Gerry screaming, "No! No!"

He jumped the fence like a bird, and the next one too. I took him back to the line of three fences and he jumped them all like a stag. When I got back to Gerry, he was livid. "You idiot," he fumed. "You don't realise how valuable that horse is!"

I replied, "He's not worth anything if he won't jump, is he?"

I rode him out again nearly every morning. He was a bloody handful. I tried all sorts of equipment on him to make him more sensible.

The race he was in at Stratford looked pretty competitive. There were some good horses in it and Rapid Pass was a 20-1 outsider. I could tell Gerry didn't want me to ride it. He was embarrassed at not being able to use a top jockey, but he'd given his word and he was a man of his word. I can't remember how the race went but he jumped beautifully and the form book assures me I won by a length and a half from a good horse called Listercombe, who went on to win at Cheltenham a few weeks later.

Gerry was beside himself, his pork pie hat at a fancy angle. Before I'd got the colours off, he came to the door of the weighing room and gave me a handful of tenners. He'd backed him, not because he thought he'd win, but he'd rather have wasted a few quid than been caught out by not backing him. He must have got plenty of 20-1, perhaps more, because he'd won about £1,000. I'm pleased to say that I kept the ride on Rapid Pass and, later that season, returned to Stratford to win the S.K.F. Hurdle For Future Champions on him.

A year later, I rode another horse of Gerry's, Track Event, in a three-year-old hurdle at Ostend in Belgium. It was a wasted trip. The horse was inexperienced and wasn't suited to their style of racing and finished last of six. It was a disappointing day. However, I did win on him next time out at Market Rasen.

Tom Jones had given me a couple of rides on bank holidays. Among the horses he'd bought that season was a hunter chaser called Fezeyot, who'd won a couple of hunter chases un the north for his Scottish owner-trainer Tom Goldie.

On the last Saturday of 1974, he had a runner in a novice chase at Newbury called Artogan, to be ridden by David Mould, the stable jockey. They finished second to a good horse of Fulke Walwyn's called Brantridge Farmer. David got off Artogan and told Tom he didn't fancy starving himself over the weekend to make the ten stone weight required for Fezeyot in the handicap chase at Leicester on the Monday. "Let Ian ride him," he said.

Tom's routine was to call you into the office every Sunday morning at 9.30 to give you your orders for the week. This particular Sunday, he said, "You can ride Fezeyot tomorrow at Leicester." The problem was that Fezeyot had ten stone dead and I weighed ten stone nine.

I went for two runs and took two laxatives and drove to the races in a sweatsuit. I went into the race having gone from 10st 7lb to 9st 12lb and felt very unwell. With my saddle I'd managed to get within a pound of the required weight, putting up a pound overweight at 10st 1lb.

It was a three-mile chase and I managed to dead-heat with Lord John Oaksey on Clonmellon. Tom Jones almost said well done to me afterwards. Lord Oaksey later sent me a photo with the inscription, "Best jockey I ever dead-heated with." Of course, I was also the ONLY jockey he ever dead-heated with!

December 1974: Me on Fezeyot leading Lord John Oaksey on Clonmellon over the last in the Broxhills Handicap Chase at Leicester. We dead-heated for first place. Lord Oaksey later inscribed the photo "To Ian - The best jockey I ever dead-heated with". Actually, I was the *only* jockey he ever dead-heated with!

Fred Flippance, the head lad, didn't like Sundays for some reason and was always in a bad mood on the sabbath. The Sunday after I'd won on Fezeyot, we'd ridden out one lot and were just sweeping up as he walked by. Someone said something and I sniggered, at which Fred turned on me. "I don't know what you're laughing at," he snarled. "You only dead-heated with a fucking amateur last week!"

Funnily enough, several years later – March 1977 to be exact – I ended up finishing second, beaten a short head, on Hardy Turk for Sam Hall in the Imperial Cup at Sandown to Acquaint, partnered by then amateur rider Nicky Henderson, now a top jumps trainer. My horse had 10st 4lb but I told the head lad I blamed him for me putting up overweight as he was late collecting my saddle from me and I didn't have time to smuggle the girths out separately. He said, "Don't tell the boss," not realising the horse would carry the extra pound anyway. I was obviously a bit above myself back at Tom's yard because Fred said it again: "Well, fancy getting beaten by a fucking amateur!"

It made no difference to Fred that Nicky Henderson and Lord Oaksey were at the time considered amongst the finest amateur riders in the country. As far as he was concerned, I'd got beaten by a "fucking amateur"!

After that Leicester dead-heat, I steadily got more rides from Tom that season, including another winning one on Fezeyot in the sponsored Mitchells & Butlers Handicap Chase at Wolverhampton in February. Having never before reached double figures in a season, I ended the 1974/75 campaign with 22 wins from 242 rides. I was on my way at last.

Back in the mid-seventies there was a craze for streaking, jumping naked over cricket stumps or running onto football pitches. So, one evening in the White Lion at Newmarket, where a whole gang of us would hang out regularly, someone jokingly said, "I wonder if anyone would dare ride a horse naked down the middle of the racecourse?"

That's when I opened my big mouth.

Thus, one very misty, early Sunday morning at around five o'clock in June 1975, having taped felt to my stirrup irons the night before, I tacked up a little filly I had, whom I'd bought for a West Midlands permit holder, Alan Rumsey, and duly headed over to the racecourse to meet my mate Tim Phillips. I'd tipped off a photographer friend who agreed to take a photo and reckoned he could get it into the Daily Mirror.

WINNING STREAK

I THOUGHT streaking was last summer's fashion, but yesterday this anonymous bareback rider thundered along the course at Newmarket (though the horse was wearing a saddle. The horseman did not display his true racing colours and the only clue to his identity is his obvious sun tan. It could have been a jockey horsing around. Or a cheeky protest about being at the bottom in the pay race by one of the Newmarket stable lads who have demonstrated for more pay. So with no visible means of support, that would explain why the rider is standing in the stirrups.

Summer 1975: My horseback streak on the Rowley Mile made the papers!

November 1975: I love this George Selwyn shot of me and Jolly's Clump at Leicester. We finished second that day, beaten five lengths by a good horse called Glanford Brigg. (George Selwyn photo)

Tim held the horse while I got my gear off. God, it was nippy for June. The dew on the grass nearly froze my feet off. I got the leg up and, apart from my hat and goggles, rode a swift canter naked past the stands and winning post on the Rowley Mile course. It duly made the papers, which caused a lot of mirth and speculation as to the identity of the 'streaker'. I don't know why but I was favourite, although Bill O Gorman and Greville Starkey were also in the betting.

I regularly went for supper with my lovely friends Captain Nick Lees and his then wife Libby. She was a very successful trainer of point-to-pointers, schooled by me and ridden by the wonderful Lucy King. Nick was clerk of the course at Leicester and Newmarket at the time.

No one mentioned the streaking incident at all, which I thought was strange, so I couldn't resist, when Nick went to do the washing-up in the kitchen, leaving his wife to entertain the guest as usual, saying to Libby, "Hey, did you hear about the galloping streaker?"

Upon which, a voice boomed from the kitchen: "Yes – and don't you ever fucking do anything like that again!"

Then we had coffee and no further mention of the incident was made. Not that night, nor ever again.

One Sunday morning before the start of the 1975/76 season, Tom called me into his office. David Mould had decided to retire and Tom wanted me to ride as his first jockey, with the exception of Zongalero, Garnishee and Tingle Creek, all of whom he felt I'd get into trouble with. Bob Davies would ride those three.

Even so, I did manage to win a couple of novice chases and an Embassy Premier Chase qualifier on Zongalero that season, although I remember turning him over at Cheltenham on one occasion when we were racing against a good mare called Grangewood Girl. Afterwards, Tom gave me a proper dressing down and told me to ride his horses more sympathetically. I deserved it too because he'd told me before about that after I'd turned over one of his, Palsboy, one day at Worcester. "You don't have to prove to me how brave you are," he'd said angrily. "These are decent horses and you don't have to ride them like some of the no-hopers you used to ride." He told me very firmly that he'd rather finish second without hurting the horse's confidence. And Tom wasn't a person to argue with.

One of my favourite horses in the yard was Sweet Joe. I won four times on him that season, including the Summit Junior Hurdle at Lingfield and the Victor Ludorum at Haydock. I'd ridden him to win on his first run at Cheltenham's October meeting, thus completing a double, having won the two-mile handicap chase on The Sundance Kid earlier that afternoon. Sweet Joe was a heavy ground horse but it was firm at Cheltenham that day. Even so, it didn't stop him bolting up by 25 lengths.

December 1975. Sweet Joe, owned by Milton Ritzenberg, was one of my favourite horses. Here we are winning the Summit Junior Hurdle at Lingfield Park

On the Wednesday before the Victor Ludorum I got a fall from a horse called Lovejoy in a novice chase in the last race at Lingfield. He wasn't a great horse but I'd won a novice chase on him at Newcastle last time out, and he was owned by a lovely man, Dick Rykens.

Lovejoy was a bit lethargic going towards the second fence so I gave him a couple of 'liveners'. He picked up okay but then fell at the fourth, fracturing my left arm. Back in the ambulance room I was being fussed over by the nurse when I heard the door open and Mr Rykens asked how I was. Another nurse told him and I heard him say, "Oh dear." The door opened again and I heard Mr Thomson Jones this time, saying, "Come on Dick, or we'll get caught in the traffic." Mr Rykens told him I'd broken my arm, to which Tom replied, "He'll be okay, he's got another one. Come on Dick!"

I was a bit concerned because of being due to ride Sweet Joe in the Victor Ludorum three days later on the Saturday. However, I rode out on the Friday morning and then managed to win on Sweet Joe with my arm still in plaster. We beat one of David Morley's good horses, Valmony, on fast ground.

I'd won on Sweet Joe a fortnight earlier on soft ground at Newcastle, beating another of David Morley's good horses, Havanus. That was the same day I'd won the novice chase on Lovejoy, so Mr Rykens was there. He told me later that he, David Morley and Tom Jones had travelled home on the train together from Newcastle. He observed that Messrs Rykens and

Thomson Jones were in very bubbly form but Mr Morley was not particularly good company!

Mr Rykens was a very wealthy managing director of some firm or another and he always drove a leased fleet car. He had a Triumph Stag, a beautiful car and, when its lease ran out, he offered it to me for peanuts. I almost took his arm off. I took it to Coventry and put a Ford police car engine in it. It had overdrive on third and fourth gears which meant that it effectively had six gears.

I always had sporty cars. Five MGs, a red Triumph Spitfire – they were usually soft top so I could put the hood down and impress the girls. I used to joke that one side had a seat belt and the passenger side had wrist and ankle straps. Wishful thinking; I'm not like that!

The Sundance Kid belonged to the well-known American owner George Strawbridge. He was a big, handsome, almost black horse, but he barely got two miles. You had to hold him up. If you got him racing too early, he'd do too much and not get home. But he had a helluva lot of speed. I'd ridden him against Tingle Creek in a gallop at least once and he was a lot better at home. If Tingle Creek had galloped like him, in my opinion he would never have been beaten. But Sundance Kid or not, no horse alive could jump like Tingle Creek.

As mentioned, I won on The Sundance Kid at Cheltenham the same day I rode Sweet Joe to win first time out. Later that season I rode him at the Festival in the Grand Annual Chase. The Cheltenham Festival was always a bit of a graveyard for me; I was always either injured and missing fancied rides or things went wrong. On this occasion I was lying second or third, having crept up and joined in just behind the leaders going to the last. I knew I had them covered, but then we fell at the last fence. I won a race at Wetherby on him the following month but it was scant consolation.

I went up to Newcastle one day to ride The Sundance Kid and a big nervous hard-pulling horse called Lewacre, who had tons of ability. I'd won on Lewacre on his previous start at Cheltenham but this time he ran appallingly. He pulled so hard he just didn't get home and we finished tailed off. I thought, "Well, the day can't get any worse." I was wrong.

Mindful of the fact that The Sundance Kid would barely get the trip, I held him up, but ended up sitting a lot further back than I wanted to, and when the moment came to push the button, he wouldn't go. He just would not increase his speed in my hands. In the event, we finished third, but he'd been well-backed and I was booed by the waiting crowd when we went back to the unsaddling enclosure. I felt awful, and to cap it all, Mr Thomson Jones gave me a piece of his mind.

A lad named Noddy Cox looked after Sundance Kid. He was a great lad, but I remember one occasion at evening stables in about 1973 or '74. The usual protocol was that you would square up your bed until the litter was in a complete square, lay your tools out along with two carrots and wait for the guvnor to come along with Fred Flippance, the head lad, to inspect them. You'd be standing your horse up, rugs off. Mr Thomson Jones would always take one carrot and give it to the horse, give the other to the lad (to feed the horse, not eat it himself!) then proceed to feel the horse's legs, ribs, sometimes its back, before waving the horse over and doing the same procedure the other side. Then, if he wanted to change anything, feed, work or whatever, he'd tell Fred, who carried a notebook and wrote it all down.

Sometimes the guvnor would be away racing, so Fred would do the evening walkabout. He'd very seldom move the horse over to look at the other side. We all came to know this but it was unfortunate for Noddy, who one evening didn't realise the guvnor had come back early and had joined Fred on his walkabout. When the crucial moment came and the guvnor waved Noddy's horse over with his stick, imagine the shame when it was discovered he'd only groomed one side of the horse. There was dust on him and a girth mark. The guvnor was furious and kept Noddy there until quarter to eight that evening doing odd jobs. Another night in similar circumstances, Noddy was caught sitting on the straw eating the carrots!

Another favourite of mine was Hardier. He was a bit strange. He lived in a stable that had carpet on the walls because he used to chuck himself about a bit. He'd been transferred by his owner, Chester Beatty, to Tom Jones. Chester was the father of Tom's second wife – he gave her a diamond mine in South Africa for a wedding present.

Tom had entered Hardier in a two-mile handicap hurdle at Market Rasen. On the Sunday morning before the race, I went to see him as usual to get the plans for the week. He rarely changed his plans and said, "We'll run. I know the course is a bit sharp but we'll find out something about him."

Injuries are, of course, part and parcel of being a jump jockey. I had a fall in a race at Doncaster four days before Market Rasen. The horse slid across my foot and broke a bone in it but I felt I was still able to carry on riding.

The weighing room at Market Rasen is quite a long walk from the paddock, but Con Byrne, the travelling head lad, suggested that he would meet me before each race, including the rides I had for other trainers, and offer his shoulder for me to lean on to aid my walk to the paddock. He was a lovely man.

Sarah, Mrs Thomson Jones the second, was asked about the chances of the yard's horses that day to which she replied drily, "I don't hold out much hope. Our jockey only has one leg."

Well, fast forward to the race. We were coming to the last couple of hurdles and Hardier started to hang left-handed, so I pulled my stick through and then he hung badly right. I pulled the stick through again; he hung left again, and so this continued all the way to the line. We won by a neck and, as I pulled up, I thought to myself, "Wow, I didn't think I could ride like that. I reckon the boss will be pleased."

As I slid gingerly to the ground, Mr Thomson Jones, after smiling and exchanging pleasantries with the owners, turned to me and said, "If you'd dropped your stick at the last, you'd have won that by four lengths, you c...!"

I recall another occasion on which I incurred the guvnor's wrath. It was the only time I rode in Ireland, on Adam's Well in a handicap hurdle at Punchestown. During the race I was surrounded by Irish jockeys who proceeded to carve me up so I couldn't get out. Said Tom after the race, "It's a long way to come to watch you make an arse of yourself!"

Hardier was sent chasing the following season. He jumped fences well. He was a big horse with plenty of spring. I won a couple of fairly big races on him: the November Novices' Chase at Sandown and the Hurst Park Chase at Ascot. But he was a bolter; you just had to let him do his own thing and not upset him – and the slightest thing could and would upset him.

The Ascot race was a two-runner affair over two miles. The other horse was trained by Bill Marshall and ridden by Steve Jobar. We set off and I went straight to the front. At the first fence I heard a crash behind me as Steve's made a mistake. Same thing at the second fence. We went past the stands and turned out into the country. At the first fence down the back I heard an even worse crash, glanced over my shoulder and saw that they'd fallen.

I thought at that point then that I'd just settle Hardier into a canter and pop him round in his own time. Unfortunately, at Ascot the road carrying the car with the roving TV camera on its roof comes very close on the bend and it suddenly loomed up behind me. Hardier shit himself and took off. I was turning round shouting "Fuck off!" at the driver in a vain attempt to get him to back off but I don't think he could lip read. The faster Hardier went, the faster the car went, right up our backside. But we managed to stay upright and went on to finish alone. I looked at the time later and we were only eight seconds off the track record.

I rode into the paddock and Mr Thomson Jones said, as he always did when we won, "Alright Ian," then continued, "Why the fucking hell did you go so fast, you idiot? Didn't you realise the other horse had fallen?"

I tried to explain about Hardier being frightened by the car coming up behind him but he was having none of it. "Go and tell your fairy stories to the fairies," he thundered. "They might believe you!"

Even the other jockeys in the changing room questioned me. "Why did you go so fast?" Then one of the senior jockeys told me that no one was bothering to watch a one-horse race on the closed-circuit TV in the changing room until someone shouted, "Look! Watty's getting fucked off with!" It made their day because sometimes I would be asked to ride some of the stronger horses just because I happened to be that bit stronger. A few of the lads back at home at the yard had realised what had happened. One of them said to me the next day, "That car didn't help you much, did it?"

There's a circular canter on the Links, about a mile and a quarter round, that we used to canter steadily around. It was the old National Hunt course – racing ceased there in 1905. They used to race left-handed but we cantered right-handed round it.

Tim, Mr Thomson Jones' son, was riding Hardier one day. He was towards the back and we were all cantering round steadily, well-spaced apart. I think I was on Tingle Creek. We started to pull up and then, suddenly, came Hardier and Tim, really tanking along. They went round a couple more times before Tim managed to pull him up and turn him round. Tim was a bit angry and gave Hardier a bit of a jerk in the mouth, which caused the horse to take off again, flat out the opposite way.

By the time he eventually got back to us, the horse had broken two blood vessels. Tim was embarrassed and Tom looked like he was about to explode, but he managed through clenched teeth to acidly say, "Thank you, Tim. You've just done a fortnight's work in five minutes!"

After the horse was eventually put down, they performed a post mortem on him and he was found to have a large tumour on his brain. Poor old horse. No wonder he was a bit odd.

I rode a few winners that season for Rex Carter, a well-respected man who trained a dozen horses at his farm near Fakenham. Des Briscoe was his regular jockey and always spoke very highly of him. I'd known of Rex for several years but never ridden for him until he asked me to ride one or two, as Des didn't ride over fences. I won a race on Redbin for him at Nottingham. Redbin was a lovely horse, a superb ride, so well-mannered, just the sort of horse you would expect somebody like Rex Carter to have.

I won a couple of selling hurdles on another of his horses, Summer Serenade, who was really far better than selling class but won when the money was down. She was one of three horses owned by George Tufts, a grand bloke, a working man done well. He'd initially had his horses with Fiddler Goodwill at Newmarket, then sent them to Rex Carter but I continued to ride them.

I'd ridden Summer Serenade for Fiddler at Nottingham one day and finished fourth. I'd disputed the lead at the last but got run out of it on the flat. Talk about Fiddler on the Roof; Fiddler *hit* the roof. "What the bloody hell were you doing finishing fourth? You've shown the horse up and you've done the owner's each-way money," he raged. But what could I have done, hoicked it back to finish ninth or tenth and risked losing my licence?

Even so, I thought the world of Fiddler, he was such a character. When he put a saddle on a horse, it rarely moved because, as he used to say, "I put it where it's doing to finish". A lot of trainers, Tom Jones included, used to put the saddle too far forward on the withers. By the time you'd done a circuit of the paddock, the saddle had slipped back to where it was going to settle, so the girths were a bit loose. Once or twice, Tom used to moan at me for tightening the girths when I got on. I didn't like to say anything because I felt it would have been wrong to criticize his saddling.

I often used to drive Fiddler to the races. One strange thing about him was that, when we were going uphill on a section of dual carriageway and I wanted to overtake the vehicle on the inside lane, Fiddler would always tell me not to overtake on a hill because there might be something coming the other way. When I explained it was a dual carriageway, he replied that there might be someone old or drunk driving on the wrong side of the road. Another curious thing was that he always thought it lucky if you passed under a railway bridge at the same time that a train was going over the top. "Oh great," he used to say, "we'll have a winner today!"

Legend had it that ordnance survey maps of Newmarket contained a spot where Fiddler used to park his bike by the Conservative Club every lunchtime when he wasn't racing.

His daughter, Linda, was one of the best riders when women were first allowed to take part in races in the early1970s. She was leading lady rider in 1973, thanks to a horse named Pee Mai, owned by Chris Barber-Lomax. She won four races on him that year including the Ladies' Derby at Ripon, which in those days was run on the same day as the Derby itself. Pee Mai used to take off with her, belt off in front and the others couldn't catch them.

I made the perfect start to 1976 by winning the four-mile Bass Handicap Chase at Cheltenham on New Year's Day aboard a lovely horse called Jolly's Clump, an out and out stayer.

I was due to ride him in the Brooke Bond Oxo National at Warwick later that month but I had a fall at Market Rasen three days beforehand and broke my collarbone. I was slightly gutted because I knew the horse had a great chance, but I reasoned that if there was any horse I could ride over fences with one hand, it was him. I rang the guvnor and told him I felt I would be fit to ride. He said, "Okay, well I want to see you ride him out first on Friday and I'll make my decision then."

The important thing to remember with collarbones is that you have to be quiet and not move them too much. The head lad, Fred Flippance, didn't leg me up that morning, he actually lifted me into the saddle. Anyway, I rode him out and cantered past the guvnor with no problems and he said, "Okay, you can ride him."

I arranged to see a surgeon at Bury St Edmunds Hospital on the Saturday morning so that he could give me an injection into the collarbone. His name was John Bracegirdle and he was a great bloke. I asked Neale Doughty, who was with Bill Marshall then before moving north to ride for Gordon Richards, if he'd drive me there and also to the racecourse in my MG, in

January 1976: Jumping the last fence on Jolly's Clump (far side) alongside Bryan Smart on Gylippus prior to winning the Brooke Bond Oxo National at Warwick, despite the minor inconvenience of a broken collarbone.

January 1976: Tom Jones and I with the sponsor's representative after the 1976 Oxo National. In the background, though I didn't realise at the time, is Angela, a beautiful girl inside and out, who was to lose her life in a car crash.

April 1976: Jumping the Chair (right) on Jolly's Clump in the 1976 Grand National.

order that I could keep as still as possible. I have to say, it was a good thing I had an empty stomach that day because Neale took quite a few chances!

We arrived at Warwick about half an hour before the race and I got changed into my colours. Jolly's Clump was a real honest gent of a horse. Unfortunately, he stumbled slightly on the way to the start and pulled my collarbone out again, even though John had strapped me up well. Because I'd had the pain killers injected it didn't really hurt that much. I took my time with him and took it up going to the last. Up until then, Bryan Smart, who rode the second, Gylippus, thought he was home and hosed.

The pictures of the presentation – they presented me with a whip, which I've still got – show me with one shoulder about six inches lower than the other. I didn't look particularly well. I heard quite a while later from Libby Heath, the great point-to-point trainer, that John Bracegirdle and his lovely daughter Tanya were so pleased to hear that we'd won the race that day.

A sad and slightly spooky postscript to that story was that I'd been seeing a lovely girl named Angela. I'd known her since she was a little girl – her older brother went out with my sister. She came and lived with me when she was seventeen and she worked in racing for Fiddler Goodwill, a trainer I rode for. I think her parents approved, but when they moved away to Warwickshire they took her with them and, as usual for those times, with no mobile phones, we just lost touch and drifted apart. Then one night her brother rang me to tell me she had been killed in a car crash.

Forty-five years later I was sent a photograph of me at the presentation of the prize for winning the Oxo National, one that I hadn't seen before. There in the background ... was Angela. I hadn't known she was there that day. What grieves me is that not only did I not get the chance to say hello to her, I didn't get the chance to say goodbye either. I was in an awful lot of pain and Neale thought it best we got away as soon as possible, so we left the course fairly shortly after the race.

She was a beautiful girl, inside and out.

I rode Jolly's Clump in that year's Grand National, my first ride in the race. He didn't have great legs and there was even a doubt about him taking part, but the owners had flown over from America. In the race, he didn't feel his normal self and he was feeling his legs from a long way out. I should really have pulled him up but I kept going because the owners were there and we eventually got round in thirteenth place.

In November 1976 I was offered the ride on Zeta's Son in the Hennessy Gold Cup at Newbury. I got a call from Peter Bailey eight days before the race. He told me Ron Barry had recommended me for the horse as he thought my style would suit him. This would be my first ever ride for him.

I travelled over to the yard at Childrey, near Wantage on the Wednesday to ride a bit of work on the horse. Old Bill Denson, the head lad there, rode upsides me on Strombolus. As we pulled up, Bill called over to me and said, "That horse will go well for you. Not many people ride him on a long rein." To be honest, I just rode him as I found him.

November 1976: On Zeta's Son, winner of the Hennessy Gold Cup at Newbury. My highest profile winner. It was the only time I rode him in a race.

The weekend coincided with the Colonial Cup International Chase in America. Peter had a runner in that, The Bo-Weevil, so he went there rather than Newbury. So too did Michael Buckley, Zeta's Son's owner, who also had a part share in Grand Canyon, trained by Derek Kent, who was entered in the Colonial Cup. My horse wasn't all that fancied. Peter's beautiful stepdaughter, Caroline, represented him at Newbury that day.

When the race started, Peter Haynes set off at a blistering pace on Le Robstan. Almost all the others belted after him but I knew the horse well and knew he wouldn't be able to keep up that gallop. I bided my time, then began to make headway once we reached the straight. Tamalin, with Jonjo O Neill on board, was in front between the last two fences, but I picked him up at the last and won by a couple of lengths. It was the biggest win of my career. Michael Buckley also enjoyed a day to remember, because Grand Canyon won the Colonial Cup.

Funnily enough, it was the only time I rode Zeta's Son. I was offered the ride another day and for some reason was unable to take it, I was also offered the ride on him in the 1977 Grand National but I'd already committed to Sage Merlin. In the event, both horses fell that day. Sadly, Zeta's Son's fall was a fatal one.

Towards the end of 1976 Tom had bought a horse called John Cherry to go hurdling for one of his big owners, Milton Ritzenberg. His colours of green and black checks are among my favourite. It was a very expensive purchase for a hurdler in those days, £29,000, a fact that made it into the papers. He'd won that year's Cesarewitch, ridden by Lester Piggott. He wasn't a big horse, under sixteen hands and light chestnut in colour. I can imagine Tom felt under a bit of pressure for the horse to be successful.

He was five, coming on six by the time we got him and had already developed a sense of cunning. I remember one morning when we were schooling. The usual routine was to canter over the first schooling hurdle several times in a circle behind the lead horse before heading down to come up over the three.

Well, we did that and then coming into the first in the line of three, the horse stopped. Bear in mind Tom did not like you to give the horse any encouragement when it came to schooling. In his view there would come a point in a race when they would have to be able to sort themselves out.

He was furious that the horse stopped. "Don't let it do that again," he shouted. So off we went and I re-presented him at the first hurdle, upon which the horse stopped again and I fell off. I landed on my feet on the other side of the hurdle and called out to Tom, "Can I give it a kick now?" That caused him to throw his hat on the floor and shout at me, "You can fuck off. You're neither use nor ornament!"

Wearing Milton Ritzenberg's green and black checked silks.
They were among my favourite colours

Later on that morning, after I'd returned home to get ready to go racing, I rang the office. I'd been offered a ride on a horse on the Saturday and I wanted to check with the guvnor that it would be okay to accept it. "Yes, yes, that's fine," he replied amicably before going on to observe, "That old horse made you look a right c... today, didn't he?"

I did win a couple on John Cherry. His first race for us was in a conditions race at Haydock. Tom did really well to find it. Because of the horse's age he would have been lumbered with a huge weight in a novice hurdle, 11st 12lb, and he was only a small horse. The conditions race was over two miles off a weight of 10st 9lb. Because the horse had won over two and a quarter miles on the flat, people felt he might not be fast enough to win a two-mile hurdle race. Even so, he started a warm odds-on favourite. His main rival was a horse called Blue Chrome, ridden by Martin Blackshaw, a lovely man who trained successfully in France after he finished riding. Sadly, he was killed in a car crash there.

John Cherry absolutely flattened the fourth last hurdle, but we turned into the straight cantering. I was tracking Blue Chrome and between the second last and the last hurdle I drew alongside Martin, who looked across at me and said, "Fuck off!" I duly did and won the race easily by ten lengths without ever coming off the bit.

I won on him again next time out at Kempton's Christmas meeting. Half an hour later I rode Strombolus for Peter Bailey in the Christmas Hurdle, finishing behind Dramatist, Night Nurse and Birds Best. Talk about a high-class race. Next on the card was the King George VI Chase, won by Royal Marshal II. I finished fifth of the ten runners on Canadius, trained by Peter Easterby.

In January 1977 I won the Embassy Handicap Hurdle at Haydock on Sea Pigeon for Peter Easterby, of which, more later. That same month I rode a horse named Lowndes Square to win at Leicester for permit holder Michael Banks. It was only a minor race but it meant a lot to me personally because I was righting a wrong from five years earlier. I'd ridden Tutor's Best for Michael's father, Sidney Banks, at Huntingdon and I rode al ill-judged race. I was going through a bad patch and, being over-anxious, went to the front far too soon. I found out later that Mr Banks had sworn he'd never use me again. Lowndes Square was my first ride for the family since then, so I was genuinely pleased for them to be able to atone for having messed up on Tutor's Best. Incidentally, Sidney Banks is still commemorated today by way of a novice hurdle race run in his name at Huntingdon.

In March I won Haydock's Greenall Whitley Chase on General Moselle for Harry Wharton. I followed up on him in the valuable Wetherby Handicap Chase on Easter Monday. I felt like I'd finally reached the top table. And by then I'd won half dozen times on Tingle Creek.

SEVEN

TINGLE CREEK

Tingle Creek had been a top steeplechaser in America prior to joining Tom Jones in 1972. His chase victories there included the Broad Hollow at Belmont Park, the Indian River and the Tom Roby, both at Delaware Park, and the Noel Laing Handicap at Montpelier, Virginia.

I rode him almost every day at home but I never schooled him over a fence. Tom said of schooling him, "He knows more about jumping than you'll ever know." I know what he meant. He was a nightmare but he knew everything. So, when I rode him for the first time in a race, finishing fourth in the Benson and Hedges Chase at Sandown in November 1975, it was the first time I'd jumped anything with him.

December 1975: The first of my seven wins on Tingle Creek, the Castleford Chase at Wetherby. Ken Bright's photo brilliantly captures his amazing scope. (Ken Bright photo)

January 1976: Photographer George Selwyn stood on the roof of a workman's hut to get this great photo of Tingle Creek jumping the Pond Fence at Sandown. (George Selwyn photo)

May 1976. Tingle Creek and I taking the open ditch at Nottingham on the way to winning the Colwick Hall Handicap Chase, conceding two and a half stone to his rivals.

He used to get wound up anyway but Tom would deliberately wind him up the day before a race so that he would get to the races and just bolt. The only choice you had with Tingle Creek was which direction you went in; you didn't have an awful lot of choice about the speed. I used to give the starter's assistant, old Albert Jenkins, a couple of quid to just tickle Tingle Creek's back legs with his long whip, to make sure he went steaming off.

He didn't really jump the fences as other horses did. He'd gallop over them, literally run over the top of them. He was extremely clever and could fiddle a fence if he needed to. But when he stood off, he stood off miles. He was something else. Steve Smith Eccles once said of him, "He goes long, very long – and fucking hell!"

David Mould has often said to me, "Those two-mile chasers, they all get forgotten." People forget just how great a horse he was. Nothing could touch him on good or firm ground. He was unbeatable and ran like an out-of-control car.

His eyesight was fantastic. I remember one summer night, following evening stables, Tom Jones would have his horses out on the Severals, having a pick of grass. He'd wander round from horse to horse and then we'd take them back in. This one time, Tingle Creek was munching grass when, all of a sudden, he stopped and stood there like a statue, like he was made of cement. He was watching a fly walk along a piece of grass. That's how good his eyesight was.

Following that first ride on him at Sandown, where he finished fourth, I was reunited with him at Wetherby on Boxing Day in the Castleford Chase, in which we made all and won by ten lengths, giving a stone and a half or more to the opposition. Two weeks later, we won the Express Chase at Sandown, again giving weight all round, beating the future dual Two-Mile Champion Chase winner Skymas by five lengths.

But for all his class, he just didn't act at Cheltenham. I rode him in the 1976 Two-Mile Champion Chase when the ground was firm, which appeared ideal. We led to the top of the hill, but when we got there you could see half of Gloucestershire in front of you and it was like he sighed and just ran flat from thereon. He didn't really get a yard over two miles and perhaps the uphill finish didn't play to his strengths. We finished fourth behind Skymas, the horse he'd beaten easily when conceding weight at Sandown.

We ended that season winning three minor handicap chases, beating sole rival Number Engaged by a distance at Towcester on Easter Monday; winning by eight lengths at Wetherby when giving two and a half stone to our four rivals; then by ten lengths at Nottingham, again conceding two and a half stone all round.

We kicked off the following season, 1976/77, by winning the Virginia Gold Cup Chase at Stratford, as usual giving two and a half stone to the others. Our next target was the Harrison Construction Chase at Worcester, which he'd won unchallenged the previous year in the hands of Bob Davies.

He was odds-on to win the race again but we were collared on the run-in by Brian Ellison's mount Tex, to whom Tingle Creek was conceding no less than 40lbs, taking into account Brian's 5lb claim. Tex was a good horse in his own class. Tingle Creek stood off too far at the fence at the end of the back straight, losing a lot of momentum at a vital stage, enabling Tex to take advantage of the huge weight concession. Tingle Creek jumped the last really well, whereas Tex was flustered, but on the run-in the weight began to tell.

Trying to concede a stone and a half to a couple of good horses in Spanish Tan and Early Spring proved beyond him in his next two races at Sandown and Kempton.

About ten days before the 1977 Cheltenham Festival, Tom asked me if I thought I could hold Tingle Creek up in a race. I told him that if there was one place it might be possible, then it was Cheltenham. But we never got the chance to try. I had two booked rides: John Cherry in the first race of the meeting, the Sun Alliance Novices' Hurdle, and Tingle Creek in the Champion Chase. The going that year was soft bordering on heavy. It poured with rain. Poor John Cherry got stuck in the mud and ran an awful race. Tom wisely then took Tingle Creek out of the Champion Chase.

The last couple of races I rode him in, he wasn't quite as exuberant as he'd been in his prime. He was eleven years old by then and maybe age was beginning to catch up with him.

The final time I rode him in a race was in a handicap chase at Fontwell Park on 19th September 1977. The meeting had been transferred there from Plumpton. By then he'd long been pretty much public property and there was a big crowd there. His presence had brought extra people through the turnstiles, just to see the great Tingle Creek.

As usual, he was conceding lumps of weight all round. There were four runners, one of whom was ridden by the lady rider Nicky Ledger, who I knew very well. However, it appeared she didn't know Tingle Creek so well and evidently wasn't familiar with his style of running, as down at the gate she asked me what my plan was for the race. I told her I'd bowl along.

She said, "I'll probably be in front of you early but please don't chase me."

I replied, "If you're within twenty lengths of me by the third fence, I'll buy that horse!"

Due to the figure-of-eight configuration of the Fontwell chase course, Tingle Creek couldn't see a fence initially, so he wasn't as fast off the mark as usual. I could imagine the other riders thinking that he was past his best and not the horse of old. But when he took the bend and saw the line of four fences, he just took off. He went from five lengths clear to a fence clear, made all and won unchallenged by twenty lengths.

Speaking of lady riders, I do remember one occasion when I was cantering down to the start at Huntingdon and I happened to be following a

September 1976: Tingle Creek's owner Mrs Helen Whitaker with her star after his victory in the Virginia Gold Cup at Stratford, as usual giving two and a half stone to the others.

September 1976: Jumping the last at Worcester ahead of Brian Ellison on Tex, to whom Tingle Creek was conceding no less than 40lbs. Tex was a good horse in his own class and collared Tingle Creek on the run-in.

October 1977: Fort Devon (Bill Smith) leading Lean Forward (James Evans) and myself on Casamayor over the water in the Hermitage Chase at Newbury. I really loved Casamayor; he was such a handsome horse.

lovely dark-haired girl, and it became apparent that she wasn't wearing any underwear. Those white breeches do show every line, especially on a sunny day, so when we pulled up, I couldn't resist mentioning this fact.

The poor girl was mortified and blushed a bright shade of scarlet. "How can you tell?" she asked. "Well, the sun was shining on your backside and I could see everything," I replied. I think I rather unwittingly scuppered her chances because she jumped off at the back of the field and never moved position throughout the race. Too embarrassed, I think.

However, the following day we lined up for a race at Lingfield. She gave me a big smile and said, "Hey, I'm wearing apple catchers today!"

That Fontwell victory on Tingle Creek was the 45th and last winner I ever rode for Tom Jones. He was winding his jumpers down by then and I'd accepted a retainer as stable jockey for Peter Bailey. I was also riding a lot for Earl Jones, who trained at Hednesford, in Staffordshire.

It was sad in a way, because some of the best and most enjoyable days of my life were when I was riding out for Tom. I do remember a tale of a rather lovely married lady who used to ride out second lot after she'd taken her children to school. She rode very well; used to ride all the big, strong horses, trotting round the roads. Anyway, she and a senior jockey used to tack up their horses then disappear into the rug room where all the horse rugs were laundered and kept, whereby they would lay a Whitney down for a bit of unbridled passion.

December 1977: Winning on Prince Rock at Chepstow. I won the four-mile Bass Chase on him at Cheltenham's New Year meeting, fulfilling a carefully laid plan his trainer Peter Bailey and I had hatched between us.

I lost the ride on Tingle Creek because he was engaged to run at Sandown but I had to go to Worcester that day to ride another former American chaser, Casamayor, for Peter Bailey. Steve rode Tingle Creek; he won and I never got back on him again.

Casamayor was such a handsome horse. I really loved him. He was very easy to ride and two and a half miles was his best trip. He was owned by Raymond Guest, the owner of Grand National and Gold Cup winner L'Escargot and Derby winners Larkspur and Sir Ivor. The race I rode him in at Worcester was the ATV Today Chase, in which his rivals included the dual Champion Hurdle winner Comedy Of Errors, who was jumping fences in public for the first – and only – time; and Broncho II, winner of the Welsh Champion Chase six months earlier, trained by Tony Dickinson and ridden by his son Michael.

Casamayor was always holding the upper hand. Comedy Of Errors chased us up the straight but finished the race six lengths in arrears, with Broncho II a further eight lengths back in third and the rest well beaten.

But my favourite horse of Peter Bailey's was a wonderful little staying chaser called Prince Rock. I won two long-distance races at Chepstow on him towards the end of 1977, the Johnny Clay Memorial and the Terry Wogan Handicap Chase. Of all the great horses I rode and the big races I won, the occasion I'm most proud of is riding Prince Rock to win the four-mile Bass Chase at Cheltenham's New Year meeting, the race I'd won two years earlier on Jolly's Clump.

Peter and I had been talking about the race for ten days or so and planning the tactics. Prince Rock wasn't very big and he wasn't a spectacular jumper, he used to get in close, but he was safe. I knew I could take my time on him and he'd outstay them. It all went like clockwork. Paul Barton on Master Upham went storming off, which was perfect for us as it spread the field out. I crept and crept, joined Paul at the last and took it up on the run-in to score by a length. On reflection, I'd say that race was my proudest moment in racing.

Prince Rock was a thin-skinned horse who marked easily. Unfortunately, I'd marked him a bit during the race and the stewards wanted to talk to me about it. However, they were busy so they said I should come to them after the next race.

Back in the weighing room, the trainer Toby Cobden came in panicking because he had a runner and his jockey, Sandy May, had been hurt and was unable to ride it. Nicky Henderson was there and he said to me, "If he asks you, you should ride it because I think it will win." He did ask me and I duly took the ride, but we fell and, as another horse came by while I was on the floor, it kicked me and broke my leg.

In the ambulance room I kept saying, "No, no, it's only badly bruised." For some reason, they wanted me to provide a urine sample, but due to the amphetamines I took to suppress my hunger pangs I was dried up, so when Richard Linley came in, I got him to pee in the bottle for me.

I managed to limp into the stewards' room. They told me I'd hit Prince Rock sixteen times and fined me for excessive use. In my defence, he was bone idle and you had to keep him at it. As I'd given him his first crack at the second fence, sixteen times over four miles hardly seemed excessive. While they were giving me a dressing down, I spent most of the interview standing on one leg, not through nervousness, because of my broken leg. Then I fell over and they had to get me a chair. But still I insisted it was only bruised as I was staying with Vic Soane that night, then planning to go schooling at Peter Bailey's and also due to ride Strombolus in the novice chase the next day. I didn't want to miss that. He had a great chance.

The next morning, I had a hot bath but the pain was horrendous. I managed to get my jodhpurs on, struggled to get my boot on, got to the yard and was legged up onto a horse but I couldn't stand up in the irons. There was no way I could ride in a race. Bob Champion took my place on Strombolus and won.

I'd driven up to Cheltenham the day before with Dick Rykens, who, as I've mentioned earlier, owned Lovejoy, the horse on whom I'd broken an arm three days before winning the Victor Ludorum on Sweet Joe. Mr Rykens was blind in one eye so I'd often drive him to the races. He lived at Saffron Waldon and would drive over to me in Newmarket and then I'd take over in his car.

I managed to get back to Cheltenham racecourse to meet him – he'd stayed elsewhere the previous evening – as I was to drive him home as planned. He was looking very nervous as I had to use my whip rather than my foot to push the accelerator down. Once it was down, I could position my foot on the pedal and hold it there. It was a bit uncomfortable but we got back to Newmarket safely.

I was keen to get back from my broken leg to ride a horse called Ballymore for Peter Bailey in a three-and-a-half-mile chase at Nottingham. Three weeks beforehand I was hobbling about intent on riding and rigged up an elastic bandage from my ankle to my crown jewels as support. Each day I'd walk up and down Warren Hill, the steep gallop in the middle of Newmarket that runs up to Warren Place. The idea was to keep my wind clear and build up cardio fitness. There were no gyms in those days and I couldn't run or ride out.

I managed to get back in time to ride the horse. On the day I wore a boot one size bigger than normal on that foot. We got round and finished second, but I was so out of breath that I thought my lungs were going to burst out of my chest.

December 1977: Riding Strombolus at Cheltenham. It's the fence in front of the stands on the new Course. Strombolus didn't normally jump this high but he'd been frightened by Diamond Edge who was leading when hitting the fence. You can see the bits of birch flicked up by Diamond Edge flying above us.

In March 1978, two months after my Cheltenham fall, I went to Newbury for a handful of rides. I hadn't ridden a winner since Prince Rock's Bass Chase but I had two good chances, Major Thompson in the novice hurdle and Alverton in the novice chase, both owned by Snailwell Stud and trained by Peter Easterby. They both won.

I'd finished riding for the day and was heading back to the car park – I'd travelled to the races with Mrs Brudenell-Bruce, the owner of Snailwell Stud – when I was accosted by a lady. She berated me about Major Thompson and said it was a disgrace that a son of Brigadier Gerard was running over hurdles.

I said, "Excuse me, madam, but he won very comfortably, beating a lot of Lambourn horses". She snapped back at me, "That's not the point. He's far too well-bred to be running over hurdles".

I excused myself and went to find the car in which I was to get a lift home. I have to say it was a sparkling effort by Major Thompson. He should really have gone on to be a Champion Hurdle winner. Jonjo O'Neill said he was the best he'd ever ridden – and he rode Sea Pigeon – but I guess Major Thompson just didn't have the heart for it.

I was reminded of that incident forty years later when I was invited to a lunch at Worcester Racecourse to celebrate their 300th anniversary of racing. There was an impressive collection of retired jockeys there including Jonjo, Stan Mellor, John Francome and Richard Pitman, plus a couple of the top Flat jockeys – Worcester had staged Flat racing until 1966. I was very keen to attend as I was the youngest of the group allocated to my table. I was sat next to one of the top Flat jockeys of his era and I told him the story of how I'd been verbally abused when leaving Newbury Racecourse after winning on Major Thompson. I told him who the lady was and asked him why he thought she'd said what she did. Without even looking up from his soup he replied, "Because she was a fucking old cow".

The struggle with weight had been a continuous one throughout my career. I tried everything: amphetamines, diuretics – I could lose four pounds in half an hour on those. Many was the occasion I'd be driving with so many clothes on I could barely move. I tied baler twine round my ankles to keep the sweat from running over the footwell off the car, the heaters on full blast. When I travelled with my fellow jockeys, they would often be sitting there in just their underpants and, I must admit, we got some strange looks as we drove through towns.

At the start of what would turn out to be my last season, I rode a horse called Spy Net at Huntingdon for David Dale. I was struggling to make the weight that day so I had my smallest saddle. "We don't need the breast girth, do we?" I asked the trainer, so he left it off and I cheated my way through the scales. I do remember the saddle was wobbling all over the place and by the time we finished it was so far back I was almost sitting on the tail. We won all the same, but it showed the lengths I was having to go to in order to do the weight.

August 1978: Returning after winning on Spy Net at Fontwell. I'd struggled to make the weight and left off the breast girth. As a result, the, saddle slipped and I finished the race almost sitting on the horse's tail.

EIGHT

SOME RANDOM MEMORIES

I nearly changed the course of horseracing history!

I was due to ride a horse called Sage Merlin for trainer John Bingham in the 1977 Grand National. I'd won a handicap chase at Haydock on him in March. He was a good horse but he wasn't very big, barely 16 hands or so. However, he'd sailed round Haydock so we didn't feel Aintree would be a problem.

I walked the course in the morning of the race with Charlotte Brew, who was about to make history as the first woman ever to take part in the Grand National, riding her hunter chaser Barony Fort. Someone took a picture of us, her in the ditch me looking down. I was wearing a very dapper leather jacket and a pair of bell bottoms, which caused a lot of amusement amongst my friends and family. The picture appeared in a Liverpool newspaper – I wish I could find it now.

The big moment came and I took Sage Merlin down and showed him the first fence. It terrified him; he could barely see over the top of it. I had to give him quite a bit of encouragement to get to the start. I got my girths checked and by then I reckon he'd started to think a bit because he started to back away, back towards the paddock. I didn't want to hit him but he just kept reversing.

As luck would have it, there were a load of protestors there with placards between the starting tape and the Melling Road. They weren't objecting to the National, it was about some scouse fellow who was in prison and they wanted him to be let out. Because of this, the starter was focusing on them rather than me and, fortunately, some kind chap hopped over the railings and led me back to the start.

I called over to Charlotte to come and line up with me and I'd look after her on the way round. We planned to go round the outside to keep out of trouble.

Sage Merlin never took to it at all. He was scared but he still jumped magnificently. However, he was pulling so hard that by the time we got to Valentine's I was sitting in second place behind the leader, Boom Docker. It felt like he was running out of fear. I was thinking, "I've got to get a breather into him or we'll never get home."

April 1977: Sage Merlin and I fall at the Chair when lying in second place in the 1977 Grand National. We almost changed the course of racing history by bringing down Red Rum.

Boom Docker and Sage Merlin were well clear as we came onto the racecourse and jumped the first two in the straight. Then we approached the fifteenth fence, the Chair. I was aiming to get a nice straight line at it, but in my mind thinking I hadn't got a hope in hell of getting round that next bend, even if he cleared the Chair. Sage Merlin jumped the fence, then buckled onto his joints on landing. I jumped up and grabbed hold of him, for a split second thinking I could get back on him. Then I saw a wall of horses approaching so I let go sharpish and ran to the rail. But we almost brought down Red Rum. He was right behind and just managed to sidestep us. Otherwise, that would have been that.

Boom Docker refused at the first fence out in the country and Red Rum went on to make history by winning his third Grand National. But how close Sage Merlin and I had come to bringing down the great horse.

Sage Merlin was never the same after that, which was a shame as he'd been a good jumper beforehand. He fell with me on his next start in the Midlands Grand National at Uttoxeter. Jeff Pearce rode him a couple of times early the next season and won on him at Huntingdon. I might have ridden him in that year's Mackeson Gold Cup at Cheltenham but I was claimed to ride Corrieghoil for Earl Jones, so Jeff rode him again. Sadly, he broke a leg at the water jump and had to be destroyed.

My first ride over the Grand National fences had been a disaster. I rode a horse for Harry Wharton called Levadon in the 1975 Topham Trophy. He had a fatal heart attack going into the wings of the first fence. He never took off, just chested it. It was a very hard fall and I was carted off to Walton Hospital. I stupidly discharged myself the next morning. It took me all day to get from Liverpool to Newmarket because I still didn't really know where I was and kept getting on the wrong train.

When I was working at Tom Robson's, I lived, along with four other lads, in the local pub at Cliburn, the Golden Pheasant. Myself and Ramsey shared the back room overlooking the car park, which had been cut out of the hill behind so it was level with our bedroom window. Brian, John and Fred shared the front bedroom.

I remember one morning when all five of us overslept, a result of overindulging the night before, I imagine. Tom was either always very early, waiting for us to arrive in the yard, or we didn't see him until 10.00am some mornings. No rhyme or reason to it; that's just how it was.

I suddenly became aware of Tom's whole body coming through our bedroom window, puce with rage and bellowing at us to get our backsides to work.

It must have been a funny sight to see; five skinny lads in various stages of undress running the hundred yards down the village street to the yard. There were houses both sides of the street plus the post office.

That evening in the pub it seemed the whole village knew about it. The jockey boys, as we were known from then on.

Mention of the Golden Pheasant reminds me of another incident. Five girls were regular customers at the pub. I fancied them all but one particular girl kindly agreed to spend the night with me in a hotel up on Shap Fell.

As mentioned earlier, when riding I really struggled with my weight. I'm now a trim 12 stone 7lb but in those days I was trying to maintain a riding weight of around 10 stone 7lbs. I took amphetamines every day to suppress my appetite.

Trying to be clever I took two pills thinking it would enhance my performance but unfortunately it had the opposite effect. Lovely girl as she was, she said, "Don't you worry, that's my department," and we had a great time. We had a bit of a giggle about it afterwards. A bit embarrassing for me but she said she was happy. Must have been easily pleased, thank God!

People ask me if I miss the riding and I tell them no, but I miss the drugs!

Sometimes when riding out, a person can get caught short. It's easier for the blokes – you can just hop off, have a pee behind a bush and jump back on again. However, one day there were a few of us riding out including a girl called Jacquie and an Irish lad whom I won't name as I think he's still about. The lad suddenly announced he was desperate for the loo, but not just a wee, the full hog. We heckled him a bit but in desperation he dismounted and led his horse behind a large bush in order to do his business. We couldn't hold the horse for him as they were young racehorses and likely to strike out at each other.

Jacquie was looking up at the sky, the stars, anything to save embarrassment. Anyway, as the lad started to do the deed, he let out a loud noise rather like a gunshot. The horse was so startled it took off dragging the poor lad out from behind the bushes, trousers and pants round his ankles and still clutching the dock leaves he'd picked in the absence of loo paper. At least he didn't let go of the horse. Poor Jacquie really didn't know where to look.

Riding in a big field of two-mile hurdlers one day at Teesside Park, a jockey named John Toland was riding a horse and it wouldn't come out of the paddock. The rest of us headed down to the start and waited for him. Eventually someone said, "Here he comes," but we could see he was being bolted with. He was completely out of control.

Like idiots, we all moved over in front of the first hurdle, out of their way, but the horse carried on flat out and ended up on the chase course. He then proceeded to jump the water jump backwards before John managed to wrestle him to a standstill and bring it back to the start. Then, to add insult to injury, when the race started, the horse fell at one of the hurdles.

Another day, I remember I rode in the novice chase at Uttoxeter during heavy rain. At the far end of the course Roy (R. F.) Davies and I both fell. I was nursing some sort of injury to my arm but other than that I was fine, but Roy had hurt his back. Two elderly St John Ambulance men came to collect us but the driver wouldn't reverse the ambulance the last fifty or sixty yards to where Roy lay, as he was afraid he'd get stuck in the mud.

The two old St John boys decided it would be a good idea to put Roy on a stretcher and carry him to the ambulance. The one holding the feet struggled to bend down to get the handles, then he had terrible trouble standing up to lift the stretcher. By this time, Roy was fed up with getting wet, so he got off the stretcher and said to the old boy, "Here, you get on the stretcher and I'll carry you!"

The St John Ambulance people do a great job. However, I remember one day at Sedgefield in January 1969 when I could have done without them. It was a bloody awful, wet day. I was riding a big, lanky horse for Peter Pittendrigh called Man o' War in a novice chase. He was presumably named after the great American champion racehorse who dominated the racing scene there just after the Great War, but unfortunately, he didn't possess the same level of ability, although he had won a few races. By this time, he was eleven years old and was having his first run over fences.

I was leading the field alongside Graham Macmillan (who went on to win the race) when Man o' War fell at the fence just past the stands. It wasn't a proper fall but he went down on his knees and didn't give me a chance of staying on him. One of the horses behind us wiped his feet over my head and I was a bit dazed.

Two elderly St John Ambulance guys loaded me onto a stretcher and headed off towards the weighing room. There was a gate in the corner, through which they left the course and went onto the tarmac. Once on the tarmac, they started to jog across it. The old boy at the back stumbled, shot me off the stretcher, and I landed flat on my face and broke my nose. There was a bit of blood but they wiped it up in the ambulance room, put a plaster on my nose, and I didn't feel too bad. I still managed to ride in the next race, finishing second on The Celestial Traveller.

During my career, I think I fell at every fence at Sedgefield bar the water jump.

January 1969: I'm in second place on Man o' War behind Graham Macmillan on Kirkhill at Sedgefield. A split second later I was on the floor. The fall wasn't a bad one but the St John Ambulance man dropped me off the stretcher while taking me to the medical room and I broke my nose!

One day, about forty years ago, my car was parked outside a restaurant in Bedford and I spotted a lady struggling to park her car next to me. Just as I was thinking, "I could park a horsebox in there," she got out and left something under my windscreen wiper. When I'd finished dining and returned to the car, I read the note. It was fairly abusive and said, "Because you have parked like an arsehole, I have had to park three streets away. Arseholes like you should take a bus!"

I thought it was hilarious so I kept it. I've photocopied it hundreds of times and used them all around the country. I keep them in my car should the occasion arise where I can place one on someone else's car. Bob Champion has had one, which apparently left him fuming.

I visited Paddy Broderick's widow Nan when her daughter Alyson turned up. So she got one too. That evening I got a message saying "if I were as old as you, I wouldn't need to buy a bus ticket. I'd have a pass." A bit extreme, I thought!

On another occasion, I was having coffee in town with my good friend Cathy Warren. I'd met Cathy when she was head lad to David Morley and we're still great friends today. She now works for Juddmonte at Banstead Manor, on night duties looking after Kingman, Frankel and Enable, which is some job to have.

While we were chatting over our coffees, we spotted Derek Thompson parking up just in front of my car before going off to do an errand. That gave me the idea for a 'leg pull', I placed a parking ticket and eagerly awaited his return. He came back, saw the ticket and grabbed it off the windscreen. As he read it his face became more and more stony and he looked up and down the High Street as if to seek the perpetrator. He hadn't spotted Cathy and me sitting in the car there. I tooted the horn and he came over and we exchanged a few good-hearted insults before he fell about laughing. He didn't tear it up but took it away with him for future reference.

As I've already mentioned, I've known Bill O'Gorman since we were at Newmarket Grammar School together. Bill's wife Elaine had a lovely old horse she'd been given called Charbon. He was her pride and joy. Bill was training at Graham Place and was having some work done there. One day he'd hired a firm with a mechanical digger. He nodded at Charbon when Elaine was busy grooming him and said, "Shall I get them to dig him a hole while they're here?" She went berserk!

When Bill's father was training at Shalfleet, a beautiful yard with big inside boxes, Bill and I found a huge dead rat one day. Elaine absolutely hates rats – don't we all? – so we tied a bit of string to its tail and lay it across the door when she was grooming Charbon, who was in training then. She spotted it and screamed, then Bill began to pull the string and the rat was going backwards across the doorway. Again, she went berserk. I think Bill got a thump for that. We'd considered putting it into Charbon's feed manger but, having seen Elaine's reaction after the dragging incident, it's probably just as well we didn't.

Speaking of rats, there was a lad called Tommy Mahon. He was a good bloke in many ways and would help anyone who wanted help riding out racehorses. He'd won the Ascot Stakes at Royal Ascot as an apprentice in the early 1950s and I believe went on to ride 200 winners in Sweden before a serious accident there ended his career and caused him to return to England. Bill was about to move his horses into the stables at Graham Place but there was a bit of a rat problem. I had an airgun and Bill and I thought it would be a good idea to go and shoot some of them. Tommy said he would come with us.

We went up to the stables when it got dark. When we shone a light at the rats, they ran towards us; it was quite scary. We did this a few times until Tommy said, "This is no good; watch this," and, as a rat ran towards him, he grabbed hold of it and bit its head clean off. He wiped the blood off his mouth and nodded at us. That was it. We were speechless.

Poor old Tommy fell on hard times. He was found years later, curled up dead in a bus shelter in Newmarket. There but for the grace of God go any of us, I guess.

I'm not exactly sure when fellow jockey Jeff Barlow and I actually met but I think it was probably in the early seventies. He was working for Edward Courage, breeder and trainer of that wonderful family of horses which included Spanish Steps and Royal Relief. Jeff wanted to move stables so I arranged for him to start work at Tom Jones with me. He actually came to live with me in my lovely flat in Park Lane. It was great, really handy for the High Street. Parking was a bit hit and miss but we coped and we had some great times. I also owned the flat next door on the ground floor and rented it out to an American couple – they had a beautiful daughter I seem to recall. David Minton, the bloodstock agent, lived above us in his own flat.

Opposite, also on the ground floor, was the lovely Jan, who used to go to school with my sister. Jan was the person who got me into buying property and putting down roots. We were very good friends. She was a very confident and driven girl who had her pick of men, and I can remember the day very clearly when she lectured me. We were having coffee one lunchtime in Cambridge in a restaurant called the Golden Egg. I was getting quite a few rides by then but wasn't able to spend the money on wine, women and song due to my severe weight problems, although I did waste a bit on a few cars. What really sticks in my mind about that day is that I was wearing an expensive suede bomber jacket (they were the height of fashion back then) and was sitting sideways on the chair, but failed to notice that my elbow was resting on top of a trolley full of creamy desserts, half of which ended up stuck to my jacket. We made a hasty exit.

A change of occupation. I was asked by a motor bike clothing firm to model their new sheepskin coat. It cost about £400 – and that was in 1977. My career as a male model was a brief one!

I did take notice of her, though, and bought a building plot in the village of Isleham. I engaged a local builder to help me design and build a house and it was finished about 1975. I named it Tingle Creek and it still bears that name today. A mate called Mick Rowe lived there for a time – he was a flying groom then – but after he moved out it was empty for a while until some student squatters took it over.

I did ask them politely to leave but they just ignored me. At that point I went back into Newmarket town to collect a few racing mates to help press the point a bit further. Unfortunately, during the discussion one of the students slipped down the stairs and broke his collarbone. They left then.

When I was with Tom Jones, there was a lad named Christy O'Connor that worked there. He was in his sixties. Tom respected that and treated him a little different to the rest of us because of it. He was a great lad but a bit too fond of a drink. He looked after Tingle Creek and also a really good horse called Swift Shadow. But he was nearly always pissed.

Before we rode out in the morning, he used to go off to the loo and keep us all waiting. One day someone put molasses all over the seat and he came roaring out of the loo with his trousers at half-mast, cursing and swearing. Tom told him to shut up and get on with it, so he had to ride out with his long-johns full of molasses.

Before I arrived there in 1973, there had been a story in the paper about a grey horse at Tom's called 'The Guinness Horse'. Tom had told them the story that the only way he could keep this horse eating was to sprinkle Guinness on its feed. The horse won races so this story made the papers. Christy looked after it and it was his job, on the way back to evening stables each day, to collect a bottle of Guinness, top off, from the off-licence, put it on Tom's account, and give it to Fred Flippance, the head lad, for feeding time. Fred would then mix up the feed and hand the bottle of Guinness to Christy for him to sprinkle on the horse's feed when he put it in his stable.

One night, Christy was taken ill before feeding time so someone else went to feed his horses. Fred handed him the bottle that Christy had brought and he went off with it to sprinkle on the feed as directed. As he poured from the dark Guinness bottle, he realised that liquid coming out of it was water. It turned out that the horse hadn't a clue what Guinness tasted like, and Christy had been drinking seven bottles of Guinness a week courtesy of Tom Jones.

Christy had a son who was known as Little Johnny. When I won on Tingle Creek I gave Christy a photo to hang on his wall. Many years later, long after Christy had died, I happened to be at York races when this big chap of about eighteen stone came up to me, dressed smartly in a suit and tie looking every inch the successful businessman it transpired that he was. He introduced himself ... it was Little Johnny.

"I've got that picture of Tingle Creek you gave my Dad," he said. "He was so proud of it." I was touched.

I remember one tale involving a senior jockey – the name must be kept secret so as not to offend the living – who'd been invited to dinner with a particular owner that he rode for, a man of high rank in the military who happened to have the most attractive and considerably younger wife. We will call her Calendula. The senior jockey and Calendula also happened to be engaging in extra marital activity at this period of time.

As the evening drew on, the Colonel – as we will call him – was getting more and more inebriated and the subject changed from talking horses and racing to him rambling on about other things. Eventually, he indicated that they should adjourn to the drawing room, sit by the fire and consume port.

The senior jockey and Calendula had been giving each other the eye all night. As she sat by the fire, she hitched up her skirt every few seconds, tormenting the hapless jockey with an eyeful of her cracking legs. Then the Colonel said, "Damn it, Calendula, we need more port. Go and fetch it will you, there's a good girl."

Calendula rose and gave a knowing look to the senior jockey, who gave her a few minutes before excusing himself, citing the need to have a wee.

He found Calendula, wanton and waiting for him in the cellar and he proceeded to take her from behind. But, as he was riding his finish – they must have been away awhile – the Colonel was calling outside the door, "Where are you with that damn port, Calendula?"

He was trying to open the door. As luck would have it, perhaps not for Calendula but certainly for the senior jockey, as he was trying to open the door it kept banging poor Calendula on the head, until the Colonel gave up and shambled off again, muttering away.

The senior jockey re-joined him shortly after and then a flushed Calendula appeared, apologizing for taking so long to find the right bottle of port. She had taken a bit of a bang alright, and not just to the head.

Despite a reputation of being able to endure pain, I did harbour an irrational fear of going to the dentist, so I'd suffered broken teeth for a couple of years before finally getting round to visiting the dentist in Newmarket to get them fixed.

To take my mind off things I focussed on the comely dental nurse and made a point of chatting her up every time the dentist left the room to fetch more instruments. One day, when I was leaving, I came across her on the stairs and our eyes met knowingly. I leaned in for a cheeky kiss and went on my way.

On my next visit, when the dentist left the room, I asked her if she was planning to go to the downstairs loo. She smiled at me: "If you want me to …"

She was married to a policeman but we engaged in a few knee-trembling sessions in the downstairs loo until word reached me that the policeman had got wind of things and was threatening, along with his copper mates, to get me fitted up and put away for ten years if I didn't back off. I backed off.

Hugo Bevan, clerk of the course at Windsor, Towcester, Worcester and Huntingdon, is a lovely man. I remember one day at Worcester during a very wet spring in 1977. Worcester's track runs right beside the River Severn and half its meetings had been abandoned. I was surprised it was on because the course used to get waterlogged and conditions could be very slippery on the bends.

That particular day there were ten races, a lot of runners, a lot of jockeys. As was the usual form, us jockeys were in the dressing room beforehand. Half an hour before the first race, Hugo walked in and banged on the table to get everybody's attention.

"Now listen jockeys," he began. "We all know what the conditions are like out there. If I'd called an inspection this morning the Stewards would have abandoned the meeting, so I'm just asking you all to be extra careful today. I've made one or two adjustments around the course to make it safer. Have a look at the course plan on the way out and you'll see where I've made the changes. Please don't take any unnecessary risks." He carried on in this vein for a while, then looked round at everyone.

"Right then, anyone got any questions?"

There was a brief pause and then Jeff King, who was at the back of the room, put up his hand up and said, "Yes, I've got one."

You could see from Hugo's face that he was pleased that a senior jockey was going to ask a valid question, the answer to which could be of valuable help to some of the more inexperienced jockeys amongst us.

"Yes, King, how can I help you?"

"When was the last time you had a shag?"

Of course, we all fell about laughing. An in fairness, Hugo laughed too. Then he rolled his eyes and said, "Thank you, King," as he walked out of the room. And that was that.

NINE

EARL JONES

Earl Jones was born in Ireland. He'd served his apprenticeship there before coming to England in 1939 for "a bit of a holiday". The 'holiday', which included war service with the Royal Army Ordnance Corps, was to last almost fifty years. 'Earl' was merely his Christian name, not a title. Apparently, the journalist and BBC paddock commentator Clive Graham, a friend of Earl's, was once asked if Earl was a member of the aristocracy, to which he replied bluntly that Earl was no lord, and the only similarity was that he drank like one.

I'd heard of Earl but had never met him. The word was that he was a top trainer who didn't put up with any nonsense from his owners, lads, horses or jockeys. In that order. All his horses ran from the front; apparently you didn't have a lot of choice about it.

Earl was a brilliant trainer. He had a loose school with fences on a pulley system so he could adjust their heights. The horses never got used to them. They didn't know what height the fences were going to be and Earl said it made them think and look at the fences and be careful. He rarely had a faller.

The other jockeys referred to him as 'Killer' Jones, due to the fact that most of his horses pulled really hard and were often ferocious jumpers. You couldn't make mistakes with him. He'd been a jockey and knew the score.

The very first time I rode for Earl was on a horse called Ballygarvan Brook over fences at Worcester. He was only a four-year-old. Earl's instructions were to give the horse a good education. "We don't need to win today," he told me.

Before I went to weigh out, David Cartwright said to me, "Have you ridden that before?" I replied that I hadn't. "Make sure you've got a short girth; there isn't much of him," David went on. "I'm really surprised they are running him over fences because he was pretty sketchy over hurdles." Just what you need to hear to fill you with confidence!

There were about fourteen runners in the race. Earl always wanted his runners to run handy but maybe I was thinking a bit because I was a bit slow out of the starting gate. Anyway, we got round okay and finished about fourth or fifth. I wasn't very happy with myself and was a bit embarrassed as I slid off the horse in the unsaddling enclosure. I started to give Earl some rubbish about being left flat-footed at the start but he waved away my excuses. "You will give him a ride next time then, will you?" he said.

The next time I rode the horse was at Stratford on 30th December 1975. This time the instructions from Earl were, "Have him up in the first two or three and if you have to hit him, make sure you don't miss!" This time we won the race and followed up over the same course in February.

After that first win, Earl came to see me in the changing room and said, "I've had my lads Johnny Hawkins and Paddy Connors getting a few ready to win. You'll do. I'm fed up with putting up yellow-livered bastards!"

I gave him some old bullshit or other and then said, "I know what you mean guvnor. If I start to see the red light, I'll let you know." He replied, "If you start to see the red light, I'll know six months before you do!" What a great saying that is. And you know, he was dead right. Us older jockeys can usually see straightaway when someone who was once brave has started to ride more defensively.

One frosty day at Uttoxeter it looked like they were going to abandon the day's racing. The first race was a novice chase, the second was a novice hurdle. Earl said to me "They're going to have an inspection. Make sure you go out there and tell them that, in your opinion, it is safe. We'll win the first two." So that's what I did.

Reluctantly, they raced. I did win the first amongst a lot of complaints that the ground wasn't safe. The hurdle race was even worse. I didn't win it and there were a lot of fallers during the race and three slipped up whilst pulling up at the end ... and two of those were loose horses.

The meeting was then abandoned.

Probably the best horse I rode for Earl was Tasco. I won a couple of Wolverhampton novice chases on him, both times by fifteen lengths, early in 1976. He was a great stayer over three miles. If only he'd had decent legs he would have been a really good horse, but he had legs like glass.

I rode him in that year's Sun Alliance Chase at Cheltenham and we fell several fences from home, so I couldn't say whether we would have won or not, but I was pretty fed up about it. I'm not sure what happened to him after that.

Corrieghoil was another good one. He'd been a decent hurdler for Fred Rimell before being trained by Earl. He was a fine, aristocratic type of horse with the loveliest head. He was on the small side, not quite sixteen hands, but as genuine as they come and always tried so hard for you. He wasn't the sort of horse to make the running but he had a devastating turn of foot.

I won five handicap chases on him between November 1976 and September 1977, including the Ken Boulton Memorial Handicap Chase at Uttoxeter. He carried 12st 7lb that day and he didn't look like he weighed

February 1976: Winning on Tasco at Wolverhampton. Tasco was potentially the best horse I rode for Earl Jones. Behind us is Michael Dickinson on Guiding Star. Tasco won by 15 lengths.

much more than that himself, so I didn't give him much chance, particularly in tacky ground. I had a real lump in my throat when he won that race. I was also pleased to have won it because Ken Boulton was a solid, though unfashionable, jockey who had died following a fall at Uttoxeter in May 1965, a year before I rode my first winner. I didn't know him but, even so, winning a race named in memory of a jockey who'd lost his life in a racing accident does engender a level of respect and also reminds you of the dangers inherent in race-riding.

I rode Corrieghoil in that year's Mackeson Gold Cup at Cheltenham. He was in with a good chance two out but weakened in the straight and finished fourth. It was a shame he was a bit too small to be really top class.

One of the worst races I ever rode – maybe THE worst – was at Uttoxeter in May 1977. I was first jockey by then to Earl Jones and also to Tom Jones. Both named Jones but very different men and both were excellent trainers in their own way.

I had three rides for Earl that day. He said he thought we might have three winners: a handicap chaser called All Spirit, a novice hurdler who I think was called Connotation, and a novice chaser whose name escapes me. I'm sure that I got beaten on the novice chaser. The handicap chaser was a wily old horse but with ability if you caught him on the right day. The race was over three and a quarter miles.

I took my time through the race, jumped into the lead at the last fence and landed running. I knew I had the second horse well beaten so I thought I'd make it easy for the old horse to cheer him up a bit. I stopped pushing him, expecting to coast it to the line, and the old bugger virtually dug his toes in to stop altogether. A 51-year-old lady, Mrs Sheilagh French, riding a horse called Royal And Ancient, who'd been a fast finishing third at the time, was galvanised into action to get up on the line and beat me by a short-head.

I was distraught. Earl was angry. Actually, that doesn't come close to his reaction. I lodged a futile objection, claiming that she'd touched me in the final strides. She hadn't, of course, and the stewards took all of ten seconds to throw it out, so I lost my deposit and, to add insult to injury, they fined me £10 for objecting to a lady.

Earl was absolutely furious. Before I mounted the third horse in the paddock, he looked at me with his steely grey eyes and said, "Now for Christ's sake don't fuck this one up." The third horse did win but it didn't really make it a better day for me. It was ages before Earl forgot it. Well, before he stopped going on about it anyway.

I was down to ride a horse called Civil List for Earl one day at Cheltenham in April 1976. He sticks in my mind now but I'd never heard anything of the horse beforehand. I could see that he was very small – he only looked as if he were 14.3 or 15 hands as he had a very hollow back – and I remarked to Earl as we watched him go round the paddock, "Not much of him is there?"

In an extremely rare move, he took the horse off the lad who was leading round once I was mounted and let us out on to the course himself. "When you take it down to the start, make sure you hang his head over the rails," he said, "or it will fuck off with you." He added, "You'll be in front by the first."

I looked up at the boards as we went by and we were 20-1 at that stage. As I cantered down I could feel the horse wanted to bolt. As predicted, we were in front by the first. It was a big field of about 25 runners. He zoomed round and we led most of the way. It was firm ground and when the horse was wrong at a hurdle, he just kicked it out of the ground and smashed it to pieces. And he did that a couple of times. We won by 25 lengths and when I came in I saw the price had come into 5-1 or 6 -1, so Earl obviously had the money on.

We went to Uttoxeter with the horse three weeks later and did the same again, making all and winning by twelve lengths. The next time, though, the other jockeys had got wise to our tactics and didn't let us get away from them so much and we got beaten.

One day, Earl remarked, "Civil List would make a grand little chaser." I didn't say much but in my mind I thought, "Jesus Christ, you want me to ride that over fences?"

"I'll get you over here to give him a little pop," Earl went on. That was a rare occurrence too. I never, ever went there to school or ride out. He had two lads in the yard, Johnny Hawkins and Paddy Connors, who was the stable jockey, who did all that. Paddy is a grand bloke. Years later, he used to lead me in our cars from different venues in Birmingham to the M6 after our annual Grand National preview get together, organised by Chris Pitt, so that I didn't get lost. That was in pre-satnav days.

Anyway, I duly went up to the yard for the schooling session. I wasn't looking forward to it. The schooling field was like nothing I'd come across before. The first fence wasn't a fence at all, it was a mound of rocks and stones, like those stone walls you see in Yorkshire. It was covered in a tarpaulin, was about three feet high.

"That's a funny obstacle," I observed to Johnny Hawkins. "Yes," he replied, "they don't hit that twice!"

Off we went. And we fair took off. The horse that Johnny was riding went like absolute shit off a shovel. The second and third were plastic fences and as we pulled up I thought we were going to get a right bollocking for going so fast. We were absolutely trapping. But when we got back to Earl, he said, "Right, go again, but this time a bit faster!"

After the schooling session we ran him in a novice chase at Worcester. I wasn't looking forward to it at all but he settled – the fences made him back off a bit. I was third over the last but then he broke a leg on the run-in. Such a shame. He really didn't like fences.

Earl trained a horse called Fatherland who used to fall a lot. I think he must have had something wrong with him. He fell a few times with me but I never turned the ride down as I didn't want to damage my reputation. One day I got a phone call from Ron Hyett, who rode a lot of Earl's horses. "I've got some good news for you," he said. "Fatherland fell today and they put him down."

That said, whereby many jockeys, just before a big race like, say, the Grand National or the Cheltenham Festival, would like to ride a winner, I was always pleased if I had a 'soft' fall beforehand, so called because I didn't actually break anything. It made me feel invincible.

I rode a horse for Earl in a two-and-a half-mile handicap chase at Uttoxeter. I'd never heard of it before. The papers said it was a shocking jumper. He hadn't run for a long time but was previously with Fred Rimell – an expensive but disappointing purchase for him. Two or three months afterwards, the horse was bought by Earl for peanuts due to its inability to jump a clear round. Earl disliked Fred Rimell and loved nothing more than to win with one of his castoffs.

Bearing in mind that most of Earl's ran from the front, the instructions I received in the paddock were alarming to say the least. "Now listen mate, I've schooled and schooled this horse. He jumped twenty pole jumps in the loose school before I put him in the horsebox to come here. DON'T hit the front with him, as I don't know what he'll do. Win if you can but don't take any fucking stupid risks!"

Well, I thought I must be riding a tiger. Earl had never said anything like that before.

We went into the first fence in a bunch of five or six. I came out just in front so pulled him back a little just in case of problems. He became an ordinary ride and finished second, a good performance for a horse with his eyes popping out of his head!

I can't remember much else about this particular horse but I think he went wrong.

Earl trained a horse called Nemon. He'd bought it for a couple of members of the so called 'Birmingham Mafia'. As was usual practice for trainers when acquiring a horse for clients, he retained a bit of the purchase price for himself. Luck money it's sometimes called.

Nemon had had two or three 'quiet' runs and was entered in a race at Warwick in March 1978, a two-mile five-furlong hurdle. The going that day was soft to heavy, ground that was completely wrong for Nemon and would give him little chance of victory. I remember it was a particularly cold and damp day and I reasoned that, as I was unlikely to be pushing out a winner, it would be okay to put a couple of sweaters under my colours to keep warm. Generally, if I knew I was going to be getting stuck in, I preferred to be cold and unrestricted by layers of clothing.

I went out to the paddock and Earl was there. "Look mate," he said, almost apologetically, "you're going to have to do your best here."

"But everything is wrong for him," I countered. "The ground and the trip."

"I know that and you know that but they want to back him," he said, referring to the owners, who weren't in the paddock as they didn't like to be seen. They weren't dissimilar in looks to the Kray twins. "They won't listen to me and they want to back him," said Earl disconsolately, "so ... just do your best."

I did my best, but to no avail and we finished down the field, about seventh. I rode in and Earl just shrugged.

A few days later I got a phone call. A voice at the other end of the phone asked if I was Ian Watkinson of such and such address. I confirmed that I was. It was the Birmingham Constabulary. "We've had a spot of bother up here, concerning your trainer Earl Jones," he said. "I'm not at liberty to go into any detail but, listen, if anyone knocks on your door tonight or tomorrow, don't answer it."

It happened to be a Saturday so the following morning, as was my usual practice, I got up early. No-one about, schooled the horses I'd arranged to school, then returned home and stayed in for the rest of the day, until I received a phone call from Earl's wife.

The owners were unhappy that Nemon hadn't won and had also got wind of the fact that Earl had kept some of the purchase price for himself. They weren't happy about that either and took it upon themselves to shoot Earl in the left knee with a twelve-bore. Kneecapped him.

I went and saw him in Staffordshire General Infirmary Hospital but he didn't really want to discuss it. He was a very tough man.

He was never the same again after that. He suffered a stroke later that year. He handed in his licence and, with nothing to keep him any longer in England, returned to his native home of Wexford and we lost touch from thereon. He died in June 2003, aged 83.

TEN

SOME OTHER TRAINERS

I was walking into Southwell racecourse one day when I spotted a local trainer, Peter Green, hanging around the weighing room. As I saw him it crossed my mind that he had a novice chaser that always fell, but I hadn't noticed its name in the paper that morning. So, when he approached and asked me if I could ride his horse in the novice chase, I said, "Yes, of course, no problem." I would have said yes anyway – I had my reputation to consider.

His horses were moderate and, for some reason, whenever the bell went in the paddock for jockeys to mount before a race, some of the horses I rode for him would go berserk and you couldn't catch the bloody things. It got to the point where I would say to him, "How about if I get on this before the bell goes?"

Back in the weighing room, the valet, Peter Saint, said, "Why on earth are you riding that? It will fall, definitely." It transpired this was indeed the novice chaser that kept falling.

I prepared myself as I usually did in these situations, by putting my shoes into my kit bag instead of under the bench. This stemmed from the occasion after I had a fall at Teesside Park and had to return from Middlesbrough Hospital by train wearing hospital slippers because my shoes weren't in my bag. A bit embarrassing.

I duly cantered down to the start and realised this horse had limited power in his hindquarters. I was the most experienced jockey to have got on the horse thus far and perhaps the previous riders had not wanted to say anything, or hadn't realised. And here I was, about to line up in a novice chase.

The starter that day was a young chap, maybe a bit inexperienced, so I called out to him, "Sir, this horse is lame behind. I think we should withdraw." He said, "Right, well, trot it up for me let's have a look." I trotted this thing back and forth and all the other jockeys were shouting, "Yes sir, that's lame behind," but the starter said, "It doesn't look lame enough for me to authorize its withdrawal," to which I replied, "Well how lame does it have to be?" Then I lined up.

March 1977: The Jimmy Harris-trained Market Sage and I part company in spectacular style at the last flight in Haydock's Victor Ludorum Hurdle.

We scrambled over the first then crashed through the second, the ditch, and fell. And there I was walking back, watching the race. I did tell Mr Green what the problem was and the horse never ran again.

I remember riding a horse for Michael Chapman at Catterick. For some reason, I was convinced it was a hurdle race. In those days they used the same start for both the hurdles and chase courses, so when I cantered down and saw that the hurdle course had been dolled off, I was puzzled.

I called over to Albert Jenkins, the starter's assistant, who was checking the girths, and asked him. "Oh," he said, "let's have a look." He pulled the racecard out of his pocket. "Merry Boy," he read, as that was the horse's name. "Two runs over fences, one pulled up, one fall, so it must be fences." A great bloke, Albert, a former jockey. He was the only person I knew who could get 50mpg out of a Volvo, whereas most people were lucky to get 22. I had a lift back from the races with him one day. Frustrating doesn't describe it.

Mr Chapman had told me to ride the horse from the front, but cantering down he'd not felt like a front-runner. They're normally pulling you down to the start.

I gave him a chance and turning into the straight I was lying second. I then jumped past Maurice Barnes, who was in the lead. The water jump at Catterick was in front of the stands in those days and my horse was definitely a bit windy. Maurice headed me again and I went to go past him between the water jump and the finish. The horse hesitated; he just wasn't brave enough to go for the gap. I knew he still had plenty of petrol so I dropped my hands and made out that Maurice had squeezed me up.

As we pulled up, the tannoy announced that there would be a stewards' enquiry. Maurice looked at me and said, "What's that all about?" I shook my head. "I don't know," I replied, but when I got back to unsaddle, I objected to him.

We were called into the stewards' room where they showed us the TV footage. I was beaten a length or half a length and you could see there was room, albeit not much. They interviewed Maurice first and he said, "I knew he was there but I thought he had enough room." When I went in, I lied through my teeth and they awarded me the race.

I felt a bit sorry because Maurice and his father Tommy were nice people. In fact, Tommy had given me my first four winners over fences on Punion. But Maurice's horse wasn't trained by Tommy. If he had been, I wouldn't have objected, but as it was, my loyalties lay with the people I was employed by on the day.

I was having a rotten time of it in the fourth season of my career. Tom Robson had packed up training; I wasn't getting on the good horses; half of them fell and I kept getting injured. I was almost at the point of chucking in the towel.

A lovely bloke named Charlie Bailey, who ran the transport cafe on the A66, had a share in a horse that ran in the name of a gypsy lady from Appleby. He said he'd be very happy for me to ride it and that he would talk to the trainer.

Charlie came back to me shortly after and said, "Sorry, the trainer said he doesn't want a broken-down jockey who's lost his nerve." Not what you want to hear when things aren't going well.

I was really quite hurt by that remark. The trainer only lived about four miles down the road from me. He'd never asked me to school for him or ride out or anything. He obviously thought I was crap.

About six years later, when I was based down south and riding good horses, I travelled north to Wetherby to ride a couple for Tom Jones. That same trainer came to me before the first race and asked me if I'd ride his filly in the second division of the novice hurdle. He explained that they'd been stopping the horse, but today the race was to be run over the shorter, tighter old course – I think the new course was flooded – and they felt it would suit her and that she would win. "There'll be a few quid in it for you," he nodded. He'd obviously had a few quid on her himself. As he walked away I can remember thinking, "I've got news for you."

It looks as though I'm in secret contemplation of the follies of the world!

She was my last ride of the day. The trainer gave me plenty of instructions in the paddock about where I should put her in the race and what to do, then he legged me up and wished me luck. I thought to myself, "You're the one that needs the luck!"

It was a big field and I made sure I didn't put the horse into the position where she would have any chance at all. To be honest, I don't think she would have won anyway. We finished about sixth or seventh. The trainer looked absolutely furious as I returned to the unsaddling area.

"You weren't off a bloody yard," he raged as I took my tack off. As I looped my girth over the saddle, I looked at him and replied, "You obviously watched the race then." Then I turned and walked back to the weighing room. He couldn't very well report me to the stewards, could he? He was the one who'd told me they'd been stopping the horse.

At the other end of the scale, a permit holder, Donald Pearman, from Compton, near Lambourn, contacted me out of the blue one day. He'd been persuaded to buy a horse – I think it was called William Penn – who was a decent handicap hurdler. The idea was to send him three-mile chasing. He'd a run over fences a couple of times but I don't think he'd ever completed. In fact, the horse refused to jump and gallop. Not ideal for a novice chaser!

Mr Pearman had been told that I was the bloke to get the horse going over fences and he asked me to go down to his stables. It sticks in mind that he asked me to arrive with an empty fuel tank and he would fill it up when I arrived. This was the first and only time in my life I've been told that. I duly arrived and he filled my tank up as soon as I got there.

The staff and he had built one fence in the paddock. ONE fence. They brought the horse out of the warm-up field where a lad had been riding him around pending my arrival. I promptly took the saddle off and put it back on again. They looked at me in a funny way but I explained it was a habit of mine whenever a horse had been tacked up by someone I didn't know.

I could see the problem: he was a small, handsome little horse but he wasn't built for the hurly-burly of three-mile novice chasing. Perhaps he felt that was beneath him as he was a decent hurdler. At the first attempt he refused, so I got stuck into him with my stick so that he was more afraid of me than the fence. After that we jumped it several times in different styles, then I got off him and asked when his next entry was. "Next Saturday at Warwick," came the reply. "Okay," I said. "Declare him and I'll ride him."

The day came and I cantered him down with the others and, during the 'girth checking' few minutes, I warmed his backside for him – it was a cold day! – and did so again over the first plain fence and the open ditch. After that he seemed to get the hang of it and we got round safely. Mr Pearman seemed delighted and gave me a present equal to two or three times the riding fee.

Unfortunately, I was unable to ride him the next time due to other riding commitments so his regular jockey, James Evans, got back on and won two or three chases on him.

Later that season, Mr Pearman had a runner in a valuable two-mile chase at Wincanton that James was due to ride. The race cut up to a walkover so Mr Pearman went to the stewards, told them what I'd done for him and asked for their permission to let me take the ride instead of James. I thought that was such a grand gesture. It was the only walkover of my career. I never did ride for him again and I was very saddened to hear of his death some years later.

ELEVEN

NIGHT NURSE AND SEA PIGEON

Peter Easterby had one of the powerhouse stables during the 1970s and 80s. Based at Great Habton, near Malton, he trained two dual Champion Hurdle winners, Sea Pigeon and Night Nurse. They were among a vintage crop of champion hurdlers, the likes of which we won't see again in the same era: Persian War, Bula, Comedy Of Errors, Night Nurse, Monksfield, Sea Pigeon. All multiple Champion Hurdle winners.

I rode Sea Pigeon on three occasions and won on him each time. I first rode him in the Embassy Handicap Hurdle at Haydock in January 1977. He carried 12st 2lb that day, conceding weight to all his fifteen rivals. He was a horse that had to be held up till the last possible moment, so I dropped him in behind and, although he made a couple of mistakes on the way round, I was able to bring him through to lead on the run-in. He quickened clear so fast that he ended up winning by seven lengths. It was an amazing performance.

Fast forward to Cheltenham 1978. I was due to partner Sea Pigeon in the Champion Hurdle and Alverton in the Arkle, both for Peter Easterby. On the Monday I took a ride on a horse of Pam Sly's at Southwell called Captain Kenneth in a maiden chase. I knew the horse and I was quite happy. I had several rides that day, all on horses in whose jumping ability I was confident. Unfortunately, Captain Kenneth fell three out when leading.

The course doctor wanted to send me to hospital. I was in a helluva lot of pain, not helped by being dropped off the first-aid table, which made my eyes water a bit, but I kept insisting, albeit through clenched teeth, it was just bruising. Jeff Pearce helped me hobble to the car and he drove me home. I figured I'd be better after a hot bath, the only problem being was that I only had a shower in my flat. As luck would have it, a lovely girl, Lavinia Thompson, who lived in a house in the same complex as my flat, offered me the use of her bath. (Even now I tease her and tell people she bathed me!) I got in it but I really struggled to get out. The warmth helped a bit but once I was cold again, I seized up.

The following morning Steve Smith Eccles turned up to give me a lift to Cheltenham. Even overnight I'd harboured hopes that I would be okay in the morning, but I couldn't move. Eventually I accepted it and rang Peter Easterby to tell him.

My then girlfriend, Cathy, drove me to the local hospital where they proceeded to x-ray me. As we sat in the waiting room I spotted an exercise bike in the corner and I informed Cathy that I was going to sit on it to try and loosen up a bit. "I'm not sure that's a good idea," she said, but I got on it until the nurse came in waving the x-ray photographs. "Get off that bike," she screamed. "Are you completely mad? You've broken your pelvis!"

At that they loaded me on to a trolley, gingerly wheeled me to a ward and carefully lay me on the bed prior to commencing my treatment of ultrasound four times a day. They also administered pain relief, which I was glad of. I've never known such excruciating pain in my life, apart from the needle going into my balls for my vasectomy!

Graham Thorner substituted and duly won the Arkle on Alverton. Frank Berry took the ride on Sea Pigeon and got beaten. I don't think I would have been. He went too soon on orders from the owner and he hit the front before the last. When I'd won on him at Haydock – and later when we won the Fighting Fifth at Newcastle – I didn't make my move until halfway up the run-in.

By the weekend I was beginning to miss my home comforts, so Cathy and I hatched a plan. At 6.00am on the Sunday morning I nicked the crutches from the fellow in the next-door bed, escaped through the French doors to where Cathy was waiting in the car and spent the day at home. I left a note on the pillow to say I'd be back at 4.00pm, which I was, but Matron went berserk!

I did receive a visit from Pam Sly and her husband. They brought a bottle of champagne which was a really kind gesture. Also, Tom Jones sent me four quarter-bottles of champagne. Again, very kind of him, especially as he'd had nothing to do with the horse that had given me the fall. I gave myself a goal to be back in the saddle within three weeks.

After I left hospital, under orders to take things easy, Cathy and I took a short trip to Majorca, reasoning that the warmer weather would work a miracle. Back in Newmarket, Cathy strapped my left leg and crown jewels up with an equine elasticated bandage, and I'd walk up and down Warren Hill in a vain attempt to keep my wind straight.

Two or three days after we returned from Majorca, I rode in a couple of hurdle races at Devon & Exeter, one for Stuart Matthews, the other for Peter Bailey. Neither was placed but I didn't feel too bad. Then a day or two later I rode a New Zealand-bred horse in a long-distance chase at Nottingham. I couldn't speak when I came in. My lungs were bursting and my hip was a bit painful, but at least I was back.

Later that month I got the call to ride Night Nurse in the Scottish Champion Hurdle. I doubt if there's ever been a classier renewal of that race. Jonjo O'Neill rode Sea Pigeon, who'd finished second to Monksfield in that year's Champion Hurdle. He had to give 6lb to Night Nurse, who'd won the previous two Champion Hurdles. Also in the line-up was the top-class hurdler Beacon Light, as well as the brilliant Irish-trained Golden Cygnet, who'd won that year's Supreme Novice Hurdle at Cheltenham by fifteen lengths.

Gerry Newman made the running on one of the outsiders, Seventh Son. I chased the leader then took up the running two out. Sea Pigeon was running on behind me, but then Golden Cygnet came past us as if we were standing still. That novice would have beaten us both, easily. He was cantering all over us when he fell at the last, a fall that would tragically prove fatal.

The following season I got to ride Night Nurse over fences. He'd been a prolific hurdler – I think he was awarded the highest rating ever to a hurdler. Then they decided to switch to chasing. Jonjo rode him on his first start over fences at Market Rasen but something went wrong and they parted company at the fourth fence.

A week later, Jonjo broke his right arm when falling on a horse named Red Well at Kelso. With Jonjo out of action, Peter Easterby approached me to ride the "odd horse" until he returned. There was no contract involved, it was just a temporary arrangement.

Four or five days before Night Nurse was due to have his next race, his owner, Reg Spencer, rang and asked me to come and school him. I couldn't sleep the night before that. I was so excited at the prospect of riding such a good horse. I arranged to meet the owner somewhere in Malton and he drove me to the Easterbys' yard where they legged me up and I jumped six fences on him. That went well and I was given the ride in the Bobby Renton Memorial Novices' Chase at Wetherby.

May 1978: Jumping the final flight on Night Nurse when finishing third in the Royal Doulton Hurdle at Haydock. That was the last hurdle Night Nurse ever jumped before embarking on a chasing career. (Ken Bright photo)

The day beforehand, I was riding for my retained trainer, Peter Bailey, at Newton Abbot. I drove from Newmarket to Lambourn in the morning and met up with Peter, then we travelled to Newton Abbot together. Quite a big mileage. By the time I got home late that night I was absolutely exhausted, but still excited about the prospect of going to Wetherby the next day to partner such a good horse.

Paddy Broderick had been his regular rider over hurdles but his career was ended by a head injury sustained when Night Nurse had fallen with him at the last flight in the 1977 Christmas Hurdle at Kempton. Brod was brilliant over fences. It was he who taught Night Nurse to jump. In fact, he was the best man I ever saw at getting a horse over a fence. He could get a novice round when no one else could. I remember one day at Sedgefield when he rode in both divisions of a three-mile novice chase, one for Arthur Stephenson, the other for Denys Smith. Neither horse had completed the course before but he won on both of them.

I hadn't been home long following the tiring journey from Newton Abbot when I got a phone call from Jeff Pearce. "Are you going to Wetherby tomorrow?" he asked. "If so, do you want a driver?" I must admit I almost took his arm off with gratitude. The next morning I got up early, rode out one lot for Tom Jones and then we set off to drive the 160 miles to Wetherby.

There were seven runners in the Bobby Renton, the second race of the day, including two serious rivals. One was a horse of the Dickinsons called I'm A Driver, ridden by Tommy Carmody. He'd won by seven lengths at Ayr just four days earlier. The other was a nice horse of Josh Gifford's called Roadhead, with my good friend Bob Champion riding. Roadhead had won his only race over fences at Worcester by twenty lengths.

Josh had told Bob to go really fast out of the gate and get all the others at it. But Night Nurse liked to front run, while I'm A Driver was a tearaway. We set off, and that first mile – and Bob and I still maintain it to this day – was the fastest mile in a two-mile chase we'd ever been in our lives.

A big crowd had gathered at the last fence. Most of the jockeys that weren't riding in the race had even gone there. They all wanted to watch as they knew we were going to be going quick. One of them even said to me afterwards, "If one of you had missed that last fence you'd have rolled right up to the winning post!".

I was lying second to I'm A Driver going into the backstretch and I got to within two or three lengths of him once we got into the straight, but I knew that bar a fall I'd beat him. We jumped to the front at the last and won easily by three lengths going away. I'm A Driver was second and Bob and Roadhead were third.

Paddy Broderick was there that day. He'd come specially to watch the race. He came to see me after and said how much he would have loved to have been on the horse. I don't blame him. Night Nurse was such a beautifully balanced horse. It was like riding on a big spring.

Later that month I rode Sea Pigeon on his seasonal debut in the William Hill Hurdle at Newbury. There were only four runners and Sea Pigeon was backed down to 9-2 on, effectively a steering job. I remember drawing level with Bob Davies just before the last, looking across and saying, "Bob, give me a hand I can't steady this horse," to which he replied, "Fuck off!" I won the race in a canter.

Five days later, a Wednesday, I was back on Night Nurse at Newcastle. He made all and won easily by fifteen lengths. He was such a superb horse. I was always aware when I went back up north that I could feel some of the jockeys' eyes burning into my back, thinking I was a lucky so and so. But a lot of the northern jockeys were my friends too.

Back at Newcastle on 18th November 1978, I enjoyed a great day. I won the Fighting Fifth Hurdle on Sea Pigeon, beating Andy Turnell on Birds Nest by a length and a half. Then half an hour later I rode Night Nurse in an Embassy Chase Qualifier, shrugging off a mistake two out to win as we liked. I virtually pulled him up on the run-un, yet he still won by a distance.

Then, in the last race of the day, I rode one for Johnny Haine in the novices' hurdle. He finished well beaten and the horse's connections looked at me in disappointment. All I could say was, "Sorry, but this wasn't the best horse I've ridden today!"

October 1978: On the way to winning the William Hill Hurdle at Newbury, jumping the last ahead of Bob Davies on Heluan.

People often ask me which was the better of those dual Champion Hurdle winners, Sea Pigeon or Night Nurse. I'd have to say, given the choice in a race, I'd have ridden Sea Pigeon. While Night Nurse would go a relentless gallop and got two miles well, Sea Pigeon had to be switched off. He'd have waited in behind Night Nurse, then done him for speed on the flat. He'd finished in front of Night Nurse in the Scottish Champion Hurdle when giving him 6lb, but neither would have beaten Golden Cygnet that day. But for that fatal fall, he would have been one of the all-time greats.

Many years later – it would have been late 1990s or early 2000s – when I was doing horsebox driving, I bumped into Peter Easterby in the bar at Chester. We got talking about Sea Pigeon and Night Nurse. "Yes," he said, "they were great horses. What a shame they came at the same time."

Then he told me a story about when Sea Pigeon was retired. The routine was that Peter would be in the yard and, around three o'clock in the afternoon, he'd go to Sea Pigeon's paddock and bring him in. It was routine, and the horse would always come to him when he approached. But one Sunday afternoon in the spring he couldn't get near him for about three-quarters of an hour. "D'you know why?" he said. "The clocks had changed the night before, gone forward by an hour."

Sea Pigeon was one of a dozen horses owner Pat Muldoon moved from Gordon Richards at Greystoke to Peter early in 1977. All the lads were getting their heads together deciding who wanted which horse. The girls at the yard didn't get a look in. A chap named Bob Healy initially got Sea Pigeon but he left not long afterwards under a bit of a cloud. At the time, Monica Jones had just lost one of her horses, a big, strong four-year-old who'd broken down and, sadly, had to be put down. With Sea Pigeon being left spare, the head lad, Keith Stone, first offered him to Jack Warrell, who looked after Night Nurse and Alverton. But Jack suggested he should go to Monica as she'd just lost a horse she'd thought the world of, so Keith gave Sea Pigeon to Monica.

Monica was only fifteen hands high whereas Sea Pigeon was just over sixteen. She often used to make herself late for riding out due to trying to find someone who would leg her on board. She eventually found a way round that. When she was in the box with Sea Pigeon, she used to do him loose, never tied him up. She made a pet of him and he adored her. The only time she tied him up was when he'd got his tack on and was ready to go out. She'd scramble up into the saddle, lean forward, undo the head collar and walk out of the box. There aren't many horses who would actually stand for that. Most horses, if you did that, when you leaned forward, they'd look at you out the corner of their eye and fly back, break the head collar and make a real fuss.

November 1978: Sea Pigeon's lass Monica Jones leads us in after winning the Fighting Fifth Hurdle.

Monica looked after another horse in the box opposite Sea Pigeon's. If Sea Pigeon saw her go to that other horse first, he'd get really upset and start banging the door down. How she calmed him down was to get a yard broom, put it beside the stable door and tell him not to touch it. He'd then pick it up in his teeth and swing it around like a pendulum until she'd finished the other horse and went over to him.

When a photographer from Timeform came to take a picture of him, the old bastard would not stand still. But Monica had a pocket transistor radio which she switched on and Sea Pigeon would stand quietly then, listening to the music.

Night Nurse, by comparison, was a pretty straightforward sort of horse. However, whereas he always liked to run from the front in his races, he would never lead the string through the village. One day, a wheelie bin spooked him and Jack Warrell fell off him.

There was another horse in the yard that looked very similar to Night Nurse, so, to prevent any chance of him being got at, before a big race they would change boxes and make it look as though they were guarding Night Nurse, while Night Nurse himself was ambling around in another box.

Next stop for Night Nurse was the Killiney Novices' Chase at Ascot on 16th December 1978. I'd ridden three at Folkestone on the Monday of the previous week. The last of them tried to refuse with me, but I got him going again and we finished second. I was struggling with a knee injury at the time so I stopped at a phone box on the way back and rang my surgeon, John Dandy, who was a pioneer of keyhole surgery on knees. He lived in Little Wilbraham, a village near Cambridge, and told me to call in and see him on the way back.

By the Wednesday morning I was in Ward C6 of Newmarket Hospital and by the afternoon I was having my cartilage removed. It was a neat job. I rested Thursday morning, went home Thursday afternoon, strapped myself up and rode out on the Friday. I was back race-riding at Nottingham on Monday, five days before I was due to ride Night Nurse at Ascot.

In the Ascot weighing room that day, several of the jockeys came over to look at my wound. There were plenty of "oohs" and "aahs". Night Nurse duly won as expected, beating Dramatist easily by six lengths. I can't remember much about the race because, an hour later. I partnered Strombolus in the SGB Chase. In the paddock beforehand, Peter Bailey said to me, "You need to take on Grand Canyon (a noted front-runner) as no one has ever done that before." So we did. Apparently, we really turned the taps on ... and ended up falling at, I think, the last fence down the back. It was a right purler. I was knocked out cold and, as Strombolus got up, he stood on my chest and broke my sternum. I still have the convex lump to this day. I also happened to have stitches in my knee from the operation I'd had a week earlier. I was not in a good way. Racing is full of ups and downs but not usually that close together.

Many years later, I attended a Grand National do at Aintree with a load of other former jockeys. We were all reminiscing. Neale Doughty, who'd won the race on Hallo Dandy in 1984, and I were talking about cars and he mentioned how much he'd enjoyed driving my Triumph Stag. I was puzzled. "When did you drive it?" I asked.

"I drove you home from Ascot," he replied. "You were all smashed up, broken sternum, stitches in your knee from the op, concussed, talking complete rubbish when you were conscious." It was the first I knew of it!

Luckily, I was back by Christmas, just in time to ride Night Nurse in the Astbury Trophy Novices' Chase at Wolverhampton, which he won unchallenged by fifteen lengths.

December 1978: Riding Night Nurse in the Killiney Novices' Chase at Ascot. He won easily, beating Dramatist by six lengths.

It was a harsh winter with lots of meetings abandoned due to a combination of snow and frost. It was the third week of February before I was able to ride another winner. The weather had improved by the start of March when I rode

March 1979: Night Nurse leads Silver Buck over the last open ditch in the Wills Chase Final at Haydock. Given the chance to ride the race again, I'd have done things differently, and I have no doubt I'd have won.

Night Nurse in the Embassy Premier Chase Final at Haydock. There were seven runners but only two really counted: Night Nurse and his main rival, the Dickinson-trained Silver Buck, ridden by Tommy Carmody. Night Nurse hadn't run for eleven weeks, whereas Silver Buck had recently run at Windsor, being brought down in the closing stages when holding every chance.

I will admit I'm not proud of that race, although people, including my good mate Bob Champion, have said it was the best chase they have ever witnessed, with two top-class horses racing each other.

When I rode Night Nurse at Wetherby previously I'd ridden him with a lot more patience. I think that was key. However, on that day at Haydock, Reg Spencer insisted, before I went into the paddock, that I was to lead all the way. If a jockey doesn't ride to his orders, he can expect to lose rides pretty sharpish.

I bounced off in front with Silver Buck just behind me. We were bowling along past the stands. The ground was okay, softish. As we turned and went down the backstraight, I was leading and the two of us were going like scalded cats, with the other runners trailing in our wake. I wished I could have tucked in behind Silver Buck and given my horse a breather but, mindful of my orders, we kept taking him on.

Going into the last I knew I had no petrol left. Poor old Night Nurse was dead on his feet. I gave him a few taps. Peter O'Sullevan said afterwards that I hit him too much, and I guess it does look like it if you watch the replay, but actually they were only encouraging taps. It really did look worse than it was. Silver Buck beat us by two and a half lengths.

Given the chance to ride the race again, I'd have done things differently, and I have no doubt in my mind I'd have won. But that's racing. And only five days later, my career as a jockey was ended in the fall at Towcester, so I never got the chance to make amends.

March 1979: Silver Buck and Tommy Carmody lead me and Night Nurse over the last in the Wills Chase Final.

TWELVE

AUSTRALIA

I rode what turned out to be my last winner on a horse of Hugh O'Neill's named Plastic Cup in the Eridge Selling Handicap Hurdle at Plumpton on 6th March 1979. Three days later, I headed for Towcester and that fateful ride on Regal Choice that ended my career.

Prior to that, I reckon I'd have had more than twenty fractured or broken bones during my time as a jockey. Collarbone four times, nose three times, arm in three places, wrist, pelvis, sternum, leg, vertebra, not to mention countless ribs and nine or ten concussions. A catalogue of injuries, but I'd always bounced back from them. But not this one.

I suppose I'd been lucky in a way to have ridden for thirteen years. When the stewards start calling you a 'senior jockey' and ask for your opinion on the state of the ground, that's a sign you've been around for a while, but it had only been in the last four years that people other than doctors and nurses had taken much notice of me.

After the Jockey Club's surgeon, Frank D'Abreu, had confirmed it was all over, I rang my friend Brian Radford of the Sporting Life. "I'm bitterly disappointed," I told him. "I feel tremendously fit. But the expert has given his opinion and I'm in no position to argue with him. I have no intention to end up a cabbage in a wheelchair. When I stop riding, I want to enjoy life for a few years."

Looking back on my career, I'd ridden some great horses and had some good retainers. When things really started to go my way I turned down the occasional outside ride if the horse's jumping ability was suspect. I think that was sensible and only fair to my retainers. I used to hate riding three-year-old hurdlers fresh from the flat. Most of the time, all they wanted to do was gallop and you couldn't place them properly.

My weakest point was not being able to ride a proper finish. I lost races I should have won because I was outridden by jockeys with a flat race style. Perhaps I could also be criticised for riding too many waiting races, but I liked to freewheel for as long as possible and I loved coming from behind, especially on a horse that barely got the trip.

I don't wish to compare jockeys of today with those I rode against but I find it difficult to understand today's fashion of having long reins and bumping up and down in the saddle. Surely that doesn't do anything for the balance of a horse. In my opinion, if you wanted to build the perfect jockey, I think the ideal combination would have been to have the style of Gerry

Griffin, the dash of Johnny Haine, the horsemanship of Gerry Scott and the strength of Jeff King.

I always thought that Chris Read was very underrated and should have ridden a lot more winners than he did. He won the Topham Trophy on Churchtown Boy two days before the horse finished second to Red Rum in the Grand National. Chris was a real good jockey, just not in the right yard and so didn't get the best chances.

Once I was able to do things again, I didn't stick around. Dana Mellor of JETS, the Jockeys Employment Training Scheme, visited me, but I couldn't really settle mentally. I ended up going to Australia for six years.

Mrs Solna Thomson Jones, Tom Jones' first wife, who owned Snailwell Stud – I rode their future Gold Cup winner Alverton and also the smart Major Thompson to victory – and Alan Lillingston, a former top amateur rider who had ridden Winning Fair to land the Champion Hurdle in 1963, very kindly arranged for me to go to Australia to work for a chap named Joe Manning, who ran Woodburn Spelling Station for horses in training, at Cootamundra, in New South Wales.

I flew out there in October 1980. I worked my passage over there on an IRT (International Racehorse Transport) horse plane. We had to go the long way to Sydney due to quarantine regulations. The regulations stated that no horse-carrying plane was allowed to refuel on any continent that had African Horse Sickness. Thus, I went from Gatwick to Shannon, in Ireland; next stop was Newfoundland, then Calgary, then Hawaii, then Fiji, then finally Sydney. The journey took 49 hours. I went on my own because I didn't know how things would work out. Cathy came out and joined me about two months later.

Joe had about fifteen or sixteen horses at the time We used to do a lot of pre-training for legendary trainers Tommy Smith and Bart Cummings, along with some other trainers from Sydney. We also trained a few for ourselves. We had some that weren't quite good enough for the city racetracks but were plenty good enough for the country races, which were still pretty competitive with good prize money.

Not long after I'd arrived, I remember the foreman, Stewart, a brilliant bloke, saying to me, "Hey, Pom, you want to get yourself a hat, mate. This Australian sun isn't like your English sun you know". Of course, me being me, I said, "No, I've got plenty of hair," then for two days I was holed up in my hotel room sweating, being sick, the shiver; sunstroke. I got a bit of stick for that when I returned to work.

I loved the job but it was getting a bit hot for me by December, the height of the Australian summer. I was really struggling with the heat, so I came home to England for Christmas, but not before Joe Manning offered me the job of training the horses if I went back. So I returned to Australia around February/March 1981 and commenced training there as private trainer for

Woodburn Spelling Station. Joe had shares in some of the horses but they ran under my name. I just looked after and trained the horses, whereas the office side of things was taken care of by others. We gradually built up the number of horses from eighteen to forty-five.

Joe's father-in-law worked in a government office in Canberra and he managed to get my visa papers through in just eight weeks, whereas it can take some people up to eighteen months. Through strings being pulled, I obtained permanent residency.

We only raced three times a fortnight but in my first season I trained seventeen winners. I trained 40-something in my second season, then in my third season I came third in the Southern District Racing Association's trainers' table. with 75 winners. I twice trained five winners in one day, once at Cootamundra, once at Gundagai, and, in 1983, we had a double at Randwick, the Australian equivalent of Ascot.

Tumut Racecourse was about fifty miles from Cootamundra, at the foot of the Snowy Mountains, and the river that ran past would always be icy cold. I was known as the Mad Pom for my habit of plunging into it on my way back from the races.

There were times, though, when things didn't go so well. One day I had six runners at Tumut and thought they all had good chances. We had a bad start to the day. We left home at about 3.30am to go to the stables, Cathy and our little dog beside me. On the way I ran over a kangaroo and broke its leg. I got my knife out in order to cut its throat and put it out of its misery and badly cut my hand, nearly cutting it off in the ensuing struggle. The little dog ran off into the bush and Cathy was hysterical. All the horses ran badly, only one was placed. Then, to cap it all, I was walking back from the weighing room where I'd collected the colours at the end of the day and one of the horses that had run in the previous race whipped round and kicked me. It was entirely my fault for not paying attention and it put the seal on a bloody awful day.

Among the best I trained was Black Streak. He was sent to me by the widow of a farmer. They'd originally intended to use him as a rodeo horse. I only took him to the racecourse five times, three times for races and twice for barrier trials. He won all five but in winning his last race he split a pedal bone and never ran again. I also trained a decent sprinter called Rolled Gold, who only ever won first time back from a holiday. I used to turn him out and make him think he was on holiday but it didn't fool him. He actually had to go away properly, shoes off, out 24 hours a day. I had a good mare called Act Of Faith. I ran her twice in one day at a picnic meeting. She finished third in the first race, then turned out again two hours later and won.

March 26, 1983: Black Streak, the most memorable horse I trained in Australia, winning the L. M. Boynton Memorial Improvers' Handicap at Gundagai in the hands of Gary Buchanan. (Bradley Photographics photo).

Swimming Spot On Brigade, trained by Mike Donoghue, in the man-made dam at Cootamundra

In September 1981 I made a brief return to England. There was a long-running show on Thames Television called 'This Is Your Life', fronted by Eamonn Andrews and latterly by Michael Aspell. How it worked was that a celebrity or person of note would be set up by all his or her friends or family to go to some function or another and, in the middle of it, Eamonn Andrews would appear and surprise them, holding a big red book and saying 'This Is Your Life'. The function would then become a show all about that person and their life.

In 1981 Bob Champion had won the Grand National on Aldaniti, having recovered from cancer. He thus became an instant celebrity. Living in Australia, I received a phone call in the middle of the night to say they were planning to surprise him on the show on his wedding day in October and would I come along as a surprise guest, all expenses paid. Would I? Of course I would!

They warned me that if any word about the show got out, it would be cancelled immediately. This was a few months beforehand.

I caught the small plane from my hometown of Cootamundra to Sydney on the Sunday morning, then flew BA Business Class from Sydney to Heathrow, arriving early Monday morning. My suitcase with my dinner suit in it didn't come off the conveyor belt, which was a bit of a worry as time was so constrained. Panicking slightly, I alerted the driver of the luggage truck and after about an hour it was located amongst the freight. But at least I'd got it.

Then a taxi took me to the Hilton Hotel in Stratford, where I was able to shower and get changed. I didn't go to the church for the wedding. My part was to be played in the marquee afterwards.

Eamonn Andrews pounced on Bob when he came out of the church, then proceeded to do the show with him in the marquee. Towards the end, he said to Bob, "Now, here's a voice from your past," at which point they played a tape recording of me saying, "Well, Bob, I thought I'd better collect that tenner!" My name was announced and I walked into the marquee.

The story behind the tenner was that Bob, Steve Smith Eccles and I all bet each other a tenner to give to the last one of us who got married. I still have Steve's tenner; I framed it. I'm not sure if I ever did get Bob's off him, but then he is from Yorkshire. I wasn't far behind Bob anyway, as I married Cathy in Australia two weeks later. It was great to be part of Bob's special day.

I stayed a night with my parents in Cambridge, took the train to Heathrow and was back at home in Cootamundra by Thursday morning. On the return journey, one of the stewardesses walked past me two or three times, then said, "Have you got a twin brother, or was it you when we travelled over to England two days ago?

"Yes, it was me," I replied. "I didn't like it. It was too cold!"

I saw an advert somewhere offering 'adventure' holidays with a firm called Australian Himalayan Expeditions, based in Wooloomooloo (an Aborigine name), near Sydney. I took a fancy to two of them. The first one was a five-day course learning and doing scuba diving, located at Airlie Beach, in northern New South Wales. The second involved seven or eight days camping in two-man tents on the beaches of the Whitsunday Islands, near the Great Barrier Reef, which runs for 2,000 miles off the North East coast of Australia.

What a fabulous two weeks that was. Four or five of us stayed in a little wooden shack on Airlie Beach, going to a nearby luxury hotel every day to use their pool to learn the art of using the scuba diving equipment in preparation for the Professional Association of Diving Instructors (PADI) course we were to undertake. It was five intense days of tuition. We all had to wear wetsuits, mainly to prevent chafing of the shoulders from the air tanks on our backs. It was hard enough for us males to have a pee as we were in the wetsuits all day. One of the girls on the PADI course was shocked when she asked the instructors how the girls had to relieve themselves. She was told to just pee in the suit – "it will feel warm but when you take the suit off after one or two pees, a hot shower will work wonders!" No one mentioned the number twos. We all peed in our wetsuits and soon got used to it, but I didn't ask to swap wetsuits with anyone!

On horseback in Australia

Watching work on the gallops at Cootamundra

The ship that took me on a tour of the Great Barrier Reef islands. It was the best two weeks of my life.

It was great fun and then at the end of the week we were taken by boat to Hayman Island, which was covered in Astro Turf, to take our exam in scuba diving. We all passed and achieved our PADI certificate which entitles us to hire diving equipment anywhere in the world.

The second adventure began by being taken by speedboat out to one of the 1,200 islands that surround the Great Barrier Reef. We joined a ship for a week-long cruise around the islands, stopping at two or three of the islands en route, staying at least two nights on each. Only one lad from the diving course came with me. We met the others there, ten of us altogether. We all had to pal up with one other person and share the two-man tent on the beach, so I teamed up with an English lad named Rob.

There were four girls amongst us, three nurses and a blue-film actress with a very curvy figure and no shame in admitting to what she did for a living. All of us males lusted after the girls but there was no tent swapping done at all, unfortunately. The days were spent fishing first thing in the morning to catch small tuna which we cooked over a camp fire and ate with crusty rolls or crackers for breakfast, then it was windsurfing, swimming or exploring the islands.

A funny thing sticks in my mind. On the first night we were sitting round the camp fire, as we did every night, drinking beer, getting to know each other, when suddenly, the bloke in charge, who was telling us the routine, held up a spade with a toilet roll tied to the handle and said, "This is the toilet!" The girls all said, "Oooohhh no!" (or something like that) as the meaning sank in. He told us to make sure we dug a deep enough hole because other people used the islands. He didn't want any accidents either, bearing in mind we were all in sandals or bare feet.

The girls were horrified but, fifteen to twenty hours in, we'd be sitting around eating or drinking or just lazing about when one of them would say, "I think I'll just take that spade for a walk," then bring it back, walk down to the edge of the sand for a wash, then join back in the conversation.

The nurses were great fun, the blue-film actress a little coarse but what the hell. The last day was really sad; none of us wanted to go back to the mainland after days of 38- to 40-degree heat. It was wonderful fresh air and we'd become experts at catching and cooking fresh fish. We had an endless supply of beer and wine; it was such a lot of fun.

The highlight for me was being collected by flying boat, going an hour or so further north along the reef and landing in a lagoon. We were then taken to an underwater cliff edge where we scuba-dived and snorkelled all day then dined on the boat on salad and freshly caught seafood. A motor boat was on hand to provide water skiing. We all got on well but no one kept in touch (as far as I know) despite promises that we would. One lad, an electrician from Sydney with red hair – he had to keep well covered during the day – was very amusing.

One incident I recall when we were exploring the underwater caves and there was a rush of water, resulting in us all becoming jumbled up together. The blue-film girl's body briefly brushed across my face. Funny the things that stick in your mind.

It really was the best two weeks of my life. I returned to the stables to find that Cathy had done a sterling job looking after things. Stewart, the foreman, said he hadn't noticed I had been away!

I eventually got elbowed out of Cootamundra. Although I'd continued to train winners for Woodburn and we had plenty of horses, there wasn't enough staff and the operation began falling apart, so I lost interest. Cathy and I moved to Colin Hayes' huge racing and breeding centre at Lindsay Park Stud at Angaston, about 50 miles outside Adelaide, where I worked on the stud and pre-training side.

I didn't stay there long, only a matter of weeks, then went to work for trainer Len Smith in Semaphore, about twelve miles from Adelaide. By then my marriage to Cathy was on the rocks. She stayed at Lindsay Park, I moved into Adelaide city. I stayed in a hotel for a couple of nights then shared a house with a couple of blokes, an Australian guy and an English man named Alec Morris, whose house it was. It was in an area called Croydon, a suburb of Adelaide. If I leaned out of the window, I could see part of the track that had been the venue for the first ever Australian Grand Prix. It was also near Adelaide's biggest sports ground where they play Aussie rules football. I went down there one day, hoping to learn how to play the game but they told me I was too short. In Newmarket I'd been a relative giant compared to most of the people there.

Alec was an interesting fellow, very clued up. He was three or four years older than me. He'd emigrated in the late 1960s and had done all sorts of things. He'd dabbled as a taxi driver for a while, mainly so he could get to know his way around Adelaide. He wasn't into racing as such but he'd managed a bookmaker's shop back in England, ironically at the end of the road where Cathy used to live. We got on like a house on fire. We went to see the Seekers in concert one night, still the original 1960s line-up. He also took me to a couple of singles clubs. I found it interesting that, whereas singles clubs in Britain used to have a bit of a stigma, that certainly was not the way in Australia. They called them 'singles mingles' clubs.

Alec and I have remained in touch ever since. I still see him every couple of years when he comes over to visit his daughter who lives in London.

While I was living in Adelaide, I got a call from a friend, John Williams, an auctioneer and course official of Hereford Racecourse, as he was helping organise a visit from four UK-based jump jockeys to take part in a Shergar Cup-type jumping tournament. It was the very first year they did this. One of the jockeys was my mate Steve Smith Eccles. John was to be their 'nanny' and was in charge of organising their entertainment. He suggested that as I knew the form and spoke Australian, I should join them for a couple of days at their hotel, so I did.

In the evening, at dinner, I said, "Are we ready for tonight's entertainment?" Then I left the table, went to reception and looked in the back of a book that I knew they'd have, for certain phone numbers of lively young ladies who would be willing to join us for the evening.

Shortly afterwards, a group of lovely ladies arrived and engaged in lively banter with us before someone suggested we all adjourn to our rooms. I shared a room with Steve as we were buddies and we held a glass to the wall to listen in to the antics of a very young but talented jockey, who shall remain nameless, in the room next door. We could hear him chatting away with his new-found lady friend. "Do you mind me asking how old you are?" we heard him say. Her reply was muffled; we didn't catch it but then we heard him exclaim "Christ! You're the same age as my Mum!" We did have a bit of a snigger about that. At that point, Steve and I said our prayers and got into our (separate) beds for the night.

Cathy and I eventually decided to return to Britain to take stock and see if we could make our marriage work. We came back early in 1986 but we split up soon after. I did very much want to go back to Australia, but I had to have a reason. Then I got to hear that Ron Mason, who'd formerly trained at Guilsborough, in Northamptonshire – he trained Track Spare, the winner of the first race started from stalls in Britain – but had since moved to Australia, was advertising for a foreman.

I jumped at the chance, flew back to Australia and joined him at his base at Airlie Beach, but within three or four days I knew I'd made a mistake. I found him an impossible man to work with. He trained winners but his methods were odd and I just couldn't put up with him or them. I stuck it out for about a month then left.

I'd earlier met an ex-jockey named Keith Watson, who trained at Perth, in Western Australia. I liked Keith and had admired him as a rider. We'd got on well and he'd given me his address and phone number in case I should ever need his help, so when I spoke with him and told him things hadn't worked out with Ron Mason, he offered me the chance to work for him as head lad. I accepted straightaway.

I flew from Sydney to Perth and began working for him. However, what I hadn't realised was that Keith's wife essentially ran the operation and I couldn't get on with her at all. I was head lad but wasn't allowed to make any decisions – I was really no more than a stable lad. Again, I didn't stay there long and made the decision to head for home.

During my time in Australia I'd worked for the international racehorse transport company, IRT. I used to work my passage back to England by taking horses to Singapore and Penang. The company provided me with an onward ticket, which suited us both. It meant they got a groom for peanuts; I got a flight home for peanuts. The plane would start off in New Zealand, pick me and the horses up at Sydney, then fly to Singapore, unload horses there, then carry on to Penang. I'd get off there, whereas some of the horses would be conveyed onwards to Hong Kong.

Along with my companion, I used to book into the Rasa Sayang Hotel in Penang for three or four days. It was a five-star place but we got it for crew rates. It was right on the beach, with entertainment organised by some of the local lads who hung around on the beach – they weren't allowed to set foot on the hotel lawn. For some reason, they all answered to the name of Charlie, which I thought was strange. They provided water skiing, para-sailing, high-speed speed-boat rides, all for peanuts. I loved the food there, top class in the hotel but interesting and tasty street food just down the road towards the 'entertainment area'.

I also spent time in Singapore before flying on to London, Life there was at a much faster pace; it was 24/7, and the old Bugis Street was the 'place to be'. One night, about three or four o'clock in the morning, I was with an Aussie bloke and a Kiwi girl, walking back to our hotel. There were rats the size of cats wandering about, not the slightest bit afraid of us. Actually, to call our place a 'hotel' is a touch flattering; it was more of a doss house. The bathing facilities reminded me of the Welsh experience: stand in a trough and pour water over you, soap then rinse. We took turns at washing the Kiwi!

Ted Ryder was the most famous commentator on the Australian racing circuit at the time. He would get asked to open things like fetes and new buildings – he was the Southern District Racing Association's answer to Tommo. (Bearing in mind the SDRA is bigger in area than the UK.) The Wagga Wagga racetrack even has a race named after him: The Ted Ryder Cup, which is run every Christmas time.

Ted was a big bloke, not only in personality but in stature, he must have been six foot five, but for some reason he chose to drive round in a vintage Morris Minor.

Like America, Australia has these great big drive-in cinemas where people come from miles around to sit in their cars and watch a movie on a massive screen somewhere in the middle of nowhere. I remember hearing of the occasion when Ted took a lady friend to one such a film, in the aforementioned Morris Minor.

Maybe it was a romantic film, or maybe it was always the plan, but old Ted got a bit amorous and he and the lady friend were making out on the front seat of the Morris when his knee got stuck on the horn. Of course, the sound of the horn blaring away was ruining the film for everyone else, so they began turning their lights on to see what was going on. There in the spotlight was Ted and his mistress en flagrante! How embarrassing, especially as he was struggling to get his knee out.

The good news is he did end up marrying the lady in question. She survived him by twenty-three years and used to present the prizes at for Ted's race at Wagga Wagga each year. Furthermore, the Daily Advertiser, for whom Ted worked, gave him a new, bigger car!

When I lived at Cootamundra, they held a two-day rodeo in the November. All the town's shopkeepers boarded up their windows beforehand because the cowboys would come into town for a drink and to cross swords with the local youth. Some of the fights made the local papers; the cowboys were as hard as nails. For a few days before the rodeo began, all beer was served in plastic pots to help avoid bloodshed.

Rodeos were held at Yass, Tumut, Gundagai and Cootamundra, all in New South Wales, and at Malmarella in South Australia. The daytime temperatures in December and January were often 39 to 41 degrees, making it impossible to stage rodeos, so they held midnight rodeos at Yass and Tumut, starting at 8.00pm and finishing around three or four o'clock in the morning. There was very little trouble despite plenty of drinking.

I did take part in a few rodeos: three bareback rides, one saddle bronco and one bull. But I was too old. I was about thirty-three and you really need to start at fourteen. Hitting the ground was a certainty, obviously, and no way would you mention wearing a crash helmet or you'd be accused of being gay! My best record was five and a quarter seconds. I never managed to reach the required eight seconds in order to get a score. I remember one day getting slung off and ending up under the feet of the pick-up horse, who stood on a very sensitive area, resulting in me being taken off to Canberra hospital. I did get a big kick out of it though, every bit as much as when I did my first parachute jump. And I've done 23 of those now!

One year, either 1982 or '83, we had a lad from the north of England staying with us named George Skelton. Our lodger, Guy, and I enlisted him to be in our team in the 'wild horse race'. This involved us roping one of the bucking horses, getting a saddle on it out in the arena and then one of us riding it past the judge. Because Guy was the tallest and was used to stepping onto a horse, he did the riding. George and Guy put the saddle on, I had one arm round its nose and the other round the back of its head, just behind the ears, and one of its ears between my teeth. Amazingly, we won it. However, there was a bit of bad feeling amongst the professional cowboys at us being amateurs so we gave the prize and the glory to the second-placed cowboys. At least that way we retained our teeth!

For me, Sunday mornings, driving along dusty roads through places whose names I've long forgotten, thirty degrees, listening to country and western music on the car radio, on the way to a rodeo, and the boozy drive back. I loved going to them, whether I was riding in them or not. It's the thing I miss most of all about Australia.

THIRTEEN

THE WOMEN IN MY LIFE

I've already mentioned some of the women who have passed through my life during the course of the previous chapters – Margaret, Kathleen, Jossie, Angela and, of course, my first wife, Cathy. But there are others without whom my life would be incomplete.

At the end of 1975 I started seeing a very beautiful girl who was a big part of my life for a couple of years. When I asked her if she would mind her story being included in this book, she declined and I respect that, but I will never forget her beaming proud smile as I walked in the door on the evening I won the Hennessy in 1976 on Zeta's Son. I may have never let her know at the time, obviously keeping up to my image as a tough guy, but .it meant the absolute world to me and it is something I shall never forget.

I wasn't a very good boyfriend to her and I messed her about until she wisely left, although not before cutting off the sleeve of one of my best jackets. Apparently, I only needed one arm for my favourite pastime.

Perhaps if she reads this she can forgive me. I'm truly sorry if I hurt her and am grateful for the good times we shared.

HELEN

I'd returned from Australia and was back riding out for Bill O'Gorman in Newmarket in April 1988 when I met Helen McLeod-Smith. She was a lovely, bubbly red-haired girl who was working for Martin Pearce, owner of a PR magazine, and riding out for John Winter in the mornings. She'd previously worked for Michael Stoute and looked after that great filly Sonic Lady, accompanying her wherever she ran, including trips to France and the Breeders' Cup in California.

We met when she came to help with the horses in the afternoons. One evening I asked her out for a meal. We had a great night. When it came to the time for me to take her home, I said, "You know, you're very welcome to stay." I will never forget her reply. "Why not?"

Gradually, she moved in, just returning to her home to collect clean socks, pants and breastplates. She was wonderful. It was a very happy time.

Her parents lived in Sussex; a village called Ditchling. I'd given Helen a car and she sometimes drove home to Sussex to visit them. On Friday, 8th

October, she went down to collect an answerphone she had bought me for my fortieth birthday the following day.

In those days, we didn't have mobile phones so I thought nothing of the fact that she hadn't returned Saturday morning. I went and rode out as usual. Looking back, I was aware of a couple of the lads riding out for Michael Stoute giving me funny looks. Then a friend of mine, Maxine Juster, who was on one of the fillies at the back of the string rode upsides me.

"Are you okay, Ian?"

"Yes, why wouldn't I be?"

"Only, I heard Helen was killed in a car crash last night."

I trotted back to the yard and saw Elaine, Bill's O'Gorman's wife, and I told her what Maxine had said. She caught hold of the horse saying, "Leave this to me. Go and find out what has happened."

I got into my car and drove to John Winter's yard. As I pulled up, I saw Rupert Arnold, who was John Winter's assistant at the time. His face said it all. "I'm so, so sorry," was all he said. I'll never forget my fortieth birthday.

I cannot, maybe do not want to, remember what I did or said next. I know that my mate Bob Champion came to see me every day to make sure I was okay.

Helen was only 24. She is buried in Ditchling Churchyard. I would have married her.

CLAIRE

I met my second wife, Claire, at the British Racing School. We hadn't been married very long when her mother came to stay with us for a few days. She did this regularly. One evening we shared a bottle of wine and I also drank a couple of small cans of beer. "You like a drink, don't you?" observed the mother-in-law.

Me being me, in the morning I decided to make a statement. After I'd got up at the crack of dawn and gone to do the horses, I returned home for breakfast and mother-in-law was pottering round the kitchen making tea and what have you. I got the cornflakes out of the cupboard and put them in a bowl, then proceeded to pour a can of beer all over them.

This gesture backfired as mother-in-law didn't leave the room so I could surreptitiously ditch the cornflakes into the bin and pretend I'd eaten them. She carried on fiddling about clearing up, occasionally glancing at the said bowl of cereal and then at me.

In the end, I had no choice but to wolf them down. Not to be recommended. I went back to work and when I came back after, Claire followed me. "Mum has just told me what you did. She said I've married either a complete berk or an alcoholic." I looked at her. "What did you say?" I asked.

"Well, I told her you're not an alcoholic!"

Clare and I had one child, Camilla, and our second, Max, on the way. It was always in the back of my mind that I needed to provide for them all. Being considerably older than Claire, I worried that she would be left a widow and unable to provide for my kids. We had the nice house in Newmarket and I had a couple of flats that I let out, but you are only worth what you are making, and as I only had a couple of horses in to do, plus riding out, I worked nights for a company called Kings Transport, whose business was freight forwarding.

I'd set off at about five o clock in the evening. The job involved driving a truck to this massive warehouse in Birmingham. It was the size of two football pitches. You had to take a piece of paper called a manifest that detailed where the parcels for your area were, put them on a pallet, wrap it in clingfilm-type stuff, and the fork-lift drivers would load it on to the truck. Then it was back to the depot in Newmarket and I'd be home any time between five and nine in the morning.

Some of the blokes sold powdered drugs to help keep themselves awake. I knew what they were as I'd used them in my riding days to keep my weight down. I'm ashamed to say I did use them occasionally to help keep awake for driving. I saw some awful things. One night I witnessed a lorry driver silhouetted against flames, unconscious at the wheel of his cab on the M6, with a burning car underneath his lorry. The police were unable to reach him as the car was petrol and in danger of exploding at any minute, whereas a diesel car wouldn't have exploded.

It was 1994. There was a BBC TV show called 'Noel's House Party', hosted by Noel Edmonds. Claire said she'd like to apply for tickets to be part of the studio audience.

"Of course," I agreed. "No problem. You get them and we'll go." I was always up for a bit of action.

There was a part of the show called 'The Big Pork Pie' in which a member of the audience would be named and shamed for some deed they'd committed, all while seated on a cardboard pork pie with a wedge cut out of it. Total humiliation in front of a studio audience and millions of TV viewers. Claire thought I deserved to go on it.

Plenty of research went into this show. They sent a woman up to secretly assess me and make sure I was the right sort of person; the type who could take the forthcoming embarrassment without having a mental breakdown, I imagine.

I came home from doing the horses one day and there was this woman sitting there talking to Claire. Claire was pregnant at the time and had been attending classes for that sort of thing. I didn't go, obviously. I'd done my bit.

I assumed this woman was from there. Claire introduced her and I charmed her with my usual, "Oh yes ... Claire said you were a right old bag but you're not!"

Unbeknown to me at the time, the woman then looked at Claire and gave her the thumbs up. Ideal fodder for the show.

The day came and we drove down to London and arrived at the TV studio car park. Claire spoke to the chap on the gate, the barrier lifted and we parked up. Then we went in and were given tea and coffee and a biscuit. I can remember thinking proudly to myself, "She's got this well organised." I didn't say anything to her though.

We were taken past a long queue of people and through some doors and there was a vast theatre full of people, absolutely packed. The usher then showed us a couple of seats. "That's lucky," I remarked to Claire. "I like to have an aisle seat with my gammy leg." I still hadn't clicked on to this at all.

The show began and then came the bit where Noel Edmonds would walk into the audience with his microphone. He was saying, "People are always teasing me about my height because I'm not very tall. It's not very fair ... isn't that right, Ian Watkinson?"

To my bemused horror, the spotlight fell on me. I glared at Claire who was convulsed in giggles.

"Stand up Ian," Noel said, which I did. "What a cheek, you're the same height as me," he observed. Anyway, I followed him down to the stage and then up on the big screen came the picture of me on a horse, naked. The Streak ... the photo that had appeared in the Daily Mirror in 1975.

I sat down on the pork pie, and I shuffled right back in the seat so my feet didn't touch the floor. More ammunition for Noel. He pointed his finger at me, turned to the audience, pointing. "See, he's so short he can't reach the floor!"

Anyway, he got me to relate the circumstances of the streak and it all seemed to go down well. Afterwards, we were taken to a hospitality suite. Angela Rippon, the newsreader, was there. I remember we had a sandwich and a drink. Noel Edmonds came over to me and shook my hand and told me he was chuffed to bits and thought it had all gone well, which was nice. I was presented with a memento – a silver pork pie with the wedge cut out of it. I still have it to remind me of the occasion. It was a great bit of fun.

I do recall afterwards, this girl who worked for Robert Williams, whom I quite fancied but she never gave me the time of day, showed a lot more interest in me. Funny that. She was too late, I was already married, and anyway, a fling with her would have damaged my weight. Her parents owned a fish and chip shop.

The fork-lift drivers from the depot in Birmingham all watched the show and thought it was hilarious. When they saw me coming, they'd lean forward, standing on the pedals and pretend to be jockeys!

I did end up having a fling with another girl. Unfortunately, she took it upon herself to make sure that Claire found out. I have no wish to comment further, apart from the fact that Claire, wisely many would say, took our children and left me to return to her family.

That was probably the worst thing to ever happen to me, the second of the three lowest points in my life, the first having been the end of my riding career. And it was my own fault. She was suffering from post-natal depression. I felt neglected, when in reality, I was the one who should have been holding things together for her.

My third lowest point followed soon after, but I'll need to go back to an earlier time to explain how it began.

I sometimes used to go racing with Jeff Barlow. One day, it must have been in the early 1990s, coming home from Market Rasen – I can't remember who was driving but we were going a bit quick and we thought we'd gone through a speed trap. Jeff said to me, "If you snuff it, do you mind if I have your driving licence? Then I can go as fast as I want and I'd just blame you." It was a bizarre thing to say but he said it in all seriousness. We'd both got licenses that pre-dated those with photographs.

I'd started doing some delivery work for my saddler friend Brian Scrivener. Jeff had a place in Hollywell Row, near Mildenhall. Half a mile down the road was a livery yard. When I used to make deliveries there, I'd call in and see Jeff on the way. One day in March 1994, I was delivering something to the livery yard and thought, "I'll go and have a cup of tea with Jeff first," then I changed my mind and went to the livery yard first. When I got to Jeff's place afterwards, the lad who worked for him saw me and said, "You don't want to hang around. The police are here. Jeff's shot himself."

If I'd gone there first, I'd have been the one who found him.

A year or so after Jeff died, I got a couple of speeding tickets and I remembered what Jeff and I had talked about that day driving back from Market Rasen. It was so easy to get a driving licence in his name.

When Claire left me, I tried to put on a brave face but I got into bad company and became mixed up in their activities. Somebody put it into my mind that, having obtained a false driving licence, I could get a credit card on the back of that. That's what I did. Armed with the card, I bought things for Claire because I thought I could buy her affections back. I was stupid, absolutely stupid, but I just didn't care. Needless to say, I very soon got caught.

I'd pretty much sorted myself out by the time of the court case in 2000. But I was all too aware I was facing the prospect of a custodial term.

I was working for Dave Thom then, driving horseboxes. I'd known him for over thirty years and had ridden for him since the early 1970s. Dave stood up for me as a character witness at the trial. He spoke of my time as a jump jockey and said to the judge, "You've got to remember, sir, that these are not ordinary men. They live on adrenaline. If it's a matter of walking the line or not walking the line, they will walk the line."

Bill O'Gorman told me later that Dave probably thought that that was the case but, in his opinion, having known me since I was ten years old, the reason I acted as I did was because of the head injury, even though it had happened fifteen or sixteen years earlier. Bill reckoned I'd been a completely different person since then and that it was a change of personality that made me break the law.

Whatever the reason, Dave's words must have had some resonance because the judge handed me an eight-month suspended sentence, suspended for eighteen months. I was ordered to pay £5,000 compensation plus £150 prosecution costs. I was very, very lucky. The level of my stupidity haunts me to this day. However, if anything good could come out of something like that, it was two-fold.

Firstly, I'm so glad to say that Claire and I now have a very amicable relationship and are both hugely proud of our kids, Camilla and Max. She is a wonderful woman and mother and there is nothing in this world I wouldn't do for her.

Secondly, my third wife, Karen – we weren't married then – was there for me when I'd reached my lowest point. I'd felt suicidal before the court hearing, but she said to me, "How would your kids feel if they found out their father hadn't got the guts to face something like this?" That hit me like a brick.

KAREN

I met Karen when I went to collect a horse from her employers at that time, Richard and Auriol Wilson, near Ipswich. All I can remember was that the horse needed some attention. Karen used to come up to Newmarket once or twice every week to ride out with Claire. I'd do the tacking up and mucking out, they did the riding, and both were top-class riders. When Claire and I fell out, Karen was living with us as her job with the Wilsons had petered out. I was delighted to have her on board, she rode well and was first class in every way. I wasn't thinking straight at this time; I'd made a complete mess of my life.

I was sent two fillies to break and get them ready to race in Bosnia. The box was hired, two drivers, Karen and myself, across the channel. We stayed the first night in a B&B in Baden-Baden, the second night in a disgusting flat in Vienna. The next day we were stuck on the border of Yugoslavia and Croatia virtually all day. We handed the horses over in a supermarket car park on the outskirts of Belgrade. I tried to take a photo but the officials went mad.

As we were heading back to the UK after a few awful days, the trouble with Claire was constantly on my mind. I must have been awful company. I just couldn't face the long journey by road back to England so I got the drivers to drop Karen and I on the outskirts of Budapest where I could buy flights back to England for us. At a service station I got a taxi, an ancient Lada driven by a wannabe racing driver who took us to the wrong airport – Budapest has two. By the time we got to the right one the flight to London had gone and we had to wait 14 hours for the next one. I spent ages on the phone to Claire, absolutely distraught, realising how I'd wrecked my life. She told me that she and a friend had got the locks changed on the house; two or three bagsful of my belongings had been dumped in Karen's flat, which was to be my home.

I can't remember which airport we landed at or how we got back to her flat in the High Street. Suffice to say that without Karen I might not be around. When, at my lowest point, she told me that my kids wouldn't think much of me if I didn't stay around to sort things out, that was what I needed to hear.

We eventually married at Gretna. My good friends Audrey and Bryan there to ensure I didn't change my mind. It was a great day apart from the speeding ticket I got on the way down the A1.

THE ONE THAT GOT AWAY

I met a beautiful northern girl in 1974 who had come to work in Newmarket with her then boyfriend. I felt he didn't treat her properly so I stole her and we had a very passionate few months. She then left town to go and work for Tony Dickinson back up north.

I wasn't able to see her much at weekends, as my riding career was just taking off and I needed to remain in Newmarket to school horses. On alternate Friday evenings Mr D used to ask her if she was going to Newmarket to see me and he'd wag his finger at her and say, "You shouldn't be driving all that way to see a jockey ... you won't be the only one."

One weekend she didn't return. My career was improving. No mobile phones; we just lost touch.

A couple of years ago, a friend who used to organise my flights to Spain went on strike so I had to embrace technology and get myself an email address. Another mate went to a Dickinson stable reunion, passed on my email address and, suddenly, I got an email from her out of the blue.

I arranged to meet her in a hotel bar in Wetherby, and after 45 years it was as if we had never been apart. It was pretty emotional. That said, we have five marriages, three children and five grandchildren between us now, but I'm so glad we are in touch with each other again.

WHAT THEY SAY ABOUT ME

CATHY'S STORY

I was eighteen, he was twenty-eight. I'd seen him at the races when I was working at Michael Oliver's yard, near Worcester and I knew who he was, but I didn't know he'd been making enquiries about me. At first it was nothing more than a look; a smile. Then out of the blue a phone call. A chat. We got on so well.

We arranged to meet up at the races and in a short space of time Ian asked me to move in with him in his Newmarket home. I gave my notice in and made plans.

One day, when he was riding at Cheltenham, I put all my possessions in the horsebox we had going there, including my Honda 250 motorbike, then shifted it all into a horsebox that was travelling to Newmarket and we set up home in one of Ian's flats that he owned then. He'd invested wisely as his career took off, purchasing first some land on which he built a house, plus two flats,.one of which he rented out and the other in which he was living when we met, in Park Lane, Newmarket. I started riding out for trainer Derek Weeden and then Robert Armstrong. Ian was very encouraging and supportive.

About a week after moving in with Ian, he had a fall (one of the many that were to come) and fractured two vertebrae in his back. Nothing life-changing and, luckily, nothing displaced. But it meant he had to spend a couple of days lying on his back on the living room floor. A physiotherapist came once to see him. I'm sure he should have spent far longer recuperating, but he spent much of the time on his back on the phone, planning his rides for the week after next. He was known as 'The Iron Man' and he was every bit as tough. He was passionate about race-riding but sometimes paid the price for saying yes to rides he should have turned down.

To say Ian is not romantic is an understatement. One day as we were getting in the car to go shopping, he suggested getting engaged. There was no actual 'proposal'. Then, as we were driving down Newmarket High Street, he pulled up outside Wiggs, the jeweller, and said, "Pop in there and find a ring you like. Give me a shout and I'll go in and pay for it." When I remarked I'd expected him to come in with me to a choose it, he replied "I can't, I'm double parked here." Twenty minutes later we were engaged.

Another (non)romantic time came when it was my 21st birthday. Ian took me out for dinner. I was somewhat surprised to find the table was booked for as early as 6.30pm. There seemed a sense of urgency about the whole thing. He was keen to make sure we left the house on time. At the restaurant he kept looking at his watch. We had a starter and a main course, but no pudding as Ian said there wasn't time. I had a feeling that there was some sort of surprise going to happen, maybe a party or meeting friends. What could it be?

As we turned into our road I expected to see cars parked all over the place and the house lit up as the party got started. Not a bit of it. Ian rushed into the house, put the TV on and the theme music to his beloved Coronation Street rang out.

"I thought we were going to miss it, for a minute there," he said. That was Ian. Oh well, we had a lovely meal.

After Ian's last fall, Steve Smith Eccles and Jeff Barlow came to the house to tell me he was in hospital. On arrival, the doctor informed me that Ian wasn't answering to his name. For some reason he'd decided his name was Michael. We all just went along with it and called him Michael. A few days after he came home, he asked why I'd called him Michel when his name was Ian. From then on, he was 'Ian' again. Except, he wasn't Ian. He wasn't the Ian that had left for Towcester races before the fall. Even making allowances for some of the random things that can happen after someone suffers a head injury, Ian had changed.

When we travelled to London to see the Jockey Club's neurosurgeon, it wasn't good news. Ian wouldn't be getting his jockey's licence back. He never said a word in reply. In fact, he hardly spoke for two days.

But Ian isn't one to wallow in self-pity. If he couldn't ride, he'd train – but not in the UK. He couldn't bear the thought of seeing those top horses he'd been riding run and win with someone else on board.

He got an offer from Australia, at Cootamundra, in New South Wales. He went over and loved it. I joined him out there a short time later. During our time there, another of his (non)romantic moments came one day when he asked what I was doing next Friday. "Food shopping," I replied. "Why?"

"I thought we might get married in the afternoon after you've put the shopping away. Okay with you?"

So, on 2nd November 1981, we became Mr and Mrs Ian Watkinson.

We had an amazing time in NSW. I think Ian was in the top ten trainers' list for each year we were there. He encouraged me take out a jockey's licence and, with his support, I rode a number of winners for him. He didn't make it easy; they weren't just 'steering jobs. "You've got to prove yourself out here," he told me. And yes, we did have something to prove. The Aussies weren't big on two Poms coming out and getting lots of winners.

Ian, never one to be PC, used to say that the Aussies were thick. One day, to prove this point, one of the horses out in the paddock had died due to a snake bite. Sadly, this can happen if a horse rolls on a snake, and it did happen a couple of times. We had a creek near the yard where any horses that died had to go. Within a matter of days they were reduced to skeletons due to 'blow flies'. That may sound callous but the ground was so hard you couldn't have buried a hamster, and you couldn't burn them due to the risk of causing a bush fire. Ian had the job of putting a chain round the horse's leg and dragging it to the creek. As he passed the yard, one of the yard girls asked Ian if the horse was dead. Ian replied, "Well I'm not fucking teaching it to lead!"

After a couple of years in NSW we moved on. Ian had accomplished all he'd set out to do in a short time. We went to Colin Hayes' massive racing yard and breeding complex in Adelaide, South Australia. But Ian was restless and it wasn't really what we wanted.

Furthermore, our relationship was starting to crack. We split for a short time but decided we wanted to make a go of things again, but not in Australia. The decision to return to the UK to buy and run a pub seemed a great idea. We came home and Ian booked us on a landlord's residential course due to commence a few weeks later. In the meantime, I started riding out for Robert Armstrong again and Ian starting clipping horses to keep himself busy. Sadly, it was during this time that I was informed Ian was being unfaithful.

After all we'd been through and done together, the fact we'd stayed together through his difficult times following injuries and, of course, the head injury, with all the associated problems that brought with it, including some personality changes, this act of betrayal was something that could not be forgiven. I left. We were divorced in 1988.

However, we remained good friends throughout and still are to this day. I go to Newmarket once a year to stay with friends. Ian and I meet for a coffee and catch up. We recently spoke about our past during the discussion of this book, and both agreed we wouldn't change a thing about our time together.

Here's a final story. I remember Bob Champion coming to stay with us when he was recovering from chemotherapy. He was wearing a toupee then as he'd lost his hair. We had a cat at the time and I suddenly became aware of the cat 'killing' this toupee on the living room floor. Aghast, we rescued it and sneaked it back into Bob's room whilst he was having a shower. Shortly after, he appeared downstairs wearing it. As he turned to walk away, we noticed there were lots of chunks out of it, but decided not to say anything to Bob!

CLAIRE'S STORY

I was nineteen years old and working at the British Racing School when I met Ian. He came to clip the horses and it was pretty obvious from day one that he was the most wonderful horseman. In fact, over the years the only person ever to come close that I have seen is the dual Grand National-winning jockey Leighton Aspell.

I was pretty shy then and Ian's cheekiness – his naughtiness – was very attractive to me, along with his horsemanship. He drew me out of myself and it was not long before I was totally besotted by him. In the old cliched terms, he literally swept me off my feet. We met in the November and were married in the following June. People did warn me to stay away from him; after all he was forty-two then and had a bit of a reputation as a womaniser and aggressor. But that was like a red rag to a bull for me; it just made me want him more.

He took me to meet some special friends of his, Ken and Norma Bright, and proposed to me while we were there. I laughed ... I didn't quite believe him. In fact, on our wedding day I looked at the marriage certificate and said to him, "You said you were thirty-nine," to which he replied, "No I didn't, I said I was nearly forty." Typical Ian.

He had a yard at the time, working with difficult horses and youngsters and he asked me to help him. They were really happy days. I would get on these unbroken or young flat horses that he felt he was too heavy for, but with him at the end of the lead rope I was 110 per cent confident that he wouldn't let anything happen to me. We became a great team.

I remember one occasion when a man was working on a barn roof. Ian was working with a difficult horse and asked him to stop. The man just said. "I've got a job to do as well, mate," and there was a bit of swearing. Then Ian went up the ladder and they had a punch-up. He was never afraid of anything but that worried me at times. I don't really like confrontation but he seemed to almost relish it. I would try to get him to walk away from an argument but if he felt there was an injustice of any sort, he would be right in there. He was bound over to keep the peace at one point for fighting. I found that side of him quite difficult, but he was never abusive to me.

In fact, it was the opposite. He wanted to look after me and protect me so much that I felt suffocated. In my own defence, I was very young at the time. We had Camilla fairly quickly. Ian's way of keeping me happy was to get me a horse and we'd go to shows and things and he would lead the horse round, do everything for me. It sounds terrible but all I began to crave was independence, my own money, my own life.

When we broke in young horses or two-year-olds and sent them back to the trainers, I would ride them for a day or two and then the trainers would ask me to ride out for them, which I really enjoyed. I'd strike up friendships with the other lads at the yard – and they were really only friendships between people with a mutual interest – but Ian would become insanely jealous and I would have to stop. I began to get resentful. I fell pregnant with Max. Looking back, I was obviously hormonal. I had my suspicions that he was being unfaithful to me, then it was confirmed to me when Max was two months old and it was all the excuse I needed. I loaded the car with the children, told him I was leaving and headed back to Sussex. I needed to do it for me.

Ian has been the most wonderful father to our children. He always provided for us. I always thought money was his God; I didn't like it, but I cannot fault the way he has made sure we never wanted for anything. Even when I met my current husband and we fell on hard times, Ian helped me out. He sold his house and bought flats for the children so they wouldn't have to struggle. I had a very close relationship with his mother and I know his father and grandfather were very hard on him, but that's how things were in those days.

I adore Ian. I'm so glad he met and married Karen. She is great, and I'm glad there is someone to look after him in his old age, although I would have done it if necessary. He is a very special man.

KAREN'S STORY

I first got to know Ian through the people I worked for, Richard and Auriol Wilson, who had point-to-pointers at Chattisham, near Ipswich, and knew Ian through racing. They always admired him as a horseman and said he was a good jockey.

We used to take some of the horses to the Links at Newmarket and Ian did quite a bit of schooling for them. They also sent some young ones to him to break in. There was one in particular that had ability but was really difficult – he was claustrophobic – but Ian managed to get him ready for the racecourse.

The point-to-pointers were roughed off in the summer and there wasn't a huge amount for me to do, so I used to go to Newmarket two mornings a week to help Ian with riding out. He had his horses at a small extension yard at Michael Jarvis' stables. I got the bug for Newmarket and Ian offered me a full-time job, with an arrangement that I could live at his flat in Black Bear Lane. I'd worked for Richard and Auriol Wilson for a long time and they were great people, but I felt I needed a change. So I ended up going to Newmarket – it was very different to the place I'd been used to.

When I arrived, Ian's marriage with Claire was going through a difficult time. It was awkward for me, being in the middle of it, and very difficult for Ian. Although I worked for him, I didn't really know him as such, not as a person, yet through circumstance we ended up living together. It's so good that Ian and Claire are now friends again. She's such a great person, a brilliant girl.

In the end, Ian didn't have as many horses so there was no longer a job there for me. Ian got me some work for Bill O'Gorman and, when that finished, I went to Pip Payne, who trained at Frankland Lodge on Hamilton Road. He was a great person to work for and I was there for eight or nine years before joining the Newmarket vets Greenwood Ellis, where I still work today.

Ian isn't particularly good at Christmas and birthday presents. Some of the presents he's given me are a bit, well, erm...

On one particular birthday he said, "I've got a surprise for you." We got in the car and drove up the hill to the cemetery. I thought, "What the hell's going on here?"

We got out of the car, walked through the gates and he marched me through the cemetery, down to the very bottom. We stood by a piece of ground and he said, "What do you think of that?"

"What?" I said, having no idea what he was talking about.

"That's your burial plot," he replied. "I've bought you a burial plot for your birthday."

That was my birthday surprise. He was a bit perplexed at my lack of enthusiasm. He said, "It's really hard to get a burial plot these days. They're running out of ground."

So now we have our burial plot booked. It's been sitting there for years, waiting for us.

I love Ian despite his idiosyncrasies and he's also my best friend. We got married in 2015 at Gretna Green and stopped off at our favourite Indian restaurant on the way home. Neither of us wanted a lavish wedding. We had a nice day, one that suited us.

THE ONE THAT GOT AWAY ... HER STORY

I was young and rather naive back in 1974 when I headed down to Newmarket with my then boyfriend. I left behind a wonderful employer in Gordon W. Richards. When I'd decided to make the move, he said, "The grass isn't always greener you know."

I went on to work with Captain Ryan Jarvis at Phantom House. It was a shock to my system. I recall my lovely housemate saying to me, as we rode out one morning, "See that flashy chestnut horse? (Tingle Creek). Well, the jockey is Ian Watkinson, and if you don't fancy him you're a rare one!"

After that I thought well, yes, there is something very appealing about him, but I was in a long line. From then on, I always looked forward to catching sight of him. My boyfriend had already started to mess me about so I didn't feel guilty. Ian did occasionally say good morning and that would make my day.

I understood Ian had many female admirers so, as time went on, my on/off boyfriend said we should move back north and try and work things out. I didn't have the confidence to stay in Newmarket alone so we headed to the Dickinsons, where, as time went on and I carried on with my work, my thoughts for Ian just wouldn't go away.

As I travelled across many racecourses, I came across Ian again with Steve Smith Eccles – I don't recall the course – and I felt like I should never have left. As time went on, I spent most of my free weekends travelling back to Newmarket to see him. My boss used to say, "I hope you don't get hurt and your heart broken. It's a long way to travel for that!"

Ian's career was taking off and after a while I thought maybe I was a distraction to him, so I stopped my visits. It was an extremely hard decision to make. I missed him but thought it was for the best.

Fast forward to the present day. A very good mutual friend always kept me up-to-date on Ian and his life, and at one of our reunions he passed me Ian's telephone number and email address. We've been in contact ever since. When I had the opportunity to meet him after 45 years, I was so nervous I felt sick, but I needn't have worried because as soon as we met it was like we had never been apart.

FOURTEEN

FRIENDS AND ACQUAINTANCES

Before moving on to events that have come to pass since my return from Australia, I want to reflect on some of the people I've met along life's racing road that became great friends and with whom I've been privileged to enjoy so many unforgettable times. There are those from the weighing room; the trainers from whom I've learned so much; and lifelong friends from others sphere of the sport; photographers, journalists, TV presenters and many others. I'd need a second book to mention them all, but here are a few humorous tales that spring to mind. Well, they make me smile anyway.

KEN BRIGHT

In the late Spring of 1975 my beautiful girlfriend of the time, Yvonne, and I were invited to stay with my great friends Ken and Norma Bright at their lovely home in Shiney Row, County Durham. I'd met Ken some years previously when he was just starting out as a photographer. He subsequently became the top racing photographer for the northern tracks and he was one of my dearest friends.

Ken and Norma's home was a gorgeous Georgian style mansion with a long sweeping driveway and a double-doored entrance hall. It was an idyllic weekend. I had a very smart green and cream Anniversary Model MGBGT at the time, set off perfectly by the beauty of Yvonne, and life was pretty good.

We were just sitting down for Sunday lunch when the doorbell rang and Ken left the table to answer the door. When he returned he was looking rather concerned and was accompanied by a large stern-looking gentleman in a suit. He turned out to be a plain clothes detective. He waved his identity card and then addressed me. "Are you the owner of a green MGBGT," and he reeled off the licence plate number. I nodded in affirmation and he went on "This car was placed at the scene of a bank robbery at Houghton-Le-Spring last night, between the hours of 1.00 and 2.00am. Can you confirm where you were at this time sir?"

Unseen by me, Ken winked at Vonnie while I stared at the police detective.

I looked at Ken. "Well, I was here, wasn't I Ken?" I replied. But Ken frowned slightly. "Well," he began. "you were still up after I went to bed, weren't you? I can't say you were definitely here..."

I stared at him in disbelief, then looked at Norma, who was looking equally serious. She shook her head. "Well, I went to bed earlier than all of them so I couldn't really say either."

"This is a serious offence, sir," the detective said, "and I'm afraid we are going to have to take you in for questioning." He looked at me sternly.

In desperation I turned to Yvonne. "Vonnie, you slept with me for Christ's sake. Tell him." She too was looking uncomfortable. "Well," she began, "we did have a long journey and I was very tired. I probably couldn't swear that you were there all night."

I was devastated. I looked round at them all. I couldn't believe that three people I loved and trusted weren't prepared to corroborate my story. I began to argue. "I'm not having this. I want to talk to my lawyer," but the detective pulled out his handcuffs. "Well, we'll need to take you into custody until he arrives from Newmarket. It would be better for you sir if you co-operate, or am I going to have to use these?"

I gave in; shaking my head. All sorts of thoughts racing through my mind. "No, it's okay," I said and got up and headed for the hall, followed by the detective and the others. I opened the first door to the front porch and, as I put my hand on the second door, Ken said, "Oh Fred, do you want a cup of tea before you go?"

I looked round and they were all absolutely pissing themselves laughing, including 'Fred' the detective. It turned out that Fred, a bona fide detective in real life, was a great friend of Ken's and they'd stitched me up good and proper. The bastards!

When I reminded Norma of this tale recently, she said, "When it dawned on you, I've never, ever heard language like it."

I remember getting a phone call some years later from Ken and Norma's son, Nick, himself by then branching into photography. I could hear the wind howling. "I'm at Leicester, it's really cold," he explained, and we talked briefly before he blurted out ... "Dad's got cancer." Poor Ken lingered on for about a year after that. He was only 53. I spoke to Norma one day and she told me he hadn't got long. I remember driving and parking my car at Ely station before taking the train up to Durham.

I walked into the ward where he lay. He was just skin and bone lying there. Apparently, he hadn't spoken for two days. He looked listlessly at me and in barely a whisper said, "Ian." That was the last thing he ever said.

He was a very dear friend to me and I'm still in regular touch with Norma and Nick.

DAVID MORLEY

David Morley was a great bloke. Sadly, he died of a heart attack at a fairly young age. He always talked with his hands, gesticulating to emphasise his point.

I rode for him one day in the early seventies at Nottingham before my career had really taken off. Bob Davies was his regular jockey but I got a call from David asking if I'd ride one for him as Bob wasn't going to get to the races in time that day for some reason. "So, would you ride it in the novice chase for me?" asked David, to which I replied "Yes, of course I will."

I was just heading out of the changing room to the paddock when Bob Davies walked in. "Oh," I said. "The boss said you weren't coming early enough to ride this horse. Why aren't you riding it?" At which Bob smiled and said, "You'll find out in a minute."

Well, we set off in the race and he jumped the first three fences absolutely fine, then when we went down to the fourth in the backstraight it became apparent he didn't really want to do it. He jinked this way and that way. I managed to get him over that one, then at the next we crashed and fell. I flew over the fence and landed the other side. The ambulance picked me up and dropped me back at the paddock and there I met D. Morley. "What did you think?" he asked. I explained that the horse had done this and then done that. He did his usual gesticulations. "Ah yes," he said, "I thought he'd do that."

Many years later, around 1986, I'd returned from Australia and didn't really have a plan. I bumped into David on Newmarket High Street. "What are you doing now?" he asked. When I replied, "Not much," he said, "Come and ride for me. I've got a few that need starting and some with problems. You can work your way through the yard."

On one occasion, I was riding a horse for David, a four-year-old, that he had some concerns about. It was a bit free, and this particular day he decided we'd take it over to the gallop known as Long Hill. Because the gallop was new to the horse, he wasn't as free as usual. Two or three times he almost hesitated. David watched as we cantered past him and then I met him at the end.

"How was that then?" he asked. "It looked fine"

"Did you notice he hesitated?" I replied.

"Yes, I did. Why was that?"

"I think he hesitated in case I'd said 'whoa' as if he hadn't heard me. I think he might be a bit deaf."

He looked at me for a bit, then, without another word, turned round and strode back to his car. When I returned to the yard the head lad, Steve, came over. "What did you just say to the old man?" he asked.

When I asked why, he replied, "Because he said that fucking idiot's still suffering from that bang on his head!"

HARRY BEEBY

Harry Beeby was a partner at Doncaster Bloodstock Sales. I got to know him when I was at Ken Oliver's and I saw him once or twice at the sales.

Round about 1989 I was renting some boxes at David Ringer's stables. I was doing a bit of breaking, pre-training, working with awkward horses, that sort of thing.

A bloke called Bell had a stud at Six Mile Bottom. He asked me to take this filly he'd just bought out of Doncaster Sales while he decided what he was going to do with her. She was quite small and in pretty poor condition. I took her on and fed her up a bit and she started to look much better. But as time went on, he never paid me.

Harry Beeby got in touch with me. "Have you got that filly such and such owned by Bell? The bastard hasn't paid us for her yet."

I confirmed that I'd got her and told him I hadn't been paid anything either. "How much does he owe you?" Harry asked.

"About £2,500," I replied.

"That's the same as me!" he exclaimed. "Right," he continued, "all the legal ways of getting money out him don't seem to be working. Bring her up to the next Donny sales and I will sell her personally myself and we can split the proceeds. It's not strictly legal but it will cost him too much to contest it in court."

Harry came over to see the filly beforehand and was delighted. "By Christ, she looks a different filly. She looks fantastic."

We duly got the filly to sales and sold her. She doubled her original selling price and we were only left £400 each short of the outstanding debt.

Old Bell was a nice old boy really but he lived way beyond his means. I went to see him and agreed to write the debt off in return for the use of a large field opposite the pub in Six Mile Bottom for the summer and I was able to graze my horse and the kids' pony there, so it was all settled amicably.

BOB CHAMPION

In February 1980, Bob Champion was in recovery from his final chemotherapy treatments and I was feeling a bit more myself after my career-ending fall. We hatched a plan to head to Miami for some winter sunshine and to avail ourselves of the Baywatch beauties that were undoubtedly waiting for us. No wonder Cathy agreed to it; she must have had an inkling of what the reality was.

Firstly, the plane journey was way too much for Bob and he was really suffering in the final hours of the flight, so the first night we stayed in a seedy hotel near the airport. Trying to find a hire car was impossible as they were all fully booked, so the next day we got a taxi to another, I'm afraid to say, seedy and pretty awful hotel. The taxi driver spent ages on the check-in desk trying to get us booked in. I think he must have been on a backhander from them. Apparently, there was no other accommodation available at that time of year.

When we hit the beach, still deluded that we were Butch Cassidy and the Sundance Kid but plainly looking more like Hinge and Bracket, to say we were disappointed would be an understatement. All we could see was hordes of leathery-skinned pensioners with an average age of about ninety. No Pamela Anderson in sight.

The only young person on the beach was the granddaughter of one of the hotel residents and, in our desperation for young company, Bob and I were vying for her attention. I went to get her a coffee but Bob snapped that he had already got her one. She plainly wasn't impressed and wandered off. Some wag later commented about our chances of pulling on the beach, given the state of our respective health that day. He reckoned we wouldn't have got a kiss in a brothel with a ten-pound note sticking out of our shirt pockets. Some people can be very insensitive!

Bob left his wig off in order to get some sun on his head but someone asked him if he was from a weird religious sect. We sat and watched TV in the evenings for want of anything better going on and gave up on the place after four days.

The highlight was the taxi ride back to the airport. We hoped to catch an early flight so we kept urging the taxi driver to go faster and faster until eventually a cop car came roaring up with blue lights flashing and pulled us over. They don't mess about in Miami and the policeman was waving a revolver. He gave us the once over then booked the driver.

All things considered; I wouldn't recommend Miami in February as a holiday when you are a young bloke looking for action!

On each of my birthdays for the last fifteen to twenty years, Bob has rung me up at five o'clock in the morning to remind me that I'm now as old as him, because I'm four months younger.

On my 70th birthday, he rang me as usual. I got my wife Karen a cup of tea, then went back to bed with the newspapers. Karen left at around ten to seven to go to work. I heard her come back in and thought she'd forgotten something. Instead, she said, "Have you looked out the window?"

"No," I replied, "why should I?"

"I think you should," she said, then off she went.

There's a road sign, Tattersalls Crescent, directly outside the flat. Attached to the sign and about 20 feet in the air were two large, gas-filled balloons with '70 TODAY' written on them. It coincided with the Tattersalls October Sales and all the traffic to the sales goes past this road sign. Hence, by the time I saw it, so had everybody else, including the former jockey Jinx James, who was the first to ring up and abuse me.

I had no idea who was responsible. I just couldn't work out who it was and I wasn't very happy about it. I accused Karen and her friend Linda but they swore blind it wasn't them who were the culprits. I didn't believe them.

It wasn't until the middle of January, three months later, that a mutual acquaintance happened to mention it, saying, "Wasn't it hilarious when Bob tied those balloons outside your house?"

Honestly, Bob was the last person I'd have thought of because it never occurred to me that he'd take the trouble to get out of bed at some ungodly hour, get in his car and drive to my house with a pair of balloons and tie them to the road sign. I reckoned he was too fat and lazy to do that. The bastard!

STEVE SMITH ECCLES

Steve had joined Tom Jones as an apprentice in 1970. He'd had a few rides on the flat and he was always going to make the grade; that was clear from the outset. I met him when I went to Tom's in 1973 and we became great buddies.

Myself, Steve, Jeff Pearce, Jeff Barlow and, occasionally, Scobie Coogan, used to travel to the races together for several years. In those days there was no A14, so to go north we had to drive down to Newport Pagnell to get on the M1.

As mentioned in an earlier chapter, when I needed to lose weight, I'd travel to the races in as many clothes as I could. On a hot day, I'd be sitting there with all the windows shut, in a sweatsuit, woolly hat and scarf, with the heater at full blast, while my fellow passengers were sitting there in just their underpants, reading the Sporting Life. Steve remembers one particular town we used to go through where the pavement was slightly higher than the road. The street was also fairly narrow. People on both sides stared at us in disbelief.

On the way back, we used to stop at a fish and chip shop. I didn't get chips because of my weight but I'd get something. Back in the car, we'd finish our banquet and roll all the paper up into a ball. Invariably, we'd pass these same two semi-detached houses with a big hedge. We used to chuck the paper out of the car window and it almost always landed on this one side of the hedge. We used to reckon that the occupant of the house whose garden it was would think, "Hello, the jumps season has started again!"

Because Jeff Barlow and Jeff Pearce shared the same Christian name, Steve came up with the bright idea of calling one of them Godfrey so we wouldn't get them mixed up. But within weeks we were calling both of them Godfrey, so we were back to square one.

Steve Smith Eccles

I don't remember much about the weeks and months following the fall that ended my career, but Steve was great and used to take me various places, not that I can remember them, but he does. One occasion he particularly recalls is when he and I were invited to a boxing evening in Cleethorpes by one of the owners he rode for to present the prizes. I was still recovering from the effects of the fall so I just mostly sat there in a daze. Towards the end of the night I was falling asleep because I wasn't used to staying awake very long. Afterwards, we were invited to stay overnight at the owner's magnificent home. We walked up the stairs, he pointed to our room and bid us goodnight.

It was a double bed, which we hadn't expected. Anyway, we got undressed and got into bed and put the lights out. Then Steve tapped me on the shoulder and said, "I thought I'd better let you know, I haven't had my leg over for a week."

I'm glad he remembers it and I don't!

DEREK THOMPSON

I've known Derek Thompson, known universally as Tommo, for over fifty years. We both live in Newmarket now but I met him when I was riding up north and he was training at Nunthorpe, near Middlesbrough, under his father Stan's name. They had a novice chaser named L'Escartier who hardly ever managed to get round. Steve Davenport and Graham Lockerbie were among her victims. I rode her one day at Market Rasen. I was lucky; I manged to pull her up before she fell.

There used to be an entertainment venue in Newmarket called the Cabaret Club. The comedian Bernard Manning, who was a big star in the seventies and eighties, was on there one night. He was a bit of a Marmite character. His jokes were usually fairly offensive and derogatory to women, but we both thought he was funny. Tommo knew him, having met him during his broadcasting career, so we got tickets and went along.

There was a group of women sitting at an adjacent table to us. As the night wore on, Bernard became more and more foul-mouthed and the jokes more risqué, but they sat there stony faced until he stopped the show and asked them why they were there as they must have heard about his reputation. He wasn't rude to them but as soon as they could they made a swift exit.

Tommo asked me if I wanted to meet him. I told him I'd like that very much, so after the show he took me backstage. He was shorter than I'd imagined, and about as wide as he was tall. We shook hands and exchanged a few pleasantries.

A few days earlier, someone had told me a joke which I thought was hilarious. I said to Bernard, "I've got a joke for you. Feel free to use it in your show." I told him the joke and thought it would impress him but his face never cracked. He listened, expressionless, looked at me seriously, patted me on the shoulder and said, "Don't give up the day job, will you?"

DON CANTILLON

Don Cantillon, now a Newmarket trainer, came over from Ireland as a pupil assistant for Tom Jones and we got on well. He definitely had a knack with horses. If there were any that needed that bit of extra individual attention, he would be the man for the job.

I actually got him his first two winners, one under rules and one in a point-to-point. Chris Wall's father, Ron Wall, trained at Colchester and he asked me to ride a horse for him at Huntingdon, but it was a bank holiday Monday and at that time there were about eight or nine race meetings held across the country. I was already booked elsewhere so I couldn't ride it. I remember saying to Ron, "We've got an amateur in the yard. He's heavy but he can ride," and put him in for the mount. In order to make the weight, on the Sunday he took laxatives and then put on as many clothes as he could that allowed him still to move and went and ran, in the sand, the two-mile gallop up Bury Side. He got home, stripped the sweaty clothes off and weighed himself but he was still too heavy, so he put them all back on and went and ran it again. He did put up a bit of overweight but still won the race.

His first point-to-point winner got me a bollocking. A lovely lady, Mrs Nick Lees, who I've mentioned earlier, used to train point-to-pointers. I schooled them for her and most were ridden by Lucy King. She had this particular horse that was an awkward one to ride so I put Don in for it as he'd told me that he had ridden winners in Ireland. The horse was called The Coalman and Don duly won on it, then in all the excitement afterwards, he confessed that it was his first winner. In fact, it could have been his first ride. I subsequently learned that if Don said it was raining, you had to look out of the window to check.

Years later we fell out. I can't remember what it was, whether I said something to upset him or what, but it was a couple of days after my fiancé Helen had been killed so I wasn't in the best form. He was a big bloke and we ended up having a scrap. He attacked me from behind and I came off worse physically. For some reason it all ended up in court. I can still see in my mind's eye the judge almost rolling his eyes at us and telling us to go away and grow up. We were both bound over to keep the peace for a year and then kept up our feud for the best part of twenty years. It was a known thing in town. If there was ever an occasion or party or anything, my friends used to joke and say, "Are you inviting Don?" I'd gnash my teeth and mutter insults. If we saw each other on the street we'd look daggers at each other.

Sometime in the 2000s, I was doing horse transport and happened to be sitting in the lorry park at Worcester. I spotted him there and I saw him notice me. Then he walked over to the horsebox where I was sitting. "What do you want?" I asked.

"What did we fall out over?" he asked me.

I shrugged. "Fucked if I know!" was my reply. He held his hand out and we shook hands. Now if we meet, we're absolutely fine.

TONY RAWLINSON

I knew Tony Rawlinson from growing up and working in Newmarket. He was the son of a jockey, also named Tony, who rode over 250 winners in Britain and spent the latter part of his career riding in Scandinavia.

I was in Australia working for Ron Mason at Airlie Beach, in northern New South Wales. Tony had gone off round the world with a Swedish jockey named Lars Kelp. One day I received a phone call from England saying that he'd rung to catch up and he'd left his number, in case I wanted to call him back. The phone number was for a café that was literally ten minutes away from where I happened to be living in Australia.

Of course, I rang the number. He answered and we chatted away for some time. I pretended I was in England. Then, as soon as we hung up, I walked round to the café. His face when I walked in was absolutely priceless.

I moved back to Newmarket sometime after that. Tony's mother lived in Newmarket and he used to come and visit her and we'd catch up. Tony was a good-looking fellow and was very charming. He'd started dating a Swedish jockey named Suzanne and was making a life for himself in Sweden. He mentioned he had some horses that needed stalls training and wondered if I'd be able to help. I duly joined him out there. I dealt with horses in both Denmark and Sweden; I'd sail between the two. We had a lot of success. I did this for about a year until they picked up on what I was doing and were able to employ their own people to do it.

Tony and Suzanne lived near Malmo in Sweden and I stayed with them. The cost of hospitality there was extortionate, so expensive that most people would go across to Denmark to buy their booze. The Swedish hotels and restaurants, accepting of this, would charge corkage to people bringing in their own. It was a completely accepted practice. I recall that the day before Tony and Suzanne's wedding, we took the car ferry to Denmark and filled up his Merc with booze for a fraction of the price he would have paid in Sweden.

One day, he had a cheque he needed to cash. For some reason, it had to be in a Danish bank and I accompanied him. There was a bit of an exchange between him and the bank tellers, lovely ladies they were. Tony spoke fluent Danish, Swedish and Norwegian. The cheque was crossed and they were adamant he couldn't cash it there. He lost his cool and the cheque was torn into 55 pieces and thrown on the floor. I think he stamped on it too for good measure.

He strode out of the bank. I followed him and we sat on a low wall. It was a beautiful day, birds singing, pretty girls everywhere, seasons in the sun. Tony looked at me and said, "Maybe I was a bit over the top". I agreed. "Shall we get a coffee?" I suggested.

"I need to apologise," he said as we drank our coffee, "if nothing else."

After we'd finished our coffee we walked back to the bank. Before he could get to his knees and grovel, the senior cashier waved him over and then showed him his cheque, which had been meticulously sellotaped together, all 55 pieces of it. I couldn't understand the conversation that happened next, but they cashed it.

Tragically, years later, I received a call while I was in Spain from Tony's brother-in-law to say that Tony had drowned in the sea in San Diego. I was shell-shocked. Apparently, things had not been going too well and Suzanne had left him. He'd taken to drinking heavily.

I was surprised that he had even been in the sea, as when we were in Australia and trying to learn to surf, the pair of us made complete arses of ourselves. He was definitely not a strong swimmer by any stretch. The day he died was the anniversary of the day Suzanne had left him, so I drew my own conclusions on that one.

He was a good bloke.

WILF

One of my very best friends is Ian Howell, also known as Wilf – he doesn't know why either.

I met him and his beautiful girl friend Julie, now his wife and mother of three fine young men, when I had a short spell as assistant trainer for the late Pat Haslam, a great bloke, around the time of the big storm of 1987. We hit it off straight away.

Incidentally, speaking of that time with Pat Haslam reminds me of an incident when they first put rails on each side of the artificial surface gallop on Warren Hill. Before that it had been an open gallop. It was the first morning they'd used it and Pat and I were sat on our horses about two-and-a-half furlongs from the start, watching the string go by. Pat was impressed with the new rails. He held his hand out and said, "Look at that; it's fantastic. It's idiot-proof."

Unbeknown to us, one of the horses had thrown his head down at the start and one of the reins had broken. Just as Pat had uttered the words "It's idiot-proof", the horse came past us. The lad who was riding him carried on all the way up the gallop without realising that one of the reins was broke until they'd pulled up. Pat just looked at me and said, "I take that back."

Anyway, back to Wilf. He worked with me when I was sorting out unruly and unbroken horses. The late Michael Jarvis sent me a filly that wouldn't behave at or in the stalls. They only get so many chances in the stalls before they aren't allowed to run if they don't comply. The great Monty Roberts had the filly for a while but to no avail. Monty did come to see her while I had her. He watched her go in, then spring out. He patted me on the shoulder and said, "Well done, son." Praise indeed from the great man.

Around this time, I had a call from a lady in the Cambridgeshire Hunt. She said that she'd heard about my reputation but she was sure her horse would beat me. They just could not stop it bucking. The moment they gave it an inch of rein, it was loose.

She said I could have it for a month. After two weeks I rang her up and asked her to bring her groom over to have a ride on the horse. She was a bit sceptical but she did it. Then she took the horse home a few days after.

Wilf is a great bloke and a brilliant rider but he has one failing. He's no good at running in the soft. We went through all the usual stages of lunging and long-reining the aforementioned horse, then we tossed a coin as to who would get on the horse and who would be on the ground with the long tom. I lost the toss.

This all took place in Michael Wigham's barn, which had a floor covering of thick, dry sand. You have to be very careful with horses in soft, dry sand as they can overreach when they get tired. It's hard work for humans also.

The horse was a huge, strong four-year-old. I said to Wilf, "When he starts performing, lash him round the hocks with the bull-whip to keep him moving forwards, and don't miss him!"

For the first couple of bucks it worked fine, but Wilf lost ground on me because he couldn't run in the soft, dry sand. The horse then put in a real 'haymaker' – it felt like he was doing a headstand – and slung me up in the air as far as my hold on the reins would allow. I landed a few feet in front of him. Before Wilf legged me back on, he took his shoes and socks off. He likened it to wearing racing plates after his boots, to help him keep up.

The horse was never any more trouble. I called it "sympathetic firmness," whereas Wilf called it "treat them like a woman." The kangaroo-hide bull-whip is hanging on my stairs now. It's a prized possession, despite being shorter than it was!

I really admire Wilf for the stoic way he handles adversity, and I'm grateful to him for the times he has led me astray.

FIFTEEN

TALES FROM THE WEIGHING ROOM

The late, great John Buckingham, master valet, friend and confidant of so many jockeys down the years, called his autobiography 'Tales From the Weighing Room'. As a tribute to him, I have given this chapter the very same title. I think it's the perfect introduction for three of my former weighing room colleagues who were – and still are – among my closest friends to say what they want about me.

Strictly speaking, not all of the 'tales' are from the same weighing room that I inhabited. Bill O'Gorman, while no mean jockey himself on the Flat and over hurdles, is best known for his skill and success as a trainer, while David Claydon rode in point-to-points rather than under rules, but they both expressed a wish to say a few words and I'm happy to give them the opportunity.

BOB CHAMPION

It must have been about 1972/73 that I met Ian. I was on about my fourth season. He'd just started getting rides in the south. We had different valets but I'd see him every day and I guess we hit it off and got on well. I invited him to come and stay at my house when he came down each week to school horses for Peter Bailey or if Cheltenham or Newbury was on. We'd go to the sauna at Hungerford with a few others, head off to the Five Bells to eat, and have a laugh.

When Tom Jones started concentrating more on the flat and Ian was retained by Peter Bailey, Peter would ring me and say, "I don't want to drag Ian all the way down from Newmarket just to school one horse. Can you come and school it for me?" I'd meet them at the schooling ground, jump on one, all tacked up and ready, and be in and out of there in ten minutes, no problem.

Bob Champion

Ian got badly injured at Cheltenham the day before Strombolus was due to run in a novice chase. I'd never actually schooled him at home but he was down to run at Cheltenham so I got offered the ride and we won. I rode him again at Ascot when Ian couldn't and we won that day too. Then there was the following season's Racing Post Chase at Kempton – it was called the Tote Pattern Chase in those days. Ian had the choice between the lovely American horse Casamayor and Strombolus. He absolutely loved Casamayor. Strombolus was set to carry 10 stone 7lb and I told Peter Bailey I'd struggle to make the weight. At a push I could do 10-8. He said that was fine as the horse had lost his form at the time. On the day I cheated and weighed out at 10 stone 11lb and we went off at 16-1. I always dropped my leathers a couple of holes on him and squeezed him along with my legs. I must admit my greatest pleasure in watching that race is hearing Julian Wilson – who was doing the commentary – say, "and Ian Watkinson has picked the wrong horse". I've sent him the DVD of that race, just in case he forgets!

We didn't see ourselves as rivals really. We both had jobs with good trainers. But we'd put each other in for rides if we were unable to ride them.

There were no agents in those days, of course, and you certainly didn't phone a trainer for rides – I think John Francome was the first to do that. We helped each other out but, make no mistake, once the tape went up we were enemies. If you got cut off at a fence it was your own fault, you shouldn't have been there. You should have been looking at what was going on.

The fastest race I ever rode in was won by Ian on Night Nurse – the two-mile Bobby Renton Chase at Wetherby, which Ian has already referred to. I was on a horse called Roadhead trained by Josh Gifford. The other one in the final shake-up was the Dickinsons' horse I'm A Driver. My horse had speed but was one paced, his best trip was two miles three furlongs but you don't get races over that distance.

Because mine had won over fences, we had a seven-pound penalty. Josh told me to jump out and get them at it and I'm telling you it was the quickest I've ever been in a race in my life. If any of us missed the last fence we would have turned 150 somersaults. All the other jockeys were down at the last fence to watch. Ian on Night Nurse won it by three lengths to I'm A Driver with me in third, a further four lengths behind.

In those days they had jockey stands at the racecourses and we all had binoculars. No sitting about in the weighing room, we'd would be out there in all weathers in our trilbies and overcoats over our colours watching what was going on. There were a lot more jockeys for fewer rides in those days. There were no superstars either. We were servants, called by our surnames. That's the way it was and we were happy with it.

The horse on which Ian had his final fall, Regal Choice, was my regular ride. I'd won on him twice, and to be honest, I've always felt a bit bad about the fact I put him in for it. But we'd do that for each other. It was a job we both loved doing and would have done it anyway despite the risks.

As Ian has mentioned elsewhere in the book, in February 1980 he and I decided to go on holiday to Miami. He'd been nearly killed and was gaga; I was bald and looking like death, recovering from cancer. What a pair!

The first night we stayed in a hotel near the airport that was so rough if you went out at night, you'd be dead. Then we found a rat-infested room in the grottiest of hotels. We couldn't find a hire car so we couldn't get out, and the average age of the people on holiday must have been around a hundred.

After three days we looked at each other and said, "Let's go home." We told our lady taxi driver we were pushed for time and she was great. She drove faster and faster until the cops pulled us over. Ian and I were spreadeagled with our hands on the roof of the taxi with revolvers pointing at our heads – we didn't say a word. They thought we were trying to kidnap the taxi driver but, luckily, she said we were okay and they let us go.

I needed to start riding out again but I was too frightened to go down to Josh's as I knew I had no strength. Ian suggested I stayed with him and rode out at Tom Jones, so I did. They put me on a horse called The Sundance Kid and I remember I was so afraid of being run away with. I was as weak as a kitten. I just managed to drop my hands and get to the end. I could hardly breathe. I was still too afraid to go to Josh's after that so I headed off to America.

As a jockey, Ian was very, very brave, too brave in many ways, but that is part of being a jump jockey. He rode some of the best horses, not just in that era but in National Hunt racing history, and did an excellent job with them over both hurdles and fences. They say good horses make good jockeys but trainers don't put bad jockeys on good horses.

When Ian came back from Australia he started breaking in horses, dealing with difficult ones, putting them through stalls. He was brilliant at it. He knew what each one needed, individually, and got it right 100 per cent of the time.

We've been good friends for nearly fifty years now. Any of his friends and acquaintances will say he is the first to be there if you need help, and I know he would be there for me. He likes his reputation as a hard man but, in reality, he's soft as muck. Just the other day, someone told me that he was in a shop where a mother told her children she didn't have the money for a chocolate bar, so he bought it for them. I wasn't in the least bit surprised – that is Ian.

JOHN FRANCOME

Ian was really the last of that hard type of jockey who would break a collarbone and go out and ride in the next race, men like Paddy Broderick. I can recall he was one of the first to have keyhole surgery on his knee at Addenbrookes; then he discharged himself, leaving a note on the bed saying, "Gone Home" and rode out the next day. I think in a previous life he would have been one of those Saxon warriors, raping and pillaging and what have you. He rode some really good horses and also managed to get a good tune out of some really bad ones.

It was a great era to be a jockey. We were blessed really; we had so much fun. Nowadays, with all the cameras on course you could never get away with the things we did. I remember Ron Barry pulling a lad's bridle off during a race, just for a laugh. We often used to jump a couple of fences on the way to the start if we thought we could get away with it. On a sunny day we'd walk back into the weighing room and someone would say, "Did anyone see the last two fences 'cos I didn't!" I don't think the world has moved on its axis but, these days, health and safety and insurance claims have made things much more bland.

Drink driving and riding was never an issue either. Some lads would be in the pub on the way to the races, then have a drink in the sauna and be half under by the time they weighed out. Then they would drive to the pub on the way back. But there were surprisingly few fatalities on course, certainly when compared with motor racing in those days when a driver got killed nearly every week.

When I think of Ian, I would say he always had a smile and was ready with a joke. He was great company. It must have been so hard for him, being such a big lad, to keep his weight under control. He and Andy Turnell used to wear those American Caliente helmets, which offered zero protection to the head but weighed very little. One of the reasons I gave up riding was because I was sick of being hungry all the time.

Ian was a real grafter and a thoroughly good lad. If you were going into battle you would definitely want him on your side.

BRIAN POWELL

I first met Ian up north, years ago in the seventies. He was based in Newmarket at the time but often rode in the north, and for some reason we hit it off. We then lost touch for many years. Ian had gone off to Australia and I was assistant trainer to Michael Dickinson who decided to send me firstly to John Gosden, who was at that time training in California, and then to someone in Australia.

Michael sent me to Colin Hayes at Lindsay Park Stud, South Australia to gain some experience there. I got picked up at the airport and the lad said he was taking me back to the bunkhouse, the communal accommodation block. As I walked through the door, someone behind me said, "What the fucking hell are you doing here?" I knew Ian's voice instantly. We ended up sharing a room there and have been in regular touch ever since.

Ian was married to wife number one at the time, Cathy, and one Sunday we all decided to go to Oakbank for the Sunday market. Ian and I decided to have a go on a camel ride. They put us up, two to a camel and I was fortunate enough to be in the front as the camel behind us took a dislike to ours and kept spitting all over a worried Ian and attacking his leg. Cathy took some photos – she found it highly amusing, as did I.

After Ian left Lindsay Park, we used to meet up in Adelaide and go to rock concerts together. We went to see Phil Collins at the height of his popularity at Adelaide Tennis Courts. I remember Ian was given some tickets by an owner of a horse for Bruce Springsteen, the number one in America at the time, but Ian had never heard of him so he gave the tickets away. Cathy said she was going to kill him for that!

I was his best man when he married his second wife Claire. She was a lovely girl but I'm afraid to say all his friends at the wedding, unbeknown to Ian, placed bets as to how long it would last because she was so young, pretty and innocent and he was that much older and very stuck in his ways. The odds were against and we didn't give it much chance. Sadly, we were right.

Brian Powell

Ian and I went on a week's holiday to Las Vegas and decided to go up a tower called the Stratosphere and have a go on the rides. It was 1,000 feet up. There was a rollercoaster that went right round the edge and a thing called the Big Shot that fired you up in to the air with the same G-force as a jet plane. There were seats for sixteen and you sat in fours. We sat with these two Japanese girls. Ian's seatbelt looked decidedly loose, so he got the security man to check it twice. The funniest thing was, as it took off, all four of us shouted, "Oh Fuck!" at exactly the same time. We felt very queasy when we got off – and these two tough former jump jockeys decided against the rollercoaster!

Ian married Karen in Gretna Green – he says he did that so it wouldn't be legal! I remember going to the pictures with them to see 'Saving Private Ryan'. When it got to the bloodiest, noisiest scene in the film, Karen nudged me to look at him. There he was, fast asleep. Another time we went to see

'Gladiator', another fast-moving, noisy and violent film, and the same thing happened. Only Ian could sleep through that lot.

Nowadays we both own places in Spain, quite coincidentally they are within half an hour of one another. If we ever meet for a quick half-pint it invariably results in the rest of the day gone and several half-pints consumed along with much reminiscing.

How do I sum him up? Well, he definitely thinks every woman in the world fancies him, or rather, he hopes they do, but deep down he knows he hasn't a cat in hell's chance half the time. He was a tough jump jockey, as hard as nails physically, but is as soft as putty on the inside. He puts up with a lot of physical pain but he soldiers on and keeps smiling and making jokes about it. He thinks he's a charmer.

A lady friend from Scotland, the wife of my former boss, who is now in her eighties, flew down to Stansted and I arranged for Ian to collect her at the airport and take her to Newmarket. She'd never met him before but now, every time I talk to her, she's full of him. "How's the lovely Ian?" she asks, as if he were her best friend.

He definitely doesn't suffer fools gladly but if he is your friend, you have a true friend.

BILL O'GORMAN

Ian and I met at Grammar School, some sixty years ago now. I had ponies, he went to learn to ride at Pat Moore's and was always absolutely fearless right from the off. He had no comprehension of danger at all.

He bunked off school and stowed away in the horsebox (his parents had no idea) to go and watch Pat Moore's horse Lizawake run in the National. George Hartigan was the owner and usually rode him but he succumbed to the press pressure to put a professional jockey on board the horse rather than ride it himself. The horse unseated Bobby Beasley at the Chair. I think they should have left George on him.

When Ian came back from up north, he went to Tom Jones as a lad. A lot of jockeys wouldn't have done that. They'd have said, 'I'm a jockey. I've had rides,' but Ian did his two like any other lad in the yard. All credit to him for that. And before long, Tom Jones could see for himself that he could obviously ride and gave him chances.

Whenever I see Ian, it's one of those rare friendships you can count on one hand, whereby it doesn't matter if you haven't seen each other in years, you just pick up where you left off, just as if you had been out to the pub the night before.

DAVID CLAYDON

I first met Ian when he was about to take his first ever ride in the Grand National on Jolly's Clump in 1976. He had a few ponies and, for some reason, had suddenly been told to vacate the grazing he'd been using and was stuck for somewhere to put them, so someone gave him my number. He rang me, said he was in a muddle and the upshot was he brought them over, then headed off to Aintree.

I was farming at Street Farm in Hundon, Suffolk at the time. I trained a few point-to-pointers and bred a few. I suppose I had about eight or ten horses, a couple of my own and some for friends. I've always been a big National Hunt enthusiast.

Ian and I got to know each other. He rode a few for a friend of mine, Hugh Collingridge, who trained both flat and jumpers. Ian invariably rode the jumpers. I would represent Hugh at the races when he had another meeting to attend, saddling the horses. Ian and I would do it between us.

If I had a young horse to bring on, Ian was always keen to help. I have to question how many other top jockeys would turn up on a cold, wet, January Sunday morning to school unraced young point-to-pointers for amateurs to ride. And he'd never expect to get paid, never asked for a penny. He did it as a friend as he did for others. He just loved bringing on young horses.

Ian is incredibly tough and a wonderful horseman with lovely hands. I remember once at Plumpton, where the fences had been rebuilt and were on the hard side. They came on for criticism from some of the jockeys. Ian won the novice chase and was quoted as saying, "I'll ride over brick walls if I have to, I've got a living to earn".

After his enforced retirement from that terrible fall, when he was acting as private trainer for Joe Manning at Cootamundra in Australia, I went to stay with him for three weeks. Ian and Cathy both worked incredibly hard. I remember they must have had about eighty horses going through there at a time. Ian would give as many lads as he could the day off on a Sunday and do all their work himself. He took me water-skiing in some filthy lake and nearly drowned me. In that lake at four o'clock in the morning, he'd strip off to the waist and go in with a horse on a lunge-line and lunge it round him for exercise, then he'd hand it over and take the next one and the next.

They would go to the races at Gundagai, Wagga Wagga, Young and several other local tracks, always taking four or five horses. Cathy was a big part of the operation; she was very good for Ian and always turned the horses out 100 per cent. They would usually have two or three winners and always won best turned out.

Ian wasn't supposed to ride because of the severity of his head injuries. However, one day he was getting, shall we say 'frustrated' at the efforts of a lad trying to get his horse to leave the yard, so he got on the horse himself.

Unfortunately, it went over backwards and put Ian in hospital. He had a massive haematoma at the base of his spine. We did, however, have to laugh when one lad, who wasn't the brightest spark, went to see him and couldn't remember which ward he was in, but asked for the bloke with the haemorrhoid up his back!

When he returned from Australia he did a lot of clipping round the Newmarket yards and in 1984 my daughter Paula started riding in point to points. Ian took so much time to give her advice and teach her about race riding. They would watch the videos and he would go over everything with her. She won several races due partly to his considerable help.

I know Ian really struggled to cope mentally with the loss of the career that he loved, the adrenaline rush it gave him and also with the severe head injuries he had suffered. I didn't see very much of him for a while, but I heard things and it would really annoy me when people would say he had lost it, that he was unkempt and scruffy whereas he'd once been really smart. It was obvious he had suffered a personality change from his head injuries. People tend to be more sympathetic if someone is in a wheelchair. If it is their head, they don't see it and become judgemental.

We are now back in touch through Facebook and we often exchange messages. He's a great bloke.

SIXTEEN

BACK FOR GOOD

When I arrived back in Newmarket from Australia, I was at a complete crossroads in my life, unsure of my next move. I'd rented my house out and was staying with my sister. I just didn't know what to do. I had a bit of experience under my belt of hotel and bar work from the times spent at the Edenhall and also the Queens Head at Tirril on the road to Lake Ullswater. I did enjoy that type of work and so I did a two-week residential course at a place near Stonehenge to learn all about the trade. At the end of the course, the senior tutor – I think all the tutors were former pub licensees – said, "Think carefully now. Do you want to re-mortgage your house then work ten to fifteen hours a day to buy it back?" I thought that was very honest of him and it settled it for me. I had a beautiful girlfriend at the time who was "keen-ish" to join me but I wasn't convinced of that either. We drifted apart and she married a footballer.

Then one day, I bumped into an old gentleman trainer friend named Hugh Sidebottom on Newmarket High Street. Hugh was well into his eighties by then and a lovely man to talk to. He later gave me a framed portrait of the 1925 Grand National winner Double Chance, ridden by Major Jack Wilson. I still have it and would never part with it.

Hugh asked what I was doing with myself and, when I replied, "Not much," he kindly offered me the use of a few of his boxes at his place at Biggin Farm, on the Newmarket side of Fordham, not far from Snailwell, to break in some horses for local trainers. I thought that sounded like a good idea.

Soon afterwards, I bumped into another trainer friend, Mick Ryan, who asked me the same question. When I mentioned the arrangement with Hugh, he said, "Great, I've got three I want you to break in for me."

Word gradually got around that I'd take horses to break and pre-train. I got some horses from Ben Hanbury and two or three other trainers. The operation steadily grew and, eventually, there wasn't enough room at Hugh's, so I moved to David Ringer's stables on Hamilton Road.

One day I was riding out on one of Ben Hanbury's when I saw Dave Thom – who I'd worked for in the early 1970s – riding one down by the Pumping Station, across the Heath from the Rowley Mile. Dave was having trouble with his horse and was complaining that he was pushed for time, as

A hairy moment schooling!

he had a job to do that afternoon, transporting horses somewhere or other. My breaking and pre-training had begun to drop off a little so I asked him if he needed a hand with his transport business.

So it was that I began driving Dave's two horseboxes, a two-horse and a four-horse. I loved it. After about a year of doing that, I bought Dave's little two-horse box off him and set up on my own. I drove horses to the races for Neville Callaghan, Michael Wigham, Pip Payne and Phil McEntee among others. I also took horses from Tattersalls Sales to various locations. I bought a four-horse box and carried on doing that until finally selling my last box in 2017. Transporting horses had served me well.

Shaun Keightley and I had become great mates after I returned from Australia. He's now a trainer with stables on Newmarket's Hamilton Road, but he was still a jockey at the time. He was riding over hurdles then with very occasional rides on the flat, and was a good, brave rider.

I was making a living riding difficult horses for people. I was riding a particularly awkward horse called Joytotheworld for my good mate Bill O'Gorman. As mentioned earlier, Bill and I were classmates in school and he was one of those kids with a photographic memory. He was a fantastic rider as well and, instead of becoming a professor, he took up riding and training racehorses.

Anyway, nobody wanted to ride the particular horse, or even have him in the string, so I used to ride him out early and trained him on his own. After a while I said to Bill, "This horse is alright, you know." Bill being Bill, he looked at me through narrowed eyes and said, "Don't tell me, he's passing those trees like they are standing still!" He can be very sarcastic.

Anyway, after I'd mentioned that I thought the horse may have a bit of ability, Bill decided he'd like to find out for himself. We headed off at lunchtime towards the gallop that runs parallel to the Rowley Mile known as Across the Flat, with him on a horse that had come fourth in the Royal Hunt Cup at Ascot. We did it at that time of day so there'd be no one about to upset my horse. He was that much of an awkward sod.

At that time, Bill would have weighed about 10st 12lb and I was about 11st 12lb. He obviously thought he was going to slaughter me because of the weight difference. We set off at a good clip and, running down towards the dip, I saw him look across at me. I hadn't moved on my horse, and then he quickened up and I went with him.

After we pulled up he asked me what weight I was and I told him. Not being one to say much, he just said, "Hmm, he's alright, but who will we get to ride him amongst all these bloody windy flat jockeys?"

I suggested Shaun Keightley, as his style was more suited to riding jumpers. The horse was given a couple of quiet runs before being entered at Beverley. Word had obviously got out as someone nicked the price and he went off at 7-2. He won it nicely.

I was standing next to Bill. All he said was, "Well, that went alright, didn't it? But as he turned into the straight, I thought it was Princess Anne riding him!"

There used to be a series of races sponsored by Coral bookmakers which culminated in the Coral Cup, a three-mile hurdle race, still run as part of the Cheltenham Festival. Shaun had a good ride on one of Martin Tate's horses, Rogers Princess, lined up for it.

On the day, the phone rang and it was his then wife Jo. "Ian, are you going to be watching Cheltenham? If so, is there any chance you could record the race for Shaun so he can watch it when he gets in?"

"No problem," I replied. I duly recorded the race and, as luck would have it, he won.

The phone rang again and it was a very excited Jo. "Did you get it? Shall I get Shaun to call in and get it on his way home?" I assured her that it would be no problem at all for me to drop it down to her myself, so I got in the car to head round there.

In Newmarket at the time there was a chap named Brian Higgs, who I've mentioned in a previous chapter. He had a shop selling ladies clothing – 'Separates', I think it was called. He also ran a video hire business from there and was known to carry a few films under the counter for the more, shall we say, discerning customer.

Schooling alongside Bernie Hutchinson. I appear to have neglected to fasten my chinstrap.

En route to Jo's it came into my head to call in on Higgsy with the videotape of Shaun's Cheltenham victory and see if he would be able to add a bit to it. Well, the end result was that just as Shaun landed over the last hurdle, the film cut to an extremely graphic close-up of a mixed-race couple going at it like hammer and tong.

I dropped it off to a very happy Jo and asked when she thought Shaun would be home. She said probably about nine o'clock. At about ten past nine the phone rang. An apoplectic Jo shouted down the phone, "You dirty bastard. I wanted to show that to my mother!"

I could hear Shaun in the background laughing like a hyena.

Shaun packed the video into his racing bag and the next time he was at the races he managed to get it played over the TV screen in the weighing room. I bumped into Hugo Bevan, the clerk of the course, and he said to me, "Have you seen that videotape of Keightley's? It's brilliant. I always know when they have got it on as all the jockeys in the weighing room are crowded round the TV!"

During the time I was riding awkward horses for people, a horse called Danube sticks in my mind. He was really well bred, being a half-brother to the Guineas winner Tirol. Colin Williams trained him in Newmarket and he had stacks of ability.

They took him to Warwick for his first run. He won easily and they all won a fortune. Colin wished he had doubled the amount he had bet on him but hindsight is a wonderful thing. Then they decided to run him up north at Thirsk. Unfortunately, in running he got hemmed in on the rails and gashed down his side. It ruined him. After that he decided he didn't much care for this racing lark. At home he decided to plant himself, whip round, anything rather than go and have a canter, so Colin had to try and come up with different ways with him.

Colin rode him himself most days but there was a particular occasion when he asked me to come and ride him, the idea being to give him a piece of work on the trials gallop, a seven-and-a-half-furlong grass on peat moss gallop, beautiful ground, like a carpet. It was situated right beside what was the old A11, with a big hedge separating the two. There were three of us: a girl and Colin on their horses and myself on Danube and we set off from Colin's yard, trotting and cantering along.

Michael Wigham, who was still a jockey then, met us up by the chalk pits on the Limekilns. The plan was for him to ride the horse the girl was riding. He parked his car and walked through the woods to where we were. The girl produced a hood which was then placed on Danube's head, completely blindfolding him, then she legged Michael up onto her horse before getting into his car and driving right round the other side of the Limekilns, near the start of the gallop, then getting out and positioning herself halfway up the gallop by a gap in the hedge.

The three of us rode through the woods, me between the other horses. He knew they were there but he kept stopping and jibbing, almost dislodged me a couple of times. He was quite a difficult horse to sit on and he was doing everything he could not to get there, but we cajoled him along to the start of the gallop.

I said to Colin two or three times, "Shall I take the hood off now?" but he kept saying "No, no, not yet, wait until we're cantering". I must admit I thought to myself, "Are you fucking mad?"

We set off trotting, then cantering and we were doing a good half speed before Colin said "righto" and I pulled the hood off and threw it in the air. We worked the horses for about six or seven furlongs and at the finish I was only three-quarters of a length behind them.

Michael, weighing about nine stone, looked across at me, was suitably impressed and said, "What weight is that carrying?"

"With tack, nearly thirteen stone," I replied, at which Michael nodded at Colin. "Fucking hell, you could have your house on that!" Colin nodded in agreement but then gloomily replied, "But the bastard won't start!"

They did run Danube in a hurdle race after that. He was a very polite horse and said "after you" to all the other horses. In fact, they were at the first before he decided to set off, yet he still finished fourth. Colin didn't persevere with him after that though. The horse really did not want to know.

Meeting the Princess Royal at Worcester in 2018 with Jimmy Lindley on my right and the late Stan Mellor on my left. (Mary Pitt photo)

I can remember the very last time I schooled a horse. I was fifty-three at the time. A trainer who lived very near my house called me one day and asked me if I would school one for him. I used to keep my horse and the children's pony there. In the mornings I'd jump on my horse and, leading the pony, would ride bareback through Newmarket to the paper shop. Lovely Jane, who ran the shop, would bring the papers out to me. On quite a few occasions one of the rather attractive young girls in the yard asked me to get her a can of Fanta. Of course, being a gentleman .... Unbeknown to her I happened to be looking over the stable next door to the one she was in with another girl who said, "Did you have to pay for that drink?" to which the lass replied, "No, he wants to give me one!" Shocking ... as if!

Anyway, I went to the Links schooling ground where one lad, Squeaker, was on the lead horse and another fellow was on the three-year-old colt that I was to ride. He was a magnificent looking horse. He had a robust physique, not too big, and his trainer felt he should be given a try over hurdles.

I was under the impression that he'd never jumped before so I took him over some little poles first before going over to the baby hurdles. He wasn't keen so I had to be fairly firm with him to get him over them. Then I went to show him the bigger hurdles and he did everything he possibly could to get out of it. He crashed through a wing and came down on his knees at which point I came off him but, fortunately, kept hold of him. I got back on and gave him a right hiding which got him going, but under protest the whole time.

I then took him over to three piles of logs which he eventually jumped but he really was not keen so I got off and handed him back to the lad with the words, "This is never going to make a hurdler as long as he has a hole in his arse!"

Squeaker said, "No, I thought he'd do that. Last week we tried and couldn't get him over anything at all. But the guvnor said not to tell you that because you would be more positive with him."

As I walked home, I reflected on the fact that if I'd been seriously hurt, no one would think I was brave or a hero; they'd think I was a complete idiot schooling those sorts of horses at my age. Unfortunately, I never got to ride the lead horses. If I did, I'd probably still be doing it now. I only got on the ones who needed teaching. So I had a bit of a light bulb moment and decided I would not school horses ever again.

I rang the trainer and told him that the horse wouldn't make a hurdler and the plans for that horse were shelved.

I had a great little apartment in Torrevieja, on the south-eastern Mediterranean coast of Spain. I bought for it about £9,000 in the spring of 1988 with Helen in mind, shortly after she and I had got together. All too sadly, we never got to go there together.

It was only small, about the size of two full-sized stables, but perfect for me and people who went to stay there. On one occasion I lent it to a couple of friends, who shall remain nameless but they will know who they are. One evening, at a local haunt, they were chatting to a lively young lady and then between them cooked up a plan. "Let's get her pissed and then we can get her back to the flat and share her." Outrageous!

She seemed pretty game for all this by all accounts, and they all had a great time in the bar before adjourning for more drinks and shenanigans. The thing was, she shagged them both to death until they could barely move, then proceeded to drink them under the table to the point they fell into a drunken stupor.

At this point, she raided their wallets, took one fellow's brand-new tennis racket and the hire car keys and made off with the car. I think there must be a moral to this story somewhere. One lad is convinced she must have poured her drinks away.

At one time I did a bit of teaching at the British Racing School. It's where I met my second wife, Claire, and also Robert Sidebottom, who was senior tutor there. He's about ten or twelve years younger than me. He used to ride on the flat for Denys Smith.

In 1990 Claire and I invited Robert and his wife Frances to join us for a holiday in Torrevieja. I rented an identical apartment to ours for them and they came on holiday with us for a week or so. We'd get up and meet up at the pool until midday-ish, then head off into town for lunch and the afternoon's entertainment. In those days the road into town was only two lanes with a large layby both sides of the road.

Every day, this – actually, quite attractive looking – prostitute would be working the layby. Rumour had it that she had a flat nearby and chaps would pull up in their cars, negotiate a fee and then she'd take them back to the flat and do the business for about £15. The medical treatment needed afterwards was not included. The exchange rate then was about a fiver to 1000 pesetas so all the English people knew this lady as 'Three Mil Lil'.

Each day we'd drive past and Claire and Frances would make scathing remarks about her, calling her a dirty old cow and denigrating any man who would stoop so low as to indulge.

Robert and I would look at each other and smirk.

Towards the end of the week, Robert and I managed to get a pass out without the ladies for a boys' night out, to talk and have a few drinks … men's stuff. I'm not quite sure what time we returned – I know had to lend Robert £35 – but the atmosphere at breakfast was decidedly cool and hadn't really improved much by lunchtime when we all piled into the car to head into town.

I spotted Three Mil Lil there in the layby and, unbeknown to the others, I flashed my lights at her, which she returned with a cheery wave. "Oh, look

Robert," I jokingly said, "she must recognise you from last night." Frances went absolutely berserk. I've never heard language like it.

However, she did come round with the £35 a couple of days after we got back.

John McCririck was ranting and raving on TV one day to the 'Noble Lord' (John Oaksey) and the others on the show about a photo of a top Formula One racing driver, which showed him on a horse without a helmet. It gave me an idea.

I borrowed a horse off Bob Champion – he was training then – and took it up to the Links. I'd arranged for a photographer to be there. Wearing just mask, T-shirt and underpants, I jumped the horse over a fence, deliberately 'calling a cab' while in mid-air. I sent the photo to McCririck to wind him up.

He sent it back by return, with the inscription, "To Watty. You look like the Noble Lord with a wig on. And you always were catching a cab! Best wishes, John McCririck". The photo hangs on the wall of my stairs today.

When I was transporting horses I was once asked to take a racehorse for a professional footballer who I won't name but he was in the Scotland team at the time. My bill came to £600 but when I asked him to pay me, he told me in no uncertain terms to F… off.

I asked another footballer-turned-trainer friend, Mick Quinn, what the form was and he replied, "He's a footballer, and they think they're doing you a favour by using you, so they aren't prepared to pay for the privilege."

I wasn't having that. Luckily, I'm good mates with an investigative journalist who looked into things for me. As far as I know, the footballer got a call explaining that a few things would find their way into the News of the World if he didn't cough up.

I got a phone call at 7.30 one morning. "Call them off. The money is in your account," he said, to which I replied, "When the bank opens at nine-thirty I'll go down and check. then I'll decide whether to call them (the press) off."

I wandered down to the bank and the money was indeed in my account. So that was the end of that.

In Newmarket there's a small pedestrian walkway off Black Bear Lane. There's a converted stable block along there with a loft space above it that was a saddler's, owned by Brian Scrivener. I recently bumped into Wally, who worked there, along with a lad called John.

I remember one day I went to drop off some stuff, rugs or tack. I had my arms full. In order to access the shop you had to climb about sixteen or eighteen wooden steps, and on this occasion I didn't have a hand free to use the handrail as I climbed up, although obviously, I used to bound up the steps two at a time with no need for the handrail anyway!

This particular day it was freezing. It was sleeting and as I reached the top step, I missed my footing and crashed all the way back down to the bottom. I'm sure that I used a few words and I went a real crash, but no-one came to my aid. I gathered all my stuff together that was strewn all about me and climbed back up again and opened the door.

John and Wally were sitting there by the fire. I obviously looked a bit dishevelled, cuts and bruises, because Wally asked, "What happened to you?"

"I've just fallen down the stairs," I replied, adding in disbelief, "I can't believe you didn't hear me."

"We heard something," said John., "but it's so cold we didn't want to open the door."

In Newmarket there is a lap dancing club called Heaven – there was a chain of them around the country at one time – and I was the proud owner of membership card number one.

I recall one particular evening, I'd just popped in for a drink, and the only remaining table happened to be near the pole. I couldn't stand at the bar because of trouble with my knees so I was glad of a seat.

Through the gloom I happened to spot a rather senior member of the Jockey Club at the adjacent table with another gentleman – Mr A we'll call him for the purpose of this story. I quietly acknowledged him. "Hi there, Mr A. I'm surprised to see someone like you in a place like this."

"Good evening Ian," smiled Mr A. "I have to say, you are EXACTLY the sort of person I would expect to find in a place like this!"

We laughed and he introduced me to his friend, a senior military man, who nearly crushed my bones with his handshake. He'd come to stay the night for some reason … "so we thought we'd just pop in here for a drink". As you do.

Another time I came across Mr A, I happened to own a lovely horse that had been too slow for racing. We called him Super although his proper name was Superbly Sharp. He was given to me by Ben Hanbury. My second wife, Claire, did loads with him: show jumping, cross country … he was such a grand horse. We kept him at Michael (Wiggy) Wigham's yard, which backed on to an area known as Hamilton Hill, and did something with him most days.

On this particular occasion, it happened to be a really hot day, so I jumped on him bareback with his headcollar on and headed off to a quiet spot on Hamilton Hill. I didn't think I'd see anybody, but then along came Mr A. "Ian," he said, "for Christ's sake, you're not wearing a hat, nor does that horse have a saddle or bridle. In fact, you're not even wearing any fucking shoes. You could easily get hurt."

I grinned at him. "If I fall off this horse, Mr A, I deserve to get hurt!" Old Super was really that much of a superstar.

A friend of mine called Max, who was in his early seventies, used to ride him out all over the Heath most days. Max was a great character. He was the most smartly-dressed man in Newmarket, always in collar and tie and with such highly polished shoes you could see your face in them. He told us that he'd ridden more winners over jumps than Bob Champion when he was in France, although we did subsequently find out this wasn't strictly true. In fact, he had never even held a licence, but we all went along with it.

To mark the celebration of fifty years of the Hennessy at Newbury, Bob and I were invited to a reception there as past winners. Bob took Max along as his guest and I met them there. It was while we were there that I got the call to say Super had dropped dead while being ridden out by a lovely lady named Yvonne as they walked along at the back of Ed Dunlop's yard. The head lad had seen him go down amongst the trees. The New Zealand vet, Peter, was on the scene almost immediately. He told me the horse had had an aneurism, a burst blood vessel, and probably knew nothing at all about it.

Rather shocked, I relayed the news to Max, who replied philosophically, "Ah well, if I have to go, I'd like it to be between the legs of a woman!"

Sadly for Max, that wasn't to be the case. He developed cancer. Bob and I used to make casseroles and things for him and go and visit him. I took him to one hospital appointment when he was in the advanced stages of the disease. The nurse was asking him some questions.

"Do you smoke?" she asked.

"No, not now," came Max's reply.

"And when did you give up?"

"Two weeks ago."

The nurse shook her head. "I'm not sure that's really going to help at this stage," she said.

He died in agony. I was with him two hours before he died. Bob and his partner cleared his house and disposed of the contents and gave me his barometer. It still hangs in my hallway and is very accurate.

These days on Facebook you see a lot about rehomed racehorses. It reminds me of a grey two-year-old I was given to sort out. He was a right awkward bastard with a real look in his eye. He came off the horsebox holding his foot up in a bit of a pathetic way, so I called him Gordon after a very good friend of mine. He was very weak – the horse, that is, not Gordon – and never likely to make a two-year-old, so I sent him up north to a friend of mine to grow and mature. When he came back the following spring, he looked magnificent, so we sent him to Neil Graham to train.

I was a bit heavy to ride him out so Neil had a delightful girl called Tracy, who would ride him out after she'd ridden her others each morning. I offered to drop her home afterwards each day and the arrangement worked well.

The way home to her house had two routes: a short, twisty way or down Newmarket High Street to the other side of town. She was a very attractive girl so I tended to take the High Street route. I mentioned to her in a jocular fashion that I did this so that people would see this attractive bird in my car and my street cred would rise. She never said anything at the time.

She used to sling her coat and jumper on the dashboard of my car for the journey home each day. One particular morning I realised she'd left a card in the window after she'd jumped out. I picked it up and read the writing. In capital letters and heavy black ink with a large arrow pointing to the driver's side, it said: "HE IS NOT GIVING ME ONE." Rather cruel, I thought!

SEVENTEEN

EPILOGUE

Looking back, there are things I'm proud of and things of which I'm ashamed, but I guess most people would say that when reflecting on their lives. Above all though, I'm proudest of how my two children, Camilla and Max, have grown into fine, responsible adults, both now having children of their own. I've always endeavoured to do what I can for them, however the credit for the way they have turned out is in large measure due to Claire, who has been the most wonderful mother throughout their lives.

I think, therefore, it's appropriate to conclude this story of my life with what Camilla (and her husband Ryan Ashworth) and Max have to say about me.

CAMILLA

My earliest memories of Dad were of him coming down from Newmarket every other Saturday to see us. He never, ever let us down. We looked forward to it so much. At half-terms and Christmases we would stay in Newmarket with him and see our Nan, his mother, which we really loved. Apart that is, from walking down Newmarket High Street. We were going to the park and we used to say we would either want a pound or ten minutes extra playtime for every time he was stopped by someone for a chat. People would cross the street specially to come and talk to him. To us, as impatient young kids, it was a nightmare.

I loved helping him at the stables where I had a pony called Honey, aside from when Max would sit up in a tree and pelt me with conkers.

I wouldn't say I'm spoilt, but whenever I told Dad I wanted something he would say, "Your wish is my command". Looking back, I guess I was a bit of a Daddy's princess.

Once, when feeding the ducks at the park a swan came and bit me on the knee. I went into full drama mode. Mum was very down to earth and said "pull yourself together, you're fine," but Dad carried me carefully to the car and made a big fuss of me. I loved that. He was always so caring if I ever fell off the pony or hurt myself.

With my daughter Camilla

When I hit my teenage years, he did phone me a bit more, always checking to make sure I was okay. I'd wind him up telling him I was going out and he would say, "Let me know you are home safe," then I would deliberately leave it until 3.00am before texting him. He'd say he wouldn't be able to sleep until he knew I was safe, so it was a bit naughty of me really. He always texted straight back.

I suppose what sticks in my mind is the time he took out of his life to spend time with us. Nothing was ever too much trouble and he was always consistent. If I was ever stuck, as a teenager and even now I'm nearly thirty, he is always there ready to help. I know I can depend on him.

He was definitely different with Max. More toilet humour and fart jokes and always playing pranks. I learned not to react to all their silliness.

The older I get the more questions I have about his previous life. He had done so much by the time he had us. Karen has always been part of our lives and she is an absolute saint. She definitely deserves a medal for putting up with him.

Since I have had my kids of my own, he has become even more of a softie. When my daughter first ran up to him and cuddled him, he was an emotional wreck and couldn't talk. Mum and my mum's mum both say, knowing him thirty years ago, they would never have believed it. He worships everything my daughter says, listens to her so patiently and is a wonderful Grandpa.

RYAN

I love Ian – but I would never tell him that. We have a great relationship. I've been with Camilla since we were fifteen and, although she has taken my name, I feel he has taken me in to his family as if I were his own son. Claire and Camilla wound him up before he met me that I had dreadlocks and tattoos and a beard. Apparently, he was seething as he drove down from Newmarket at 100 miles an hour.

When I wanted to ask for Camilla's hand in marriage, I was terrified. I rang him on some pretext of getting a part for my car in Cambridge and asked if he would be in. I took my best man with me for moral support. When we got there, he ordered in pizza for us, then he turned to me and said, "Right, there are three reasons why you're here. You either want to borrow money, you've got Camilla pregnant, or you want to marry her. Which is it?"

I stammered that I wanted to ask for his permission to marry his daughter, to which he replied, "Well I'm really glad you chose that one!" Then he shook my hand and said it would be okay.

MAX

My parents split up when I was a baby so I have no memory of Dad as a father in the way perhaps other people would call normal. What I do know is that, without fail, he would turn up every other weekend to take us out somewhere. It wasn't a big deal to us at the time, we just thought it was

With my son Max

normal. Now, as a father myself – and as a driver – I realise exactly what a big deal it was to drive all the way down to Worthing from Newmarket every other weekend, just to see us for a few hours.

He always kept within the boundaries of what was acceptable – I suppose he and Mum must have discussed it; I don't know – but it was always incredible. I mean, it was just going for a pizza or something, nothing major, but he always made it special.

I can remember so looking forward to those visits. Going to Littlehampton Beach, where he taught us to skim stones. We did it for ages. And now I do the same with my son, all the while remembering the happy times I had with my Dad.

He would take us to Spain for holidays. I would have been about seven or eight years old and the anticipation would start. You knew it was going to be brilliant, and it always was. He was never a 'helicopter' parent – he let us do things. If we got out of our depth when we were swimming or something, we had to work it out for ourselves and get back to shore. But I know he was there looking out for us. We didn't doubt it.

When Dad met Karen, he was so nervous about bringing her on holiday with us. The thing with Dad is that he always wants to please everybody and doesn't always think about pleasing himself. He really cares what other people feel. But it could not have been better, the balance between having the three of us and then having Karen along was changed in such a way. I can't explain it, except to say that it made things … even better.

My friend the late Arthur Such once described me as "an enigma" and he may well have been right about that. It's been a life punctuated by some exhilarating highs and jolting lows – hopefully I've still got a few years left to enjoy it – but I feel I've finally emerged on the other side. And I can safely say that 'The Going Up Was Worth The Coming Down'.

EIGHTEEN

THE WINNERS

No.	Date	Course	Horse	Type of race	Trainer
			1965/66: 1 win	Number of rides: 2	
1	28.5.66	Hexham	Charles Cotton	Selling Hurdle	T Robson
			1966/67: 6 wins	Number of rides: 61	
2	24.9.66	Hexham	Sundowner	Novice Hurdle	T Robson
3	17.12.66	Catterick	Charles Cotton	Selling Hurdle	T Robson
4	14.1.67	Catterick	Defender	Novice Hurdle	T Robson
5	25.3.67	Carlisle	Champ	Novice Hurdle	T Robson
6	15.4.67	Hexham	Champ	Novice Hurdle	T Robson
7	24.4.67	Ayr	Champ	Novice Hurdle	T Robson
			1967/68: 6 wins	Number of rides: 78	
8	18.10.67	Newcastle	Punion	Selling Chase	T Barnes
9	11.11.67	Wetherby	Punion	Selling Chase	T Barnes
10	25.11.67	Sedgefield	Punion	Handicap Chase	T Barnes
11	27.3.68	Ayr	Punion	Handicap Chase	T Barnes
12	8.4.68	Leicester	Marcello	Selling Chase	L Shedden
13	13.4.68	Carlisle	Sea Romance	Selling Hurdle	Jos Bowness
			1968/69: 9 wins	Number of rides: 119	
14	14.10.68	Ayr	Darkwood	Handicap Chase	J K Oliver
15	19.10.68	Kelso	Altirio	Handicap Chase	P Pittendrigh
16	26.12.68	Sedgefield	Tipperwood	Novice Hurdle	P Pittendrigh
17	25.1.69	Sedgefield	Impeachment	Handicap Chase	P Pittendrigh
18	12.4.69	Kelso	Harvest Gold	Handicap Chase	T Robson
19	16.4.69	Newcastle	Bright Lad	Novice Hurdle	T Robson
20	29.4.69	Kelso	Common Pond	Novice Hurdle	P Pittendrigh
21	1.5.69	Hexham	Pampered Queen	Novice Chase	T Robson
22	16.5.69	Sedgefield	Tipperwood	Novice Chase	P Pittendrigh
			1969/70: 8 wins	Number of rides: 127	
23	1.9.69	Cartmel	Ticket o' Leave	Juvenile Hurdle	T Robson

24	11.10.69	Ayr	Kildrummy	Handicap Hurdle	W Crawford
25	13.10.69	Ayr	Tipperwood	Handicap Chase	P Scott
26	13.10.69	Ayr	Lothian Prince	Novice Chase	W Crawford
27	22.10,69	Newcastle	Jungle Wise	Novice Hurdle	W Crawford
28	4.11.69	Hexham	Tipperwood	Handicap Chase	P Scott
29	11.11.69	Kelso	Jungle Wise	Novice Hurdle	W Crawford
30	17.1.70	Catterick	Tipperwood	Handicap Chase	P Scott
			1970/71: 1 win	**Number of rides:** 24	
31	10.4.71	Southwell	Frontiersman	Novice Chase	P Ransom
			1971/72: 5 wins	**Number of rides:** 85	
32	27.12.71	Mkt Rasen	Hey-Up	Novice Hurdle	W O'Gorman
33	5.1.72	Doncaster	Luck of the Game	Selling Hurdle	W O'Gorman
34	21.2.72	Plumpton	Carlton Hill	Novice Chase	E McNally
35	25.3.72	Doncaster	Sweet Combat	Novice Chase	P Moore
36	8.5.72	Wye	Pronto-Pronto	Novice Chase	P Moore
			1972/73: 7 wins	**Number of rides:** 136	
37	26.8.72	Mkt Rasen	Sweet Nenene	Juvenile Hurdle	D Thom
38	28.8.72	Southwell	Strong Heart	Handicap Hurdle	W O'Gorman
39	11.12.72	Wye	Lord Jason	Novice Hurdle	N Callaghan
40	16.12.72	Nottingham	Strong Heart	Novice Chase	W O'Gorman
41	26.3.73	Wye	Anaval	Handicap Hurdle	W Holden
42	5.5.73	Warwick	Foursquare	Novice Chase	J Webber
43	28.5.73	Towcester	Foursquare	Novice Chase	J Webber
			1973/74: 6 wins	**Number of rides:** 75	
44	4.2.74	Leicester	Sammy's Girl	Novice Chase	Mrs R Lomax
45	20.2.74	Catterick	Palace Hope	Novice Hurdle	A Goodwill
46	2.3.74	Mkt Rasen	Anaval	Handicap Hurdle	W Holden
47	8.4.74	Wye	Blacksboat	Novice Hurdle	A Goodwill
48	15.4.74	Fakenham	Fine Judge	Novice Hurdle	B Richmond
49	27.5.74	Fakenham	Patillo	Selling Hurdle	A Goodwill
			1974/75: 22 wins	**Number of rides:** 242	
50	10.8.74	Southwell	Caley's Harvest	Selling Hurdle	H O'Neill
51	21.9.74	Warwick	Khoda Khan	Selling Hurdle	A Rumsey
52	26.10.74	Huntingdon	Golden Days	Novice Hurdle (3yo)	A Goodwill
53	26.10.74	Huntingdon	Hazelestyn	Novice Chase	J Webber
54	26.10.74	Huntingdon	Speed Cop	Novice Hurdle (3yo)	A Goodwill
55	14.11.74	Stratford	Rapid Pass	Novice Hurdle	G Blum

56	21.12.74	Fakenham	Dingle Poke	Handicap Chase	P Felgate
57	27.12.74	Mkt Rasen	Duc d'Orleans	Four-year-old Hurdle	L Carrod
58	30.12.74	Leicester	Fezeyot (dd-ht)	Handicap Chase	Tom Jones
59	20.1.75	Wolver'ton	Golden Days	Handicap Hurdle	A Goodwill
60	1.2.75	Wetherby	Mine a Million	Novice Hurdle (4yo)	Tom Jones
61	1.2.75	Wetherby	Artogan	Novice Chase	Tom Jones
62	8.2.75	Wolver'ton	Fezeyot	Handicap Chase	Tom Jones
63	1.3.75	Mkt Rasen	Greek Ancestor	Novice Chase	Tom Jones
64	1.3.75	Mkt Rasen	Hardier	Handicap Hurdle	Tom Jones
65	18.3.75	Nottingham	Brushwood	Novice Hurdle	Tom Jones
66	5.5.75	Southwell	Frockham Brae	Novice Hurdle	P Felgate
67	10.5.75	Worcester	Tucker's Boy	Handicap Hurdle	H Wharton
68	16.5.75	Stratford	Rapid Pass	Novice Hurdle	G Blum
69	19.5.75	Southwell	Pinchario	Novice Hurdle	H Collingridge
70	26.5.75	Fontwell	Mine a Million	Novice Hurdle	Tom Jones
71	31.5.75	Mkt Rasen	Dingle Poke	Handicap Chase	P Felgate
			1975/76: 45 wins	**Number of rides:** 298	
72	4.8.75	Mkt Rasen	Chartist	Novice Chase	C Hassell
73	27.9.75	Mkt Rasen	Chartist	Novice Chase	C Hassell
74	8.10.75	Cheltenham	The Sundance Kid	Handicap Chase	Tom Jones
75	8.10.75	Cheltenham	Sweet Joe	Novice Hurdle (3yo)	Tom Jones
76	9.10.75	Cheltenham	Lewacre	Novice Hurdle	Tom Jones
77	13.10.75	Southwell	Ordnance Hill	Juvenile Hurdle	H Westbrook
78	25.10.75	Huntingdon	Saragusa	Novice Hurdle (3yo)	H Westbrook
79	31.10.75	Sandown	Hardier	Novice Chase	Tom Jones
80	5.11.75	Newbury	Jolly's Clump	Handicap Chase	Tom Jones
81	7.11.75	Doncaster	Summer Serenade	Selling Hurdle	Rex Carter
82	10.11.75	Nottingham	Redbin	Handicap Hurdle	Rex Carter
83	14.11.75	Ascot	Hardier	Novice Chase	Tom Jones
84	28.11.75	Mkt Rasen	Speed Cop	Handicap Hurdle	Rex Carter
85	2.12.75	Huntingdon	Il Magnifico	Novice Hurdle	H Westbrook
86	6.12.75	Lingfield	Sweet Joe	Summit Junior Hurdle	Tom Jones
87	13.12.75	Nottingham	General Ginger Nut	Novice Chase	Tom Jones
88	26.12.75	Wetherby	Tingle Creek	Castleford Chase	Tom Jones
89	30.12.75	Stratford	Ballygarvan Brook	Novice Chase	Earl Jones
90	1.1.76	Cheltenham	Jolly's Clump	Bass Handicap Chase	Tom Jones
91	1.1.76	Cheltenham	Zongalero	Novice Chase	Tom Jones
92	8.1.76	Doncaster	Knave of Hearts	Selling Hurdle	H Westbrook
93	9.1.76	Sandown	Tingle Creek	Express Chase	Tom Jones
94	20.1.76	Wolver'ton	Tasco	Novice Chase	Earl Jones
95	21.1.76	Mkt Rasen	Summer Serenade	Selling Hurdle	Rex Carter
96	24.1.76	Warwick	Jolly's Clump	Oxo National Chase	Tom Jones

#	Date	Course	Horse	Race	Jockey
97	7.2.76	Stratford	Ballygarvan Brook	Novice Chase	Earl Jones
98	11.2.76	Fontwell	Near and Far	Handicap Chase	Rex Carter
99	14.2.76	Wolver-ton	Zongalero	Novice Chase	Tom Jones
100	16.2.76	Wolver-ton	Tasco	Novice Chase	Earl Jones
101	20.2.74	Fakenham	Crimson Glove	Handicap Hurdle (4yo)	H Collingridge
102	21.2.76	Newcastle	Sweet Joe	Four-year-old Hurdle	Tom Jones
103	21.2.76	Newcastle	Lovejoy	Novice Chase	Tom Jones
104	6.3.76	Haydock	Sweet Joe	Victor Ludorum Hurdle	Tom Jones
105	9.3.76	Huntingdon	Invergayle	Four-year-old Hurdle	Tom Jones
106	19.3.76	Uttoxeter	General Moselle	Novice Chase	H Wharton
107	23.3.76	Nottingham	Water Pistol	Novice Hurdle	Tom Jones
108	1.4.76	Stratford	Ballygarvan Brook	Novice Handicap Chase	Earl Jones
109	7.4.76	Cheltenham	Civil List	Juvenile Hurdle	Earl Jones
110	10.4.76	Uttoxeter	Ashendene	Novice Chase	Tom Jones
111	19.4.76	Towcester	Tingle Creek	Handicap Chase	Tom Jones
112	20,.4.76	Wetherby	The Sundance Kid	Handicap Chase	Tom Jones
113	29.4.76	Uttoxeter	Civil List	Novice Hurdle (4yo)	Earl Jones
114	5.5.76	Wetherby	Tingle Creek	Handicap Chase	Tom Jones
115	24.5.76	Nottingham	Tingle Creek	Handicap Chase	Tom Jones
116	1.6.76	Uttoxeter	La Balconne	Novice Hurdle	Earl Jones
			1976/77: 43 wins	**Number of rides: 343**	
117	9.8.76	Worcester	Invergayle	Four-year-old Hurdle	Tom Jones
118	28.8.76	Mkt Rasen	Michael's Boy	Novice Chase	Earl Jones
119	28.8.76	Mkt Rasen	Track Event	Juvenile Hurdle	G Blum
120	4.9.76	Stratford	Tingle Creek	Handicap Chase	Tom Jones
121	16.9.76	Worcester	Forget It	Novice Chase	Earl Jones
122	24.9.76	Mkt Rasen	Molly's Beau	Novice Hurdle	H Collingridge
123	9.10.76	Uttoxeter	Gay Kempley	Handicap Chase	Earl Jones
124	11.10.76	Southwell	Reformina	Juvenile Hurdle	H Wharton
125	13.10.76	Wetherby	Joe Coral	Novice Hurdle (4yo)	Tom Jones
126	15.10.76	Mkt Rasen	Rossborough	Novice Chase	Tom Jones
127	29.10.76	Sandown	Stupendous Boy	Novice Hurdle	J Powney
128	8.11.76	Wolver'ton	Corrieghoil	Handicap Chase	Earl Jones
129	12.11.76	Chepstow	Sweet Joe	Olympic Hurdle	Tom Jones
130	20.11.76	Newcastle	Zongalero	Embassy Premier Chase	Tom Jones
131	27.11.76	Newbury	Zeta's Son	Hennessy Gold Cup	P Bailey
132	29.11.76	Wolver'ton	Light Master	Novice Chase	Earl Jones
133	2.12.76	Haydock	Hopeful Hill	Selling Chase	Earl Jones
134	2.12.76	Haydock	John Cherry	Pattern Hurdle	Tom Jones
135	27.12.76	Kempton	John Cherry	Novice Hurdle	Tom Jones

136	11.1.77	Leicester	Lowndes Square	Novices' Hurdle	M Banks
137	22.1.77	Haydock	Sea Pigeon	Handicap Hurdle	M H Easterby
138	24.1.77	Worcester	Friendly Builder	Novice Hurdle	N Callaghan
139	12.2.77	Catterick	Merry Boy	Novice Chase	M Chapman
140	5.3.77	Haydock	General Moselle	Greenall Whitley Chase	H Wharton
141	5.3.77	Haydock	Sage Merlin	Handicap Chase	J Bingham
142	11.3.77	Sandown	Pinchario	Novice Chase	H Collingridge
143	22.3.77	Nottingham	Oropendola	Novice Hurdle	Tom Jones
144	26.3.77	Bangor	Ousky	Novice Hurdle (4yo)	Earl Jones
145	11.4.77	Wetherby	General Moselle	Handicap Chase	H Wharton
146	12.4.77	Uttoxeter	Corrieghoil	Handicap Chase	Earl Jones
147	12.4.77	Uttoxeter	Ousky	Four-year-old Hurdle	Earl Jones
148	20.4.77	Ludlow	Light Master	Handicap Chase	Earl Jones
149	3.5.77	Huntingdon	Crimson Glove	Handicap Hurdle	H Collingridge
150	6.5.77	Towcester	North Two	Selling Hurdle	J Powney
151	10.5.77	Nottingham	All Spirit	Novice Chase	Earl Jones
152	11.5.77	Ludlow	Corrieghoil	Handicap Chase	Earl Jones
153	13.5.77	Newcastle	Pavement Artist	Novice Hurdle	Tom Jones
154	13.5.77	Newcastle	Pinchario	Novice Chase	H Collingridge
155	19.5.77	Uttoxeter	Connotation	Novice Hurdle	Earl Jones
156	23.5.77	Nottingham	Swift Shadow	Conditions Hurdle	Tom Jones
157	6.6.77	Wetherby	Boy Marvel	Selling Hurdle	L Shedden
158	6.6.77	Wetherby	Swift Shadow	Handicap Hurdle	Tom Jones
159	7.6.77	Uttoxeter	Corrieghoil	Handicap Chase	Earl Jones
			1977/78: 25 wins	**Number of rides: 150**	
160	1.8.77	Newton Abbot	Colditz Captive	Juvenile Hurdle	W Marshall
161	27.8.77	Mkt Rasen	Suviel	Novice Hurdle	S Nattriss
162	29.8.77	Huntingdon	Spy Net	Handicap Chase	D Dale
163	14.9.77	Worcester	Corrieghoil	Handicap Chase	Earl Jones
164	17.9.77	Warwick	Kelly's Hero	Handicap Chase	A Wates
165	19.9.77	Fontwell	Tingle Creek	Handicap Chase	Tom Jones
166	6.10.77	Cheltenham	The Bo-Weevil	Novice Chase	P Bailey
167	24.10.77	Nottingham	Lanka	Novice Hurdle	P Bailey
168	29.10.77	Worcester	Casamayor	ATV Today Chase	P Bailey
169	10.11.77	Wincanton	Strombolus	Novice Chase	P Bailey
170	11.11.77	Chepstow	Prince Rock	Handicap Chase	P Bailey
171	22.11.77	Nottingham	Five Bells	Novice Hurdle (4yo)	J FitzGerald
172	28.11.77	Wolver'ton	Casamayor	Handicap Chase	P Bailey
173	29.11.77	Huntingdon	Fair Kitty	Novice Chase	J FitzGerald
174	3.12.77	Mkt Rasen	Soldiers Field	Selling Hurdle	F Wiles
175	3.12.77	Mkt Rasen	Come Spring	Novice Chase	W N Guest
176	21.12.77	Chepstow	Prince Rock	Handicap Chase	P Bailey

177	26.12.77	N'ton Abbot	Dublin Express	Handicap Chase	P Bailey
178	26.12.77	N'ton Abbot	Strombolus	Novice Chase	P Bailey
179	31.12.77	Newbury	Skryne	Handicap Chase	P Bailey
180	2.1.78	Cheltenham	Prince Rock	Bass Handicap Chase	P Bailey
181	4.3.78	Newbury	Major Thompson	Novices Hurdle (4yo)	M H Easterby
182	4.3.78	Newbury	Alverton	Novice Chase	M H Easterby
183	13.3.78	Southwell	Jonswallow	Selling Hurdle	D Weeden
184	29.5.78	Fakenham	Avgerinos	Novice Hurdle	H Collingridge
			1978/79: 21 wins	**Number of rides:** 153	
185	29.7.78	Mkt Rasen	Charlotte Mary	Maiden Hurdle	J Powney
186	23.8.78	Fontwell	Spy Net	Handicap Chase	D Dale
187	31.8.78	Fontwell	Erstung	Novice Hurdle	W Holden
188	23.9.78	Warwick	Erstung	Novice Hurdle	W Holden
189	18.10.78	Wetherby	Night Nurse	Bobby Renton Chase	M H Easterby
190	18.10.78	Wetherby	King Weasel	Handicap Chase	M H Easterby
191	27.10.78	Newbury	Sea Pigeon	William Hill Hurdle	M H Easterby
192	1.11.78	Newcastle	Night Nurse	Novice Chase	M H Easterby
193	1.11.78	Newcastle	Eminence	Novice Hurdle	M H Easterby
194	3.11.78	Sandown	Skryne	Handicap Chase	P Bailey
195	3.11.78	Sandown	Hunter's Joy	Novice Chase	P Bailey
196	13.11.78	Nottingham	Groovy	Selling Hurdle	H O'Neill
197	16.11.78	Wincanton	Gay God (w/o)	Handicap Chase	D Pearman
198	18.11.78	Newcastle	Sea Pigeon	Fighting Fifth Hurdle	M H Easterby
199	18.11.78	Newcastle	Night Nurse	Embassy Premier Chase	M H Easterby
200	21.11.78	Ayr	Chokwaro	Novice Hurdle (3yo)	M H Easterby
201	25.11.78	Newbury	Skryne	Handicap Chase	P Bailey
202	16.12.78	Ascot	Night Nurse	Killiney Novice Chase	M H Easterby
203	27.12.78	Wolver'ton	Night Nurse	Astbury Trophy Chase	M H Easterby
204	22.2.79	Wincanton	Taffy	Maiden Hurdle	P Bailey
205	6.3.79	Plumpton	Plastic Cup	Selling Hurdle	H O'Neill
			Last ride		
	9.3.79	Towcester	Regal Choice (fell)	Handicap Chase	J Haine

THE MOST MEMORABLE 50

	Course	Name of Race	Horse
1	Ayr	Melleray's Belle Challenge Cup Handicap Chase	Darkwood
2	Kelso	Anthony Marshall Trophy Handicap Chase	Altirio
3	Kelso	Stewart Wight Memorial Handicap Chase	Harvest Gold
4	Ayr	Melleray's Belle Challenge Cup Handicap Chase	Tipperwood
5	Leicester	Broxhills Handicap Chase (dead-heat)	Fezeyot
6	Wolverhampton	Mitchells & Butlers Handicap Chase	Fezeyot
7	Stratford	S.K.F. Hurdle For Future Champions	Rapid Pass
8	Newbury	Lionel Vick Memorial Handicap Chase	Jolly's Clump
9	Ascot	Hurst Park Novices' Chase	Hardier
10	Lingfield	Summit Junior Hurdle (3yo)	Sweet Joe
11	Wetherby	Castleford Handicap Chase	Tingle Creek
12	Cheltenham	Bass Handicap Chase	Jolly's Clump
13	Sandown	Express Chase	Tingle Creek
14	Warwick	Brooke Bond Oxo National Handicap Chase	Jolly's Clump
15	Newcastle	Minnow (4yo) Hurdle	Sweet Joe
16	Haydock	Victor Ludorum (4yo) Hurdle	Sweet Joe
17	Towcester	Alex Fetherstonhaugh Challenge Cup Chase	Tingle Creek
18	Wetherby	Sherburn Handicap Chase	Tingle Creek
19	Nottingham	Colwick Hall Handicap Chase	Tingle Creek
20	Stratford	Virginia Gold Cup Handicap Chase	Tingle Creek
21	Chepstow	Olympic Hurdle	Sweet Joe
22	Newcastle	Embassy Premier Chase (Qualifier)	Zongalero
23	Newbury	Hennessy Cognac Gold Cup Handicap Chase	Zeta's Son
24	Haydock	Garswood Pattern Hurdle	John Cherry
25	Kempton	G. J. Novice Hurdle (4 & 5yo)	John Cherry
26	Haydock	Embassy Handicap Hurdle	Sea Pigeon
27	Haydock	Greenall Whitley Breweries Handicap Chase	General Moselle
28	Haydock	Dormouse Handicap Chase	Sage Merlin
29	Wetherby	Wetherby Handicap Chase	General Moselle
30	Uttoxeter	Charles Lewis Cup Handicap Chase	Corrieghoil
31	Uttoxeter	Ken Boulton Memorial Handicap Chase	Corrieghoil
32	Fontwell	South Downs Handicap Chase	Tingle Creek
33	Worcester	ATV Today Chase	Casamayor

34	Wincanton	Mendip Hills Novices' Chase	Strombolus
35	Chepstow	Johnny Clay Memorial Handicap Chase	Prince Rock
36	Wolverhampton	Staveley Handicap Chase	Casamayor
37	Chepstow	Terry Wogan Handicap Chase	Prince Rock
38	Newton Abbot	Mid-Devon Novices' Chase	Strombolus
39	Newbury	Old Year Handicap Chase	Skryne
40	Cheltenham	Bass Handicap Chase	Prince Rock
41	Newbury	Highclere Novices Hurdle (4yo)	Major Thompson
42	Newbury	Sam Cowan Novice Chase	Alverton
43	Wetherby	Bobby Renton Memorial Novices Chase	Night Nurse
44	Wetherby	Headley Handicap Chase	King Weasel
45	Newbury	William Hill Hurdle	Sea Pigeon
46	Newcastle	Falstone Novices' Chase	Night Nurse
47	Newcastle	Fighting Fifth Hurdle	Sea Pigeon
48	Newcastle	Embassy Premier Chase (Qualifier)	Night Nurse
49	Ascot	Killiney Novices' Chase	Night Nurse
50	Wolverhampton	Astbury Trophy Novices' Chase	Night Nurse

Index

Acquaint 51
Act Of Faith 114
Adam's Well 57
Aldaniti 116
All Spirit 91
Altirio 27
Alverton 76. 101, 106, 113
Alydar 38
Anaval 43
Andrews, Eamonn 116
Anglo 9
Arkle 26
Arnold, Rupert 125
Armstrong, Robert 131
Armstrong, Sam 41
Artogan 50
Ashworth, Ryan 173
Aspel, Michael 116
Aspell, Leighton 134

Bailey, Caroline 63
Bailey, Charlie 98
Bailey, Maurice 6
Bailey, Peter 62-63, 71-74, 102, 104, 108, 15--151
Ballygarvan Brook 89
Ballymore 74
Banks, Michael 65
Banks, Polly 16
Banks, Ralph 16
Banks, Sidney 65
Barber-Lomax, Chris 59

Barlow, Jeff 39, 84, 128, 132, 143
Barnes, Maurice 19, 97-98
Barnes, Tommy 19-21, 98
Barony Fort 78
Barry, Ron 62, 153
Barton, Paul 73
Beacon Light 102
Beasley, Bobby 5, 156
Beatty, Chester 56
Beeby, Harry 141
Bell, Harry 16-17, 29
Berry, Frank 102
Berry, Jack 16, 21
Bevan, Hugo 88, 163
Biddlecombe, Terry 21, 38
Billy Bow 26-27
Bingham, John 78
Birds Nest 65
Blackshaw, Martin 47, 65
Black Streak 114
Blue Chrome 65
Blum, Gerry 47-49
Bob's Brae 20
Boom Docker 78-79
Border Flight 5
Boss, Ron 2
Boulton, Ken 90-91
Boy Marvel 23
Bracegirdle, John 59, 61
Bracegirdle, Tanya 61
Brake, Tom 5

Brantridge Farmer 50
Brew, Charlotte 78
Brigadier Gerard 76
Bright, Ken 134, 138-139
Bright, Nick 139
Bright, Norma 134, 138-139
Briggs, Dave 36
Briscoe, Des 58
Broderick, Paddy 83, 104, 153
Brogan, Barry 26-27
Broncho II 73
Brondesbury 40
Brown, Charlie 14
Buckingham, John 150
Buckley, Michael 63
Bula 101
Bull, Phil 8
Burch, Elliott 38
Bush, Linda 39
Byrne, Con 56

Callaghan, Neville 41, 161
Casey, Terry 43
Campbell, Eric 9-16, 21, 23, 29
Canadius 65
Cantillon, Don 145-146
Captain Kenneth 101
Carlton Hill 37
Carmody, Tommy 104, 110
Carter, Rex 58

Cartwright, David 89
Casamayor 73, 151
Cedric 42
Champ 14
Champion, Bob 1, 4, 74, 83, 104, 110, 116, 133, 141-143, 150, 156, 161-162, 167, 169
Chapman, Michael 97
Charbon 83
Charles Cotton 10-11, 14, 20
Chesmore, Peter 23
China Cloud 27
Choir Boy 26
Churchtown Boy 113
Civil List 92
Clancy, Mick 30
Clarke, Bryan 19-20
Claydon, David 157-158
Clever Scot 41
Clonmellon 50
Cobden, Toby 73
Collingridge, Hugh 157
Collins, Phil 154
Comedy Of Errors 73, 101
Connors, Paddy 90, 93
Connotation 91
Coogan, Scobie 143
Corrieghoil 79, 90-91
Cosmo Walk 14
Count Verano 43

Courage, Edward 84
Cox, Noddy 55-56
Cummings, Bart 113

D'Abreu, Frank 3, 112
Dale, David 76
Dandy, John 108
Danube 163-164
Darkwood 26
Davenport, Steve 145
Davies, Bob 53, 68, 105, 140
Davies, Roy 81
Defender 14
Dempsey, Frank 6
Denson, Bill 62
Devon Blue 19
Dickinson, Michael 73, 154
Dickinson, Tony 73, 130
Double Chance 159
Doughty, Neale 59-61, 109
Dramatist 65, 108
Dreaper, Tom 26
Drumikill 30
Dunlop, Ed 169

Early Spring 69
Easterby, Peter 65, 101, 106
Edmonds, Noel 126-127
Edwards, John 40
Edwards, Roy 29
Ellison, Brian 69
Enable 83

Evans, James 100
Evans, Richard 21

Farrell, Paddy 5
Fatherland 93
Fawcett, Jeremy 14
Fetherstonhaugh, Bob 41
Fezeyot 49
Flatbush 26
Fletcher, Brian 11
Flippance, Fred 51, 56, 59, 86
Flyingbolt 26
Fooasaboot 26
Foreman 41
Francome, John 76, 152-154
Frankel 83
Freddie 23
French, Sheilagh 92
Frenchman's Cove 41
French Society 41
Frontiersman 34

Galpin, Richard 6
Garnishee 41, 53
Gaston, Charlie 5
General Moselle 65
Gifford, Josh 104, 152
Golden Cygnet 4, 102-103, 106
Golden Days 47
Goldie, Tom 49
Gongoozler 17-19
Goodwill, Fiddler 41, 47, 58-59
Goodwill, Linda 59
Gosden, John 154
Graham, Clive 89

Graham, Neil 169
Grand Canyon 63, 108
Grangewood Girl 53
Green, Peter 96
Greig, Bobby 30
Griffin, Gerry 21, 112-113
Guest, Raymond 73
Gylippus 61

Haine, Johnny 1, 21, 38, 113
Hall, Sam 51
Hallo Dandy 109
Hanbury, Ben 159, 168
Hardier 56-58
Hardy Turk 51
Harrison, Joe 4, 8
Harvest Gold 9, 30
Haslam, Pat 148
Havanus 54
Hawkins, Johnny 90, 93
Hayes, Colin 120, 133, 154
Haynes, Peter 63
Hazelestyn 47
Healy, Bob 106
Henderson, Nicky 51, 73
Higgs, Brian 37, 162
Hogg, George 26
Holden, Bill 1, 41-43
Howell, Ian (Wilf) 148-149
Hunter, Malcolm 11-14

Hyett, Ron 93
Hy-Gocean 11

I'm A Driver 104, 152
Impeachment 29

James, Jinx 143
Jarvis, Jack 5
Jarvis, Michael 135
Jarvis, Ryan 136
Jenkins, Albert 68, 97
Jobar, Steve 57
John Cherry 63-65, 69
Jolly's Clump 59-62, 73, 157
Jones, Earl 79, 89-95
Jones, Harry Thomson 2, 41-42, 49-59, 63-71, 84, 86, 91, 98, 102, 104, 143, 156
Jones, Monica 106-107
Jones, Sarah Thomson 56
Jones, Solna Thomson 113
Jones, Tim Thomson 58
Joytotheworld 161
Juster, Maxine 125

Keightley, Shaun 161-163
Kelleway, Paul 38
Kelp, Lars 146
Kent, Derek 63
King, Jeff 21, 38, 40, 88, 113

King, Lucy 53, 146
Kingman 83

Larkspur 73
Lauren, Lucien 38
Ledger, Nicky 69
Leech, John 21, 30
Lees, Libby (Heath) 53, 61, 146
Lees, Nick 53
Le Robstan 63
L'Escargot 73
Levadon 80
Lewacre 55
Lillingston, Alan 43
Linley, Richard 74
Listercombe 49
Lizawake 5, 156
Lockerbie, Graham 31, 145
Lomax, Rosemary 43
Lovejoy 54, 74
Lowndes Square 65
Luck Of The Game 36

Macmillan, Graham 82
Magic Court 9
Mahon, Tommy 84
Major Thompson 76, 113
Manning, Bernard 145
Manning, Joe 113-114, 157
Man o' War 81-82
Marcello 23
Marsh King 9

Marshall, Bill 57, 59
Mason, Ron 121, 146
Master Upham 73
Matthews. Stuart 102
May, Sandy 73
McCarron, Pat 21
McCririck, John 167
McEntee, Phil 161
McLeod-Smith, Helen 124-125
McMurchie, John 19
McNally, Eddie 37
Mellon, Paul 38
Mellor, Dana 113
Mellor, Stan 76
Merry Boy 97
Milburn, Freddie 29-30
Milburn, George 21
Minton, David 84
Moment Of Madness 6
Monksfield 101-102
Moore, Colin 5
Moore, Pat 5, 23-24, 38, 156
Morley, David 54-55, 83, 140
Morris, Alec 120
Mould, David 21, 38, 50, 53, 68
Muldoon, Pat 106
Mummy's Game 40

Nemon 94

Newman, Gerry 103
Newson, Jimmy 17
Nicholson, David 21
Nicolaus Silver 5
Night Nurse 4, 65, 101-111, 152
Norfolk, Duke of 42
Number Engaged 68

Oaksey, Lord 50-51, 167
O'Connor, Christy 86
O'Gorman, Bill 4, 6, 36, 38, 40-41, 53, 83, 124-125, 129, 156
O'Gorman, Elaine 83-84, 125
O'Gorman, Paddy 4, 36
Oliver, Ken 26-27
Oliver, Michael 131
Oliver, Rhona 26-27
Oliver, Stuart 30
O'Neill, Chris 34
O'Neill, Hugh 34, 112
O'Neill, Jonjo 4, 63, 76, 102-103
O'Sullevan, Peter 111
Our Betters 41
Owen, George 6

Palsboy 53

Pampered Queen 30
Paxman, Philip 6
Payne, Pip 135, 161
Pearce, Jeff 79, 101, 104, 143
Pearce, Martin 124
Pearman, Donald 99-100
Pee Mai 59
Pendil 43
Persian War 101
Phillips, Tim 51-53
Piggott, Lester 63
Pitman, Richard 43, 76
Pittendrigh, Peter 27, 29, 81
Plastic Cup 112
Pollard, Eve 47
Powell, Brian 154-155
Powney, John 5
Press Button B 11
Prince Rock 73-76
Provideo 40
Punion 19-20

Queen's Taste 9
Quinn, Mick 167

Radford, Brian 112
Ransom, Bill 43
Ransom, Peter 34-35, 43
Rapid Pass 47-49
Rawlinson, Tony 146-148
Read, Chris 113
Redbin 58
Red Rambler 19
Red Rum 79

Red Well 103
Reesh 40
Regal Choice 1, 112, 152
Renwick, Aubrey 14
Ribero 49
Richards Gordon W. 106, 136
Rimell, Fred 93-94
Ringer, David 159
Rippon, Angela 127
Ritzenberg, Milton 63
Roadhead 104, 152
Roberts, Monty 148
Robinson, Arnie 11
Rob Ricketts 19-20
Robson, Tom 6-17, 21, 26, 29-31, 80, 98
Rogers Princess 162
Rolled Gold 114
Ross, Fred 11
Royal And Ancient 92
Royal Emblem 35
Royal Marshal II 65
Rowe, Mick 86
Royal Relief 84
Rumsey, Alan 51
Ryan, Mick 159
Ryder, Ted 122-123
Rykens, Dick 54-55, 74

Sage Merlin 63, 78-79
Saint, Peter 96

Sammy's Girl 43
Sanvina 27
Saucy Kit 19
Sayf El Arab 40
Scott, Gerry 21, 113
Scott, Peter 29-30
Scrivener, Brian 47, 128, 167
Sea Pigeon 4, 65, 101-108
Sea Romance 31
Secretariat 38
Seventh Son 103
Sham Fight 9
Shedden, Tommy 23
Sidebottom, Frances 166-167
Sidebottom, Hugh 159
Sidebottom, Robert 166-167
Silver Buck 110-111
Sir Ivor 73
Skelton, George 123
Skymas 68
Sly, Pam 101-102
Smart, Bryan 61
Smith, Denys 104
Smith, Len 120
Smith, Tommy 113
Smith Eccles, Steve 2, 68, 101, 116, 120-121, 132, 137, 143-144
Soane, Vic 74
Sonic Lady 124
Spanish Steps 84
Spanish Tan 69
Speed Cop 47

Spencer, Reg 103, 110
Springsteen, Bruce 154
Spy Net 76
Starkey, Greville 53
Stephenson, Arthur 104
Stephenson, Willie 21
Stone, Keith 106
Stoute, Michael 124
Straight Sailing 21
Strawbridge, George 55
Strombolus 62, 65, 74, 108, 151
Strong Heart 40
Such, Arthur 175
Summer Serenade 58
Sundowner 14
Superbly Sharp 168
Superlative 40
Sweet Joe 53-55, 74
Swift Shadow 86

Tamalin 63
Tate, Martin 162
Tarquin Migol 11
Tasco 90
Taylor, Pat 11
Team Spirit 5
Tex 69
The Bo Weevil
The Celestial
Traveller 27, 82
The Coalman 146

188

The Sundance Kid 53, 55, 152
Thom, Dave 38-41, 128-129, 159-161
Thompson, Derek 83, 145
Thompson, Lavinia 101
Thorner, Graham 47, 102
Ticket o' Leave 30
Timeless Times 40
Tingle Creek 2, 53, 55, 58, 65-73, 86, 136
Tipperwood 29-31
Tirol 163
Titterington, Raymond 9-11, 31
Toland, John 81
Track Event 49
Track Spare 121
Trespasser 23
Tufts, George 58
Tuite, Kevin 5
Turnell, Andy 154
Tutor's Best 65

Valmony 54
Veitch, John 38
Vittorio 16-17

Wall, Chris 145
Wall, Ron 145
Walwyn, Fulke 50
Warrell, Jack 106
Warren, Cathy 83
Watkinson, Aileen 4
Watkinson, Camilla (now Ashworth) 125, 129, 134, 171-173
Watkinson, Cathy (now Edwards) 1-2, 101-102, 113-116, 120-121, 131-133, 141, 154, 157
Watkinson, Claire (now Rigg) 125-130, 133-135, 154, 166, 171
Watkinson, Eric 4, 9
Watkinson, Jill 4, 9
Watkinson, Karen 129-130, 135-136, 142-143, 155, 173-174
Watkinson, Max 126, 129, 134, 171, 173-175
Watson, Keith 121
Webber, Anthony 47
Webber, John 47
Weeden, Derek 131
Wharton, Harry 65, 80
Wigham, Michael 149, 161, 163-164, 168
Wilkinson, John 26
William Penn 99-100
Williams, Colin 163-164
Williams, John 120
Wilson, Auriol 129, 135
Wilson, Jack 159

Wilson. Julian 151
Wilson, Richard 129, 135
Wilson, Tom 10
Winning Fair 113
Winter, Fred 6
Winter, John 124-125
Wyndburgh 19

Zeta's Son 62-63, 124
Zongalero 53